THE **Building Christian English** SERIES

Building

Christian English

Building With Diligence

Grade 4

Rod and Staff Publishers, Inc.
P.O. Box 3, Hwy. 172
Crockett, Kentucky 41413
Telephone: (606) 522-4348

Copyright 1992

First edition copyright 1969, revision 1992

by

Rod and Staff Publishers, Inc.
Crockett, Kentucky 41413

Printed in U.S.A.

ISBN 978-07399-0515-9

Catalog no. 12404.3

12   13   14   15   16   17   —   20   19   18   17   16   15   14   13   12

Acknowledgments

We are indebted first and most of all to God, whose blessing made possible the writing and publishing of this book.

We express gratitude to each one who was involved in this work. The original edition was written by Lela Birky, and the revision by Marion W. Leinbach. Marvin Eicher was the editor, H. Lynn Martin and various others were reviewers, and most of the artwork was done by Thomas R. Anderson, Daniel Porter, and Lester Miller. We are also indebted to the teachers who used the material on a laboratory basis in their classrooms, as well as to numerous people who assisted along the way by providing finances, by encouraging those directly involved in the work, and by interceding in prayer for the work.

Various reference books were consulted in accomplishing this task, such as English handbooks, other English textbooks, encyclopedias, and dictionaries. For these too we are grateful. We have chosen to favor the more conservative schools of thought that are considered authoritative in correct English usage.

—The Publishers

Table of Contents

(Stars indicate written composition and oral work.)

Chapter 1

Subjects and Predicates

Chapter 2

Kinds of Sentences

Chapter 3

Nouns

Chapter 4

Verbs

Chapter 5

Using Verbs Correctly

Chapter 6

Pronouns

Chapter 7

Adjectives

Chapter 8

Adverbs

Chapter 9

Punctuation

Chapter 10

Prepositions and Conjunctions

Chapter 11

Capitalization and Dictionary Use

God Gave Us Language

God made man in a special way. He gave man the ability to think, and He gave him language with which to express his thoughts. Animals cannot communicate the way man does.

God gave people language so that He could communicate with them. God speaks to people through the Bible. We study language so that we can understand God's Word better.

God also gave us language so that we can communicate with each other. We study language so that we can communicate better with other people.

God gave Adam and Eve the language they used. The language was the same all over the world until God caused the people to speak other languages at the Tower of Babel. Now there are many languages in the world.

Missionaries sometimes need to study other languages in order to teach God's Word in other places. Studying our own language helps us to learn other languages more easily. Who knows? Maybe God will want you to learn another language when you grow up.

English was first spoken in England, a country of Europe. People in America speak English because many people from England came to this land. But the form of English used in America is different from the form used in England. This is so because language changes as it is used by people in different places. If people study their language and understand how it works, the language will not change so much. With fewer changes, the language is easier to use.

Doing your best in studying English will help you in many ways. It will help you to practice working and studying hard. It will help you to develop a keen mind. It will help you to speak and write more clearly when you want to share your thoughts with others. Then when you are older, you can share the truths of the Bible with others, and God will be glorified.

Chapter 1
Subjects and Predicates

1. Getting Acquainted With Your English Book

Language is a gift from God. It is a tool that you use every day, not just a subject to study in school. That is why you should prepare now to study English diligently this year. Your English book will help you to understand and use the English language in a way that is pleasing to God.

The study of English builds from one grade to the next. This year you will add to what you already know. You will also review the new things you learn. Then next year you will build on what you learn this year.

Examine your book now with your teacher to see what is new and what is review. The table of contents at the front of the book lists all the lessons in their proper order. The index at the back lists the topics of the book in alphabetical order.

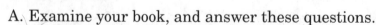
Oral Drill

A. Examine your book, and answer these questions.
   1. What is the title of your English book?
   2. What is the copyright date of your book?
   3. What company published your book? What is the address of the company?

B. Look at the table of contents to answer the following questions.

1. Which chapters teach about sentences?
2. Which chapters teach about verbs?
3. Which chapters teach about pronouns?

C. Use the index to help you find the answers.
　　1. Which pages teach about common and proper nouns?
　　2. Turn to the page that gives a definition of a noun. Read the definition.
　　3. Which pages teach about action verbs?
　　4. Find and read the definition of a verb.
　　5. Find the pages that give the definition of a pronoun. Read the definition.

D. Unscramble these sentences.
　　1. shepherd is my the Lord
　　2. shew approved study to thyself unto God

> Written Practice >

A. Unscramble these sentences, and write them correctly. Capitalize the first word in each sentence, and place a period at the end.
　　1. one ye to kind be another
　　2. trust be I not and will afraid

B. Use the index to help you find the answers.
　　1. a. Which page gives the definition of a noun?
　　　　b. A noun is the name of a ——, ——, or ——.
　　2. a. Which pages teach about helping verbs?
　　　　b. Write two sets of helping verbs.
　　3. a. Which pages teach about singular and plural pronouns?
　　　　b. Write three plural pronouns.

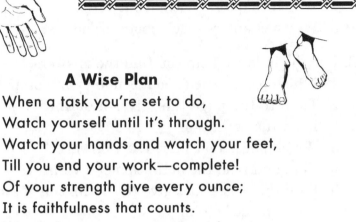

A Wise Plan
When a task you're set to do,
Watch yourself until it's through.
Watch your hands and watch your feet,
Till you end your work—complete!
Of your strength give every ounce;
It is faithfulness that counts.
Watch that you may give your heart
To your task—each smallest part.
Be as steadfast as a rock;
Watch yourself—but not the clock!

—From *Poems for Our Boys and Girls*

2. Getting Organized

Have you ever imagined what life would be like without language? We could not speak or read or write. Without language we would feel very helpless.

Your study of English will go better if you are organized and know what you need to get done. Here are some pointers on being well organized.

1. Be attentive and interested. If you are interested, you will learn more.

2. Study hard. Be ready to answer any question the teacher may ask about the lesson. Study as if you will be asked to explain the whole lesson to someone else.

3. Pay close attention to directions. Listen carefully when your teacher gives the assignment, and read the directions carefully before starting the work. Ask questions if you do not understand, or you may have to do your work all over.

4. Prepare your paper the same way every day. Use the pattern shown below or one your teacher gives you.

    a. Put your name and the date at the correct places.

    b. Write the name of the subject and the page numbers.

English	
Name	Date
Pages 18–21	

5. Keep your papers clean, and write neatly. Write careful and complete answers.

Which one will your paper be like?

6. Use correct spelling and proper English. Do not hurry through your work just to get it finished. That is cheating yourself!

7. Pay attention to mistakes you have made. Learn what your mistake was and why the right answer is correct. If you do something wrong in your lessons, you will get it wrong on the test unless you learn how to do it right.

They that wait upon the Lord shall renew their strength.

— Isaiah 40:31

Oral Drill

This exercise reviews some of the things you learned in third grade.

A. Give the answers.

1. What two things should we remember when we write sentences?
2. What part of speech shows action or being?
3. What part of speech names a person, place, or thing?
4. Give five action verbs.
5. Name the forms of the verb **be.**
6. Give the following nouns.
   a. Three that name persons.
   b. Three that name places.
   c. Three than name things.
7. What part of speech takes the place of a noun?

B. Tell which words are nouns in the following sentences. Tell which words **are** verbs.

1. John lives in Switzerland.
2. He takes cows to the high pastures.
3. Mary helps Mother in the garden.
4. The mountains are beautiful.
5. There is a large lake.

C. Give the seven main ideas of the lesson that tell how to be better organized in your study of English.

> Written Practice >

A. Prepare an English paper according to the pattern shown in the lesson. Use it to do your written assignment.

B. Unscramble and rewrite these sentences. Remember to begin and end each one correctly.
1. do each best your day
2. you the find can answers the in book

C. Copy the seven rules you should follow to be organized in your study of English. Copy only the main ideas that are in bold print.

_____

3. Learning About Sentences

A sentence is a group of words that expresses a complete thought. Every sentence has two main parts: a **subject** and a **predicate.**

Every sentence tells **who** or **what does** or **is** something. The **subject** is the part that tells **who** or **what.** The **predicate** is the part that tells what the subject **does** or **is.** In the following sentences, the first part is the subject, and the second part is the predicate.

Daniel | refused the king's meat.
The four young men | were faithful to God.

Every sentence must begin with a capital letter and end with the correct punctuation mark. A sentence usually ends with a period.

> **Remember:** A sentence is a group of words that expresses a complete thought. Every sentence has a subject and a predicate.

> Oral Drill >

A. Study these subjects and predicates. Tell who or what does or is something. What does the predicate tell about the subject?

Subjects	Predicates
1. The children	were playing happily.
2. The wise man	built his house on a rock.
3. A large tree	stood in the yard.
4. Sarah and I	picked the beans.
5. Three birds	sat on the fence.

B. Supply a good predicate for each subject.
   1. The furry squirrel
   2. My little brother

C. Supply a good subject for each predicate.
   1. picked up the cans.
   2. read us a story.

D. Tell whether these groups of words are sentences.
1. God created man.
2. The first man was Adam.
3. Eve was the first woman.
4. Could not talk with animals.
5. Adam was lonely.
6. A good helper.
7. Created Eve.

> Written Practice >

A. Match these subjects and predicates by writing complete sentences that are true according to the Bible. Be sure to begin and end them correctly.

1. in the beginning God

2. King Saul

3. the apostle Paul

4. the animals and man

5. Hannah's son Samuel

6. John the Baptist

a. were created on the sixth day

b. was in a shipwreck

c. created the heaven and the earth

d. was preaching in the wilderness

e. helped Eli in the tabernacle

f. was the first king of Israel

B. Write the numbers of the groups of words that are complete sentences.
1. Jesus loves the little children.
2. Counting his collection of pennies.
3. Did not hear her.
4. Three red apples hung on the tree.
5. On the first day.

6. All that God made was good.
7. God made plants on the third day.
8. The sun and moon on the fourth day.

C. Add what is needed to make proper sentences from the groups of words in Part B that are not sentences. Remember to begin and end your sentences correctly.

D. Divide this group of words into four complete sentences. Begin and end each sentence correctly.

Bob's book is dirty he dropped it in the lane maybe he can wipe it clean he will be more careful after this

E. Write the definition of a sentence.

---

4. Finding the Simple Predicate

Every sentence has a subject and a predicate. The **complete subject** contains all the words that tell **who** or **what.** The **complete predicate** contains all the words that tell what the subject **does** or **is.**

In the following sentences, the complete predicate is in bold print.

A rabbit | **raced across the yard.**
His home | **is in the meadow.**

The complete predicate usually has one main word that tells about the subject. This word is a verb, and it is called the **simple predicate** of the sentence. In the following sentences, each simple predicate is underlined twice.

> The men | <u>worked</u> busily.
>
> These dogs | <u>are</u> collies.
>
> Marie | <u>has</u> a new dress.

To find the simple predicate, look for the verb in the sentence. Most verbs are words that show action.

| jump | run | play | sing | think |
| read | smile | cry | look | talk |

Remember: The predicate of a sentence tells what the subject **does** or **is.**

 Oral Drill

Tell where to divide each sentence between its subject and predicate.

1. Seventy large geese flew overhead.
2. My mother sang very softly.
3. The old barn burned.
4. John hurried to the house.
5. My cousin came yesterday.
6. My brother studies very hard.
7. The serpent tempted Eve.
8. Eve took the fruit.
9. Her husband ate some fruit.
10. Adam accused Eve.
11. She blamed the serpent.
12. God punished them all.

> **Written Practice** >

A. Copy each complete predicate in Oral Drill. Draw two lines under each simple predicate.

B. Write three short sentences about things you did during summer vacation. Draw two lines under each simple predicate.

> **Challenge Exercise** >

Copy each simple subject and simple predicate, and draw a line between them. Underline the simple subject once and the simple predicate twice.

> **Example:** God sent the Saviour into the world.
> **Answer:**   <u>God</u> | <u>sent</u>

1. My little dog knows my voice.
2. The old yellow cat has hidden her kittens in a barrel.
3. The Allegheny National Forest is in western Pennsylvania.

---

5. Verb Phrases

The simple predicate of a sentence may be more than just one verb. It may be a **verb phrase.** These sentences have verb phrases.

> Rain | **was falling** yesterday.
> Elmer | **has pulled** weeds all morning.

Every verb phrase has a main verb and at least one **helping verb.** In these verb phrases, the helping verbs are in bold print.

is going	**have** caught
has been singing	**had been** lost

The main verb is always the last word in the verb phrase.

Some of the most common helping verbs are **have, has, had,** and forms of **be.** All the forms of **be** are listed here.

am, is, are, was, were, be, been, being

Be careful! A form of **be** is a helping verb only when it is used with another verb. When it stands alone, it is the main verb.

Helping verb: The Lord **is coming** soon.
Main verb: The Lord **is** my shepherd.

Remember: A simple predicate may be more than one verb. It may be a verb phrase with helping verbs.

Memorize these helping verbs: **have, has, had, am, is, are, was, were, be, been, being.**

 Oral Drill

A. Give the main verb in each verb phrase.

1. was running	5. have been seen
2. had been helping	6. has done
3. am writing	7. were singing
4. have gone	8. is leaving

B. Read the ~~simple~~ *complete* predicate of each sentence. Then read
the simple predicate. Be sure to find the whole verb
phrase.

1. Jane is going to the store.
2. Loren has visited his grandmother.
3. A strong wind was blowing today.
4. Those dogs have been chasing our car.
5. The boys are riding their bicycles.
6. We have seen her picture.
7. The rain has been pouring down today.
8. John was feeling sick.
9. We had been cleaning all day.
10. Those flowers were found in my garden.

> Written Practice >

Copy each sentence, and draw a line between the subject
and predicate. Underline each simple predicate twice. Be
sure to find the whole verb when there is a verb phrase.

Example: My brother | <u>is feeling</u> better today.

1. The girls played church.
2. First grade is going outside for recess.
3. Jerry cleaned the shop.
4. Ruth finished her work.
5. Peanuts are raised in the South.
6. Dorcas has eaten her lunch.
7. The twins are folding the clothes.
8. The boys are flying their kites.
9. We have done our best work.
10. Peas are growing in Mother's garden.
11. Mother has planted corn too.
12. We have been eating strawberries.

> Review and Practice >

A. Copy the form of **be** that you find in each sentence. Write **main** or **helping** to tell how it is used.

1. John's home is in Switzerland.
2. Mary was helping Mother in the garden.
3. The cows were in the meadow.
4. Most Swiss cows are dairy cattle.
5. The family has been working in the field.
6. They were making hay for the cows.
7. One morning snow was on the ground.
8. The children were skiing to school.

Corel

B. Fill in the blanks. See the "Remember" boxes in all the lessons you have studied so far.

1. A sentence is a group of words that express a ——— thought.
2. Every sentence has a ——— and a ———.
3. The predicate of a sentence tells what the subject ——— or ———.
4. The simple predicate of a sentence may be more than just one ———. It may be a verb ———.

A Wise Old Owl
A wise old owl
    lived in an oak;
The more he saw,
    the less he spoke;
The less he spoke,
    the more he heard.
Why can't we all
    be like that bird?
—*Edward Hersey Richards*

6. Learning to Observe and Listen

We have two ears and two eyes, but only one mouth. So we should hear and see twice as much as we say. We need to observe and listen carefully if we are going to write well. But sometimes it seems our eyes are closed and our ears are turned off when we should be seeing and listening!

With our eyes we can learn about the color, size, shape, and action of things all around us. If we simply take time to observe, we will notice many interesting things that we would miss otherwise.

The Bible says, "Be swift to hear, slow to speak" (James 1:19). Be an interested listener. Notice the things others say. Be a kind and courteous listener. Listen to others in the same way you want them to listen to you.

Be a careful listener. Listen to every word, and do not add your imagination to it. Also listen to the beautiful sounds God has put in nature for us to enjoy. Do not be a forgetful listener. The Bible says that a forgetful listener is one who does not do the good things he has heard.

Jesus pronounced a blessing on those who see with their eyes and hear with their ears (Matthew 13:16). Let us use our eyes and ears to learn more about the wonderful things God has for us to know.

> **Remember:** To be a good writer, you must be a good observer and a good listener.

A. Name some sounds you might hear on a summer night.

B. Describe your house or school building. Tell what it looks like.

C. Give the words that belong in these blanks.
1. In order to be a good writer, you need to be "swift to ———" and "slow to ———" (James 1:19).
2. You will not be a good writer if you are like this verse says: "Their ——— are dull of hearing, and their ——— they have closed" (Matthew 13:15).

> Written Practice

A. Write an interesting paragraph about something you can see. It may be an animal at home or something in nature, such as a flower. Observe the object closely, and write a good description. You may use an encyclopedia or other reference book for ideas, but write only about things you can see. Here are some suggestions.

1. My Pet Dog
2. Our New Calf
3. Our Horse
4. A Daffodil
5. Mother's Ferns
6. A Blade of Grass

B. Ask an older person to tell you about something that happened long ago. Listen carefully, and ask polite questions. Then write a story about what you heard. Be ready to read it in class.

7. Finding the Simple Subject

The **complete subject** of a sentence contains all the words that tell who or what does or is something. In the following sentence, the complete subject is in bold print.

My little yellow kittens | are growing fast.

The complete subject has one main word that tells who or what does or is something. This word is usually a noun, and it is called the **simple subject** of the sentence. In the following sentences, each simple subject is underlined.

    1. **A small happy <u>boy</u>** | sat on the bank.
    2. **Four speckled <u>fish</u>** | swam in the pond.

To find the simple subject, first find the simple predicate (the verb). Then ask **who** or **what** about the verb. Say those words together to be sure they make sense. Notice how this is done for the two sentences above.

    Sentence 1: The simple predicate is **sat.**
                What sat? A boy.
                Boy sat makes sense.
                The simple subject is **boy.**

    Sentence 2: The simple predicate is **swam.**
                What swam? Fish.
                Fish swam makes sense.
                The simple subject is **fish.**

Be careful! Not every noun in a sentence is the simple subject. The simple subject is only the noun that tells who or what does or is something.

    A cat caught the mouse.
        Both **cat** and **mouse** are nouns. Which is the simple
            subject?
        The verb is **caught.** What caught?
        A cat caught.
        Cat caught makes sense.
        The simple subject is **cat,** not **mouse.**

> **Remember:** The subject of a sentence tells who or what does or is something. To find the simple subject, first find the simple predicate (the verb). Then ask **who** or **what** about it. Say those words together to be sure they make sense.

> Oral Drill >

Tell where to divide each sentence between the complete subject and the complete predicate. Then say the simple subject and the simple predicate together.

1. The other mower works better.
2. Charles is coming soon.
3. The fleecy clouds raced across the sky.
4. A red leaf fluttered to the ground.
5. The large goose hissed angrily.
6. The frightened sheep huddled in the corner.
7. The brown corn rustled in the wind.
8. The chubby puppy ran away fast.
9. The six young geese flew away today.
10. The five young children sang.
11. The people praised the Lord.
12. The chicken's first egg was laid.
13. The rooster crows every morning.
14. The fox was stealing hens.
15. Several big fat hens were eaten.

> Written Practice >

A. Copy these sentences, and draw a line between the complete subject and the complete predicate of each. Underline the simple subject once and the simple predicate twice. Watch for verb phrases in the predicate. Check your work by reading each simple subject and simple predicate together to be sure they make sense.

>   **Example:** One little <u>girl</u> | <u>was holding</u> a doll.
>   **Check:**   girl was holding

1. Mary has come early.
2. John had been working yesterday.
3. Ten white mice scampered around.
4. This park is beautiful.
5. The five workmen are eating lunch.
6. Joan is coming back.
7. The old shed was burning fast.
8. The students are singing heartily today.
9. God created the heaven and the earth.
10. Creation praises God.
11. The pink rose is blooming now.
12. The roses smell wonderful.

B. Write the eleven helping verbs that you have memorized.

C. Write three sentences of your own, telling about some things you might see or hear in the woods. Draw one line under the simple subject in each sentence.

>   **Examples:** Tall green <u>trees</u> grow in the woods.
>   The <u>leaves</u> rustled in the wind.

8. Pronouns and Noun Phrases

You have learned that the simple subject is usually a noun. It may also be a **pronoun.** Here are some sentences with pronoun subjects.

We are drawing animals.
She has the answer.

Do you remember which pronouns may be used as subjects? They are listed here.

I, you, he, she, it, we, they

The simple subject may also be a **noun phrase.** A noun phrase is more than one word that names something. Usually all the words of a noun phrase are capitalized, as in the following examples.

Brother Frank Miller
Mount Rushmore
Thanksgiving Day

Here are some examples of noun phrases used as simple subjects.

Charles Baker | lives here.
North Carolina | is a state.

Remember that you find the simple subject by first finding the simple predicate. Then ask **who** or **what** about it. Say those words together to be sure they make sense.

Give the simple subject of each sentence. You will find pronouns and noun phrases.

1. The famous Grand Canyon is in Arizona.
2. Old Faithful is a geyser in Wyoming.
3. Donald Miller was here last night.
4. Jerry Martin came with him.
5. The snow-capped Mount McKinley is the highest mountain in North America.
6. She went to church.
7. Mrs. Wilmer Lapp came to bring lunch.
8. Sister Phoebe Martin has taught school.
9. They were walking behind us.
10. Doctor Luis Miller has moved.
11. Simon Peter was a disciple of Jesus.
12. Yellowstone National Park is a lovely place to visit.
13. The tall Mount Kenya is in Africa.
14. I am coming soon.

> Written Practice >

A. Copy each sentence from Oral Drill, and draw a line between the complete subject and the complete predicate. Underline the simple subject once and the simple predicate twice.

Example: <u>Mount Mitchell</u> | <u><u>is</u></u> in North Carolina.

B. Write sentences using these subjects.
1. Rocky Mountains   3. Miss Marilyn Foster
2. Brother John   4. Sister Carolyn

C. Write two sentences using pronoun subjects.

> Review and Practice >

A. Write **yes** for each group of words that is a sentence.
Write **no** for each group that is not a sentence.
1. Many years ago.
2. The earth is round.
3. Long ago many people
   thought the earth was flat.
4. Like a sphere.
5. A sphere is a ball.
6. The earth is a sphere.
7. God made the earth.
8. Live on it.
9. Beautifully made.
10. God made it beautiful.

Corel

B. Write words to fill in the blanks. See the "Remember"
boxes if you need help.
1. The subject of the sentence tells —— or —— the
   sentence is about.
2. The predicate of a sentence tells what the subject
   —— or ——.
3. The simple predicate may be a verb or a —— ——.
4. A sentence is a group of words that express a ——
   ——.

9. Diagraming Sentence Skeletons

The simple subject and the simple predicate together make up the **skeleton** of a sentence. In the following sentences, the skeletons are in bold print.

My **cat** | **hunts** quietly.
The little **bird** | **sings** merrily.

A sentence diagram shows how the words in a sentence work together. To diagram a sentence, begin with a base line divided into two parts, like this.

Find the simple predicate, and write it on the right half of the line. Then find the simple subject, and write it on the left half. Later you will learn how to diagram the other words in the sentence.

cat | hunts   bird | sings

Remember the three steps for finding the simple subject of a sentence. First find the simple predicate. Then ask **who** or **what** about it. Say the simple subject and the simple predicate together to be sure they make sense.

Remember: The simple subject and the simple predicate of a sentence make up the sentence skeleton.

> Oral Drill >

Say the skeleton of each sentence. Diagram the skeletons at the chalkboard.

1. Martha was helping her brother.
2. The last box was very heavy.
3. Lester Campbell is coming soon.
4. The basket was filled quickly.
5. Governor Smith is visiting the school.
6. My purse has been stolen.
7. The large Lake Huron is one of the Great Lakes.
8. My red notebook has disappeared.
9. The Mississippi River winds south a long way.
10. The Pamir Mountains have been called the "Roof of the World."

> Written Practice >

Diagram the skeleton of each sentence.

1. Fanny Crosby was born on March 24, 1820.
2. Many sad things happened.
3. She caught a bad cold.
4. It affected her eyes.
5. Then the doctor made a mistake.
6. He prescribed the wrong treatment for her eyes.

7. Soon little Fanny was completely blind.
8. She learned contentment.
9. Fanny Crosby wrote many hymns.
10. We sing many of her hymns.
11. William Doane wrote many tunes for Fanny.

> Review and Practice >

A. Write **yes** or **no** to tell whether each group of words is a complete sentence.

1. God gave us water, soil, and plants.
2. Water is one of the most important natural resources.
3. Animals and plants.
4. Need water.
5. Most plants do not grow well in a desert.
6. Ocean water is salty.
7. It is not good to drink.
8. Cannot use salt water.
9. God sends the rain that fills the wells.
10. Good wells have fresh water.

B. Use these words as simple subjects in sentences of your own.

1. father   3. apple   5. answer
2. mountain   4. friends

C. Divide these words into proper sentences.

I see a bird it is blue and white I can hear it too it must be a blue jay

Let all things be done decently & in order.

10. Compound Subjects and Predicates

Sometimes two sentences have the same predicate but different subjects. In such cases, the two sentences can be combined into one by using **and** to join the subjects. The new sentence has a **compound subject.** Notice how this is done in the following sentences.

> Ducks | are flying.
> Geese | are flying.
> Ducks **and** geese | are flying.

Two sentences with the same subject but different predicates can also be joined. The new sentence has a **compound predicate.**

> I | saw the paper.
> I | picked it up.
>
> I | saw the paper **and** picked it up.

Some sentences have both a compound subject and a compound predicate.

> Rabbits **and** birds | came **and** ate the beans.

Remember: A sentence can have a compound subject or a compound predicate. The compound parts are joined by **and.**

 Oral Drill

Join each pair of sentences into one sentence as shown in the lesson. Tell whether your sentence has a **compound subject** or a **compound predicate.**

1. Dogs hunt for food.
   Cats hunt for food.

2. The people sang at church.
   The people prayed at church.

3. Father heard us.
   Father came quickly.

4. The boys are leaving.
   The girls are leaving.

> Written Practice

A. Join each pair of sentences into one sentence with a compound subject or a compound predicate.

1. The students work hard.
   The teachers work hard.

2. Gerbils are good pets.
   Hamsters are good pets.

3. Plants were created by God.
   Animals were created by God.

4. The calf kicked.
   The calf ran.

5. John shouted.
   John ran to the house.

6. The whole family came.
   The whole family helped
      to catch the calf.

7. Uncle Ralph came for a visit.
   Aunt Elizabeth came for a visit.

8. The teacher found the key.
   The teacher opened the door.

9. The fierce wind flattened the wheat.
   The fierce wind blew down the cornstalks.

10. Oranges are good for you.
    Apples are good for you.

B. In each sentence you wrote for Part A, draw a dividing line between the complete subject and the complete predicate. Underline the simple subjects with one line and the simple predicates with two lines.

C. Join these four sentences into one sentence with a compound subject and a compound predicate. Draw a line to divide between the complete subject and the complete predicate. Underline the simple subjects once and the simple predicates twice.

Adam heard God's voice.
Adam hid among the trees.

Eve heard God's voice.
Eve hid among the trees.

> Review and Practice.

Divide the following groups of words into proper sentences.

1. Alan is my neighbor he is visiting today we have some work to do then we can play together

2. Today is Monday we have an English lesson the class will start soon I am ready we all enjoy English when we work hard

11. Diagraming Compound Subjects and Predicates

If a sentence has a compound subject or a compound predicate, the skeleton is put on a diagram that has a fork. Each subject or predicate is put on a separate line, as shown below. Also notice where **and** belongs on the diagram.

Betty and Sarah are working today.

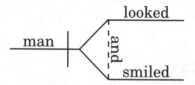

The old man looked at us and smiled.

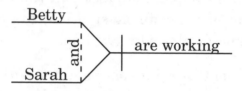

If the sentence has both a compound subject and a compound predicate, a fork is placed at each end of the base line.

Mother and Jane swept and mopped the floor.

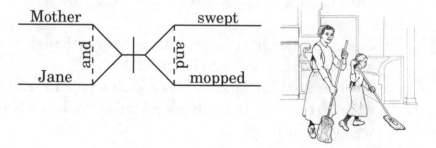

Diagram the skeletons of these sentences at the chalkboard. Include the word **and** on your diagram.

1. Amos peeled the apple and ate it.
2. The cat and the dog are sitting on the porch.
3. The boy and his sister stayed with us.
4. Mary and Nancy washed and ironed the clothes.
5. The deer saw us and sped swiftly away.
6. Peaches and plums are very sweet.
7. James and John went to the store and bought some bread.

> **Written Practice**

A. Write whether each sentence has a **compound subject,** a **compound predicate,** or **both.**

1. Esau sold his birthright and disobeyed God.
2. Jacob and Rebekah deceived Isaac.
3. Later Esau and Jacob were friends again.
4. The boy and his spotted puppy romped and played.
5. Alice held her doll and played with the kittens.

B. Diagram the skeleton of each sentence. If a sentence has a compound subject or predicate, include the word **and** on your diagram.

Example: Two ducks and five geese flew to the pond.
Answer:

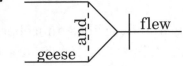

1. A beautiful green plant was growing there.
2. Mother worked in the garden yesterday.
3. The tiny baby coughed and sneezed.
4. Some plants grow in a dry desert.
5. Three lizards scurried under a rock.
6. Nancy and Edith drew pretty pictures.
7. The sparrows and swallows sang and flew.
8. Brother John and Sister Mary are coming soon.
9. The dogs barked noisily and jumped around.
10. Mount Tabor and Mount Carmel are in Palestine.
11. The horses and donkeys turned and ran.
12. The little birds are eating seeds.

---

12. The Paragraph

A paragraph is a group of sentences that develop a single topic. The first sentence usually tells what the paragraph is about. It is the **topic sentence.** The other sentences add more information about the topic. A sentence that tells about a different topic must be left out or used in another paragraph.

A paragraph has a certain form. The first line is always **indented,** or set in from the left margin. The sentences come one after another, filling up each line. The left margin is kept perfectly straight, and the right margin is kept as straight as possible.

The following paragraph describes an iceberg. The topic sentence is underlined. Three sentences are crossed out because they do not belong.

Icebergs

Icebergs are both beautiful and frightening. Some people have called them shining palaces. At sunrise or sunset, they may glow with many beautiful colors, such as orange, pink, or red. ~~My favorite color is pink. I especially like pink flowers.~~ At night, icebergs may appear deep blue or purple. Some are so large that even the largest ships look small beside them. ~~Once I saw a large ocean freighter.~~ Icebergs are also dangerous. Only a small part of an iceberg shows above the water. Ships may hit the huge part hidden beneath the water.

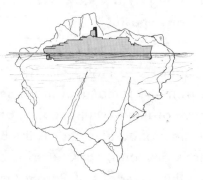

Writing paragraphs will help you in many ways. In English class, you will write paragraphs when you write letters, stories, and reports. In reading, history, or science class, you will sometimes write a paragraph to answer a question. So you should learn to write good paragraphs.

> **Remember:** A paragraph is a group of sentences that develop a single topic. The topic sentence tells what the paragraph is about. A paragraph must tell about one topic only.

> Oral Drill >

For each of the following paragraphs, tell which is the topic sentence. Tell which sentences do not belong.

Wasps

The next time you see a wasp, do not run. Go close to her, moving very slowly. See how neat she is, how shiny and clean. She looks as if she had been newly polished with wax. We use wax on our floors. A bush with sweet flowers, a grapevine with ripe grapes, or a fruit tree with fallen fruit is a good place to see wasps. Once I got stung by a yellow jacket. I got too close to the round paper nest!

Coral Islands

Some islands are made mostly of coral, which is limestone from the remains of many small sea animals. You can buy coral in beautiful colors of orange, blue, or pink. One chain of coral islands is the Bahamas. Most of these islands are long, narrow strips of limestone covered with a thin layer of soil. Porous limestone rocks are found all over the Bahamas. The islands are beautiful, but not much of the land on them is good for farming. My friend once visited the Bahamas.

> Written Practice >

A. Write the definition of a paragraph.

B. Write the following sentences in paragraph form. Underline the topic sentence. Begin and end each sentence correctly.

   Check your paragraph to see that the first sentence is indented. Be sure that the left margin is straight and the right margin is as straight as possible.

   1. The people in Peru raise and sell potatoes of many different colors.
   2. They are pink, yellow, or purple.
   3. Some of the potatoes are dried and frozen until they look and feel like wood.
   4. These potatoes, called **chuño,** are the main food of Indians in Peru.

C. The following paragraph does not have proper paragraph form. Write it correctly.

   Mushrooms are plants, but they are different from most other plants. Mushrooms are not green. They do not have leaves, flowers, or fruit. Some mushrooms are good to eat, but some are very poisonous.

13. Speaking Clearly

Spoken English is called **oral English.** Because we often need to speak, we must follow the rules for good oral English. But perhaps we talk so naturally that we do not think there are any rules! Nevertheless, we can all improve our oral English by learning how to speak properly, clearly, and pleasantly.

You cannot form speech sounds without moving your face, especially your mouth. Do not have a wooden mouth! Use your tongue, lips, teeth, throat, and nose to make the correct sounds. Do not become careless and leave out certain sounds or replace them with incorrect sounds. Say **speak** (not **spea**) and **fleet** (not **flee**). Pronounce **ing** at the end of words. Do not say **singin** for **singing.** Do not jam words together. Speak distinctly, separating your words.

Always speak loudly enough to be heard. Remember that when you speak to a group, you must speak louder than when you speak to just one person.

Remember: Be courteous and speak clearly.

> Oral Drill

These sentences have words and phrases that are often pronounced lazily. Read each sentence correctly three times.

1. It was kinda warm outside.
2. Wen will you be there?
3. I wish we woulda come sooner.
4. Do we hafta do all the problems?

5. Please gimme some paper.
6. Jacob's pilla was hard!
7. We were singin hymns on Sunday evening.
8. Are you gonna be there?
9. Grandpa is comin for a visit.
10. Father brought some tools with im.
11. I wonder if I kin help.
12. Do you wanna drink?
13. Don lef his books at home.
14. He shoulda been more careful.
15. Is that box fer us?
16. You coulda had a bad accident.
17. We were thinkin about you.
18. Why dontcha ask yer mother?
19. Achan didn't think he'd git caught.
20. That tree is a weepin willa.

Written Practice

A. In each pair, copy the word or phrase that shows correct pronunciation.

1. gonna   going to
2. kinda   kind of
3. find it   find ut
4. try to   try ta
5. wanna   want to
6. give me   gimme
7. yella   yellow
8. Come here.   Come ere.
9. coulda   could have
10. get   git
11. learnin   learning

12. sof   soft
13. when   wen
14. pitchure   picture
15. can't you   cantcha
16. fer me   for me
17. should have shoulda

B. These sentences have words and phrases that show lazy pronunciation. Write each sentence correctly.
   1. Be sure to folla directions.
   2. Where are we goin?
   3. Lookut that huge elephant!
   4. Long ago miners useta dig coal by hand.
   5. That musta been hard work.

C. Find a poem or short story that you like. After your teacher approves it, practice reading it clearly and distinctly. Be ready to read to the class.

---

14. Chapter 1 Review

> Oral Drill >

A. Use these groups of words to answer the following questions.
   a. The children are picking berries.
   b. Frank and his sister are absent today.
   c. They are sick with the flu.
   d. From the top of the hill.
   e. Three bottles fell and broke on the floor.

1. Which is not a complete sentence?
2. Which has a compound subject?
3. Which has a compound predicate?
4. Which has a verb phrase?
5. Which has a pronoun subject?
6. What are the skeletons of **a** and **c**?

B. Combine these sentences by forming compound subjects or predicates.
   1. The boys raked leaves.
      The boys burned the leaves.
   2. Carol arrived late again.
      Her brother arrived late again.
   3. Boys need good food.
      Girls need good food.

C. Tell whether each group of words is a **subject,** a **predicate,** or a **complete sentence.** Add what is needed to make complete sentences of those that are not complete.
   1. Baked cookies today.
   2. We came in and sat down.
   3. They helped us.
   4. Flies and mosquitoes.
   5. Fell down in the snow.
   6. He forgot again.
   7. The little striped kitten.
   8. Opened the gate.

D. Tell whether each sentence is **true** or **false.**
   1. The topic sentence tells what a paragraph is about.
   2. Each sentence in a paragraph should begin on a new line.
   3. Spoken English is called oral English.

4. Your tongue, lips, and teeth are the only parts you use when you speak.
5. It is all right to leave out the unimportant sounds when you speak.

> Written Practice >

A. Write the correct words to fill the blanks.
   1. Every sentence expresses a ——— thought.
   2. Every sentence begins with a ——— letter and ends with a ——— or other punctuation mark.
   3. A pair of words like **is going** or **has seen** is a ——— ———.
   4. A pair of words like **Robert Morris** or **Mount Moriah** is a ——— ———.
   5. The sentence skeleton includes the ——— ——— and the ——— ———.
   6. In order to write well, you must ——— with your eyes and ——— with your ears.

B. Copy the number of each subject, and beside it write the letter of the matching predicate.
   1. A big shaggy dog   a. is our teacher.
   2. Gwen's brother   b. shows a fall scene.
   3. This large picture   c. had bright stars.
   4. The dark, clear sky   d. has a crack in it.
   5. One of these jars   e. was barking loudly.

C. Read each group of words. Write **C** if it is a complete sentence, **S** if it is a subject, and **P** if it is a predicate.
   1. The small white flowers.
   2. Was helping Eli.
   3. Chewinks are birds.

4. Heard one yesterday.
5. Larry's shoes.
6. I caught the mouse.

D. Join each pair into a sentence with a compound subject or predicate. Underline the simple subjects once and the simple predicates twice. Draw a dividing line between the complete subject and the complete predicate.
   1. Jesus sat down.
      Jesus taught the people.
   2. The fruits are fresh.
      The vegetables are fresh.
   3. He builds doghouses.
      He sells them nearby.

E. Diagram the skeletons of these sentences.
   1. Mother made some cookies.
   2. Carol bought a gift and wrapped it carefully.
   3. The men and women sang and prayed.
   4. The moon and stars were shining brightly.
   5. Daniel and John sawed and hammered in the shop.

F. Choose and write the correct words for these sentences.
   1. A paragraph is a group of sentences that develop (one topic, several topics).
   2. (Indent, Underline) the first line of a paragraph.
   3. The left (line, margin) of a paragraph should be straight, and the right one as straight as possible.
   4. You must move your (hands, mouth) in order to speak clearly.
   5. You should speak (loudly, quickly) enough to be heard.

Building Sentences

The task of building sentences
Brings glory to the Lord,
If we will build our sentences
According to His Word;
This task is given to the folks
Who will to do the right,
Who persevere to please the Lord
And find it their delight.

The task of building sentences
That make good common sense,
Expressing clearly what we mean
And causing no offense,
Is needful preparation now
To later on explain
The blessed Word to other folks
In sentences quite plain.

The task of building sentences,
Perplexing may appear,
But step by step with diligence
The puzzles disappear;
And as we learn to build with cheer,
With patience and great care,
The Lord will bless our life and work
With blessings rich to share.

Chapter 2

Kinds of Sentences

Statement:	A bright rainbow appeared in the sky.
Question:	Did you see the pretty rainbow?
Command:	Look at the lovely rainbow.
Exclamation:	How beautiful the rainbow is!

15. Sentence Fragments and Run-on Sentences

A sentence must express a complete thought. **All gone** is not a sentence because it does not make sense by itself. Such a group of words is a **sentence fragment.**

A sentence fragment may be missing a subject. **Sent the rain** is not a sentence because it has no subject. It does not say **who** or **what** sent the rain.

A sentence fragment may be missing a predicate. **Our heavenly Father** is not a sentence because it has no predicate. It does not say what our Father does or is.

A fragment may have neither a subject nor a predicate. It may be only a phrase. **In the rain** is not a sentence. It does not say who or what is being talked about, nor does it say that anything happened.

Two sentences written incorrectly as one sentence make a **run-on sentence.** Look at this group of words.

God is good to all good gifts come from Him.

This run-on sentence can be written correctly by dividing it into two sentences. A period and a capital letter must be added.

God is good to all. Good gifts come from Him.

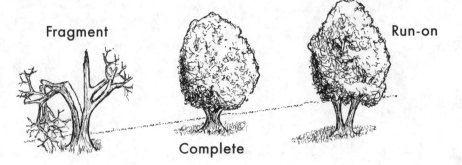

Fragment

Complete

Run-on

Study these run-on sentences and their corrections.

Run-on: It is not late we still have time.
Correct: It is not late. We still have time.

Run-on: Our cat is clever, she catches many mice.
Correct: Our cat is clever. She catches many mice.

Run-on: Jerry washes the dishes Ann dries them.
Correct: Jerry washes the dishes. Ann dries them.

A sentence must begin with a capital letter and end with a punctuation mark. The end punctuation is usually a period, but it may also be a question mark or an exclamation mark.

Remember: A sentence must express one complete thought. A sentence must begin with a capital letter and end with correct punctuation.

 **Oral Drill**

A. Tell which are sentences, which are sentence fragments, and which are run-on sentences.
1. Has taken the wrong coat.
2. The other rake is newer.
3. Martha made some cookies, you may have a few.
4. I found the book.
5. Playing in the lane.
6. My brother has a tent I can borrow it.

B. Make complete sentences from the sentence fragments in Part A.

C. Tell how to correct the run-on sentences in Part A.

Written Practice

A. Read these groups of words. Write **S** for each sentence and **F** for each fragment.
   1. The tall green tree behind the barn.
   2. Cypress trees grow in wet places.
   3. Grow in swamps.
   4. Are beautiful and useful.

B. Write **S** for each sentence, **F** for each sentence fragment, and **RO** for each run-on sentence.
   1. The rain fell.
   2. We didn't mind the rain it wasn't cold.
   3. Thankful for the rain.
   4. We are late, the moon is rising.
   5. At nine o'clock.
   6. We will go home the children will go to bed.

C. Correct each run-on sentence by writing it as two separate sentences. Use proper capitalization and punctuation.
   1. I was with Moses, I will be with you.
   2. The priests carried the ark they went first.
   3. The soles of the priests' feet touched the water, it parted and stood in a heap.
   4. The priests stood in the Jordan the people passed over on dry ground.
   5. Twelve men gathered stones to make a heap, these stones were piled up at Gilgal.
   6. The stones were for a memorial they would help the Israelites remember that great day.

> Review and Practice >

Diagram the sentence skeletons.
1. The strawberries have grown well.
2. May and John were picking strawberries.
3. Ellen and Mary hulled and washed them.
4. Baby Julia was eating strawberries.

---

16. Statements: Sentences That Give Information

A sentence that gives information is a **statement.** A statement is a telling sentence. It states a fact. It does not ask a question but rather gives information.

> I have kept the faith.
> Have I kept the faith?

The first sentence is a telling sentence or statement. It tells something. The second sentence is not a statement. It does not give a fact. Instead it asks a question.

Sentence fragments are not statements. They do not give facts in complete thoughts. Telling sentences must state facts in complete thoughts.

> Keeping the faith.

This is a fragment. It is not a statement. It does not state a complete thought. A statement must express a complete thought.

A statement must begin with a capital letter and end with a period. Study these examples of statements.

God is always faithful.
He keeps His promises.
In my Father's house are many mansions.
The heavens declare the glory of God.

Remember: A sentence that gives information is a statement. A statement begins with a capital letter and ends with a period.

Oral Drill

A. Say **yes** or **no** to tell whether each group of words is a statement.
1. Living in Jerusalem.
2. Which book shall we read first?
3 English is Jane's favorite subject.
4. Have never seen the ocean.

B. On the chalkboard, diagram the skeleton of each word group that is a statement.
1. Shirley is going to Guatemala.
2. Will see many new things.
3. Do you enjoy watching wild animals?
4. The platypus lives in Australia.

> Written Practice >

A. Read each group of words. Write **S** if it is a statement, and **N** if it is not a statement.

1. Noah and his sons built an ark.
2. God sent a great flood.
3. Covered the whole earth.
4. Did Noah's family enter the ark?
5. Who shut the door?
6. Rained and rained.
7. For forty days.
8. God took care of Noah's family.
9. The water began to go down.
10. The ark rested on Mount Ararat.
11. Noah offered a sacrifice to God.
12. A rainbow in the sky.

B. Diagram the skeleton of each statement. Do not diagram sentence fragments or questions.

Example: The flood covered the whole earth.

Answer: flood | covered

1. The great rainstorm lasted for forty days.
2. The huge ark held all the animals.
3. Did Noah feed the animals?
4. Hibernating in the winter.
5. The wicked people sinned against God.
6. God destroyed them with a flood.
7. Noah preached faithfully.

C. Write three statements of your own, telling about things you might see at a zoo.

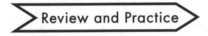

Review and Practice

Read these groups of words. Write **S** for each sentence, **F** for each sentence fragment, and **RO** for each run-on sentence.

1. A big black bear.
2. She has a cub it is playful.
3. Jesus wept.
4. Loves me.
5. God is love.

---

17. Diagraming Statements

A diagram shows the different parts of a certain thing and how they fit together. Here is a diagram showing the different parts of a flower.

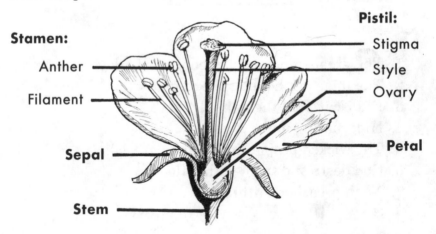

In the same way, the diagram of a statement shows its different parts and how they fit together. To diagram a statement, first find the simple predicate. Then ask **who** or **what** about the simple predicate. The noun that answers this question is the simple subject. Say the simple subject and the simple predicate together to be sure they make sense.

The simple subject and the simple predicate together form the skeleton, and they are the first words to write on a sentence diagram. Write the simple subject on the left half of the sentence diagram, and the simple predicate on the right half.

Mother was baking a cake for the neighbors.

Mother	was baking

When you are finding the simple predicate, look for a word that shows action or being. Remember to watch for verb phrases, and put the whole phrase on your diagram. Here are some examples.

are working   have been going

In verb phrases, the helping verbs usually are **have, has had,** or some form of **be.** The eight forms of **be** are listed here.

am, is are, was, were, be, been, being

Remember that in some sentences forms of **have** and **be** may be used as main verbs rather than helping verbs.

When you are finding the simple subject, watch for noun phrases. Here are some examples.

Brother John Martin   Sister Sylvia

The subject pronouns are **I, you, he, she, it, we,** and **they.** These pronouns can be simple subjects in sentences.

> Oral Drill

A. Diagram the skeletons of these sentences at the board.
   1. A platypus has a leathery bill.
   2. They had been there.
   3. Uncle John is coming tomorrow.
   4. We have had much rain.

B. Diagram the skeletons of the statements. Do not diagram the fragments, run-on sentences, or questions.
   1. Augustus Caesar was the emperor.
   2. On which day was Jesus born?
   3. We do not know, the Bible does not say.
   4. A platypus lays eggs.
   5. A big orange balloon.

> Written Practice

A. Diagram the skeletons of these statements.

Examples: a. Joshua led the children of Israel.

b. Jericho was a wicked city.

Answers: a. <u>Joshua</u> | <u>led</u>

b. <u>Jericho</u> | <u>was</u>

1. The Israelites walked around Jericho seven times.
2. They obeyed the Lord.
3. They went around the city for six days.
4. They had been walking quietly.
5. Then the people shouted loudly.
6. The priests blew trumpets.
7. The walls fell down flat.
8. Rahab was saved.

B. Diagram the skeletons of the statements. Do not diagram the fragments, run-on sentences, or questions.
   1. At the edge of the dark stream.
   2. A raccoon was washing its food.
   3. Raccoons wash their food by instinct.
   4. Noah was a righteous man.
   5. He preached faithfully, the people did not listen.
   6. What did the people do?
   7. Kept on sinning.
   8. Rain fell for forty days and nights.
   9. The ark rested on Mount Ararat, it may still be there.
   10. Eight people were saved.

> Review and Practice >

Write a statement of your own to answer each question.
1. What time did you get up?
2. How many boxes of berries did you pick?
3. Can you pick four boxes in one hour?
4. What treat will Mother make for supper?

18. Questions: Sentences That Ask for Information

A sentence that asks something is a **question.** A question is a sentence that needs an answer. It asks for information.

Every question must begin with a capital letter and end with a question mark.

There are different kinds of asking sentences. Some questions can be answered with **yes** or **no.**

> Does air have weight?
> (**Yes,** air has weight.)
>
> Are all mushrooms good to eat?
> (**No,** not all mushrooms are good to eat.)

Some questions begin with words such as **who, whose, whom, what, which, when, where,** or **why.** They may be called **wh** questions.

> **Wh**ere is the new book?
> **Wh**at new mercies of the Lord have you seen today?

Remember: A sentence that asks for information is a question. A question begins with a capital letter and ends with a question mark (?).

> Oral Drill

Tell whether each group of words is a **question** or a **statement.** Tell what end punctuation each should have.

1. What is a fossil
2. Fossils are prints left in stone
3. How were fossils formed
4. Were they formed in the Genesis flood
5. That could well be so

> Written Practice >

A. For each sentence, write **Q** if it is a question and **S** if it is a statement. Also write the correct end punctuation that each sentence needs.

    Examples: a. God sent a flood upon the earth
               b. Was God punishing the wicked people
    Answers: a. S .
               b. Q ?

1. Did you know that fossils have been found on top of mountains
2. Fossils of fish and other sea animals have been found there
3. How did they get there
4. The great flood may have put them there
5. Many animals died suddenly
6. They were buried beneath rocks and mud
7. They had no time to decay
8. Predators had no time to eat them
9. What are predators

B. Write three questions that you might ask an older person about long-ago days.

>Review and Practice>

A. Reach each group of words. Write **F** if it is a sentence fragment, **RO** if it is a run-on sentence, **S** if it is a statement, and **Q** if it is a question.

   1. Were Jacob and Esau twin brothers

   2. Were twin brothers

   3. Isaac was their father

   4. Rebekah loved Jacob Isaac loved Esau

   5. Esau was a hunter, Jacob worked in the tent

   6. What did Esau make that
      Isaac liked

   7. Isaac was getting old he
      could not see

   8. Rebekah and Jacob
      deceived Isaac

   9. Was greatly displeased

  10. Jacob had to leave home,
      Esau was angry

B. Write one statement and one question about each picture below.

> Challenge Exercise >

For each of the following statements, write a question that can be answered with **yes** or **no.**

> **Example:** Frank went to Boston.
> **Answer:**   Did Frank go to Boston?

1. The children found arrowheads.
2. Beth received a letter.

---

19. Diagraming Questions

A question can be diagramed. Like all sentences, a question has a simple subject and a simple predicate, and it expresses a complete thought.

To diagram any sentence, remember to find the verb first. Many questions have a verb phrase (a main verb and at least one helping verb). You will need to find **all** the parts of the simple predicate. In the following sentence, the simple predicate is in bold print.

> When **is** Julia **leaving**?

In questions the word order is **inverted.** The subject does not come before the verb. Sometimes the subject comes after the verb, and sometimes it comes between the helping verb and the main verb.

To diagram a question, we need to change the word order. Study the following examples.

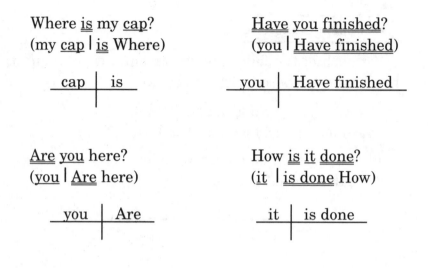

Where <u>is</u> my <u>cap</u>?
(my <u>cap</u> | <u>is</u> Where)

cap	is

Have <u>you</u> <u>finished</u>?
(<u>you</u> | <u>Have finished</u>)

you	Have finished

<u>Are</u> <u>you</u> here?
(<u>you</u> | <u>Are</u> here)

you	Are

How <u>is</u> <u>it</u> <u>done</u>?
(<u>it</u> | <u>is done</u> How)

it	is done

To diagram a sentence, remember that it helps to find the verb first. Be sure to find the whole verb phrase if the sentence has one. Then find the subject.

> **Oral Drill**

Change the word order of each sentence. Then diagram the skeletons at the board.
1. Are you helping?
2. Where is your coat?
3. Why are you spilling paint?
4. What are you doing?
5. Where has Robert worked?
6. Where were your dogs last night?

> **Written Practice**

Diagram the skeleton of each sentence.
1. Is your brother coming?
2. When are you painting the roof?

3. Have you seen the bill of a platypus?
4. Where has Father gone?
5. Are you washing dishes this morning?
6. Was it snowing?
7. Were the children playing outside?
8. Why is the horse in the yard?
9. Are you trying to catch him?
10. Has Kevin been helping you?

> Review and Practice >

A. Diagram the skeletons of these sentences.
   1. A parrot was in the cage.
   2. Is he talking?
   3. Are the books on the shelf?
   4. Are the children reading them?
   5. Heavy smoke poured out.
   6. Was the barn burning?
   7. The leaves were burning.
   8. Have you raked them?
   9. John was raking leaves yesterday.
   10. Was it a large pile?

B. Read each group of words. If it is a fragment, add words
   to complete the sentence. If it is a run-on sentence, divide
   it into two sentences. Use correct capitalization and
   punctuation.
   1. Has taken the wrong coat.
   2. A tall green tree.
   3. The rain fell, the wind blew.
   4. On the sand fell flat.
   5. The house on the rock.

> Challenge Exercise >

Write four **wh** questions for each of the following statements.

> **Example:** Today Luke brought a new bat to school.
> **Answers:** What did Luke bring to school?
> When did Luke bring a new bat to school?
> Who brought a new bat to school?
> Where did Luke bring a new bat?

1. Betty and Alma sent a book to Frank yesterday.
2. Uncle Ben will take us to the zoo tomorrow.

---

20. Combining Sentences

You know that two sentences written incorrectly as one sentence make a run-on sentence. But short, choppy sentences do not make good writing either. There are proper ways of combining sentences so that the writing is smooth and pleasant to read.

One way to avoid choppy sentences is by writing sentences with compound parts. A sentence may have a compound subject, a compound predicate, or some other compound part.

> **Choppy:**   Brother Marvin arrived early.
> His wife arrived early.
> **Combined by a compound subject:**
> Brother Marvin and his wife arrived early.

Choppy: Elmer caught the ball.
              Elmer threw it to Doris.
Combined by a compound predicate:
    Elmer caught the ball and threw it do Doris.

Choppy: We saw ducks on the pond.
              We saw geese too.
Combined by another compound part:
    We saw ducks and geese on the pond.

Sometimes two whole sentences can be combined by using words like **but** and **and.** When this is done, a comma is placed before **but** or **and.**

Choppy: Cain tilled the soil. Abel took care of
              sheep.
Better: Cain tilled the soil, but Abel took care of
              sheep.

Choppy: Abel offered a sheep. God was pleased with
              it.
Better: Abel offered a sheep, and God was pleased
              with it.

Short, choppy sentences are tiresome because they often repeat many words and phrases. Such repeating can be avoided by taking words from one sentence and putting them into another sentence. Study the following examples.

Choppy: Tabby is a small orange cat. She is a cat
              with green eyes that shine at night.
Better: Tabby is a small orange cat with green
              eyes that shine at night.

Choppy: The cow was a strange-looking animal. She had large, wild eyes. She had long, curved horns.

Better: The strange-looking cow had large, wild eyes and long, curved horns.

Remember: Do not use many short, choppy sentences in your writing.

> **Oral Drill**

A. Tell how to combine these groups of sentences.
1. Dogs are interesting animals. Cats are interesting animals.
2. They have unusual habits. They have unusual manners.
3. Some are shy. Others are affectionate.
4. The wind was fierce. It blew the dry leaves. They went across the lawn.
5. We saw three deer. They were eating apples. They were in the orchard.

B. Look at the paragraph in Written Practice, Part B. Discuss ways to combine the sentences in that paragraph.

> **Written Practice**

A. Combine these sentences.
1. Dogs learn rapidly. Dogs forget slowly.
2. Mother had baked some cookies. She baked some pies.

3. The puppies were playing. The kittens were playing. They were on the porch.
4. There is a letter. It is for you. It is on the table.

B. Rewrite this paragraph. Combine some sentences to make the writing smoother.

Suppose you looked into a mother black bear's den. Suppose you looked in the middle of winter. You might see something that surprised you. You might see two little cubs. Each one might be only about eight inches long. Each one might weigh only half a pound. When baby bears are born, they have very little hair. Their eyes are closed. They stay in the den until they are about two months old. Then it is springtime. They are ready to come out into the warm sunshine. They come out with the mother bear.

>Review and Practice>

Write complete sentences to answer these questions.
1. How many topics should each paragraph speak about?
2. Which sentence in a paragraph tells what the paragraph is about?
3. What is spoken English called?

> Challenge Exercise >

Combine sentences 1–3 as shown in Example A, and sentences 4–6 as shown in Example B.

Example A: A man stood on the bridge. He was tall and young.

Combined: A tall young man stood on the bridge.

1. The children picked strawberries. The berries were juicy and red.
2. We watched the rabbits. They were playful and little.
3. Jesus healed the man. The man was poor and blind.

Example B: The children raced through the tall weeds. They did not see the pipe.

Combined: Racing through the tall weeds, the children did not see the pipe.

4. Jesus sat in a boat. He taught the people.
5. Father spoke quietly. He explained our mistake.
6. We drove down the road. We saw several deer in the meadow.

---

21. Commands: Sentences That Tell You to Do Something

You have learned that two kinds of sentences are the statement and the question. Today you will study a third kind of sentence. It is the **command.** A command is a sentence that tells you to do something.

Be careful
Give cheerfully.
Sit up straight.

The subject of a command is **you,** but it usually is not stated. When the subject **you** is not stated, we say it is **understood.**

Sometimes **you** is stated in a command. In many Bible commands, **thou** or **ye** is used instead of **you.**

You come with me.   Be ye thankful.

Sometimes the subject of a command includes **you** and another noun or pronoun. Then the command has a compound subject.

You and Sarah wash the dishes.

The verb in a command is often the first word. Sometimes it is the only word. A command may begin with **please, never,** or **always,** but these words are not nouns or verbs. They are not part of the skeleton.

(you) Help me carry the box.
(you) Come.
(you) Always do what is right.

A command begins with a capital letter and ends with a period.

Remember: A sentence that tells you to do something is a command. A command begins with a capital letter and ends with a period.

A. Read each sentence, and tell what kind it is. Tell what end punctuation each one needs.
   1. God is our refuge and strength
   2. Can the blind lead the blind
   3. Trust in the Lord with all thine heart
   4. Even a child is known by his doings
   5. Be thankful unto Him
   6. Be ye kind one to another

B. Give the subject and the verb in each of these commands.
   1. Never throw books on the floor.
   2. Always close the doors in the winter.
   3. Please help me.
   4. Know ye that the Lord He is God.
   5. Be thou an example.

> Written Practice >

A. Write whether each sentence is a **statement,** a **question,** or a **command.** Also write the correct end punctuation for each sentence.

   Examples: a. Rose bakes cookies
               b. Does Rose bake cookies
               c. Bake some cookies

   Answers: a. statement **.**
               b. question **?**
               c. command **.**

   1. Show me your hands
   2. Did you wash them

3. The Bible speaks of clean hands
4. Praise ye the Lord
5. Keep looking up
6. The Lord is my shepherd
7. Be still, and know that I am God
8. Obey your parents
9. What shall we do now
10. You and Martha sweep the floor.

B. Write the subject and the verb of each command. If the subject is understood, write **(you).**
   1. Always tell the truth.
   2. Be ye doers of the Word.
   3. Pray without ceasing.
   4. Never be a talebearer.
   5. Come thou into the ark.
   6. You tell us the story.
   7. Please bring me a drink.
   8. Talk ye of all His wondrous ways.

C. Write three commands that your teacher might give you.

> Review and Practice >

Write the word that belongs in each blank.
   1. The —— of a sentence tells who or what the sentence is about.
   2. The —— of a sentence tells what the subject does or is.
   3. The simple —— of a sentence is always a verb.

22. Diagraming Commands

A command expresses a complete thought. For that reason, a command can also be diagramed.

To diagram a command, first find the verb. Study the verbs in the following examples.

<u>Pray</u> every day.   <u>Trust</u> in the Lord.

When the subject **you** is understood, put it in parentheses on the sentence diagram.

<u>Close</u> the door.

(you)	Close

When **you, ye,** or **thou** is stated, diagram the command in the same way as a statement.

<u>You</u> <u>answer</u> the telephone.   <u>Be</u> <u>thou</u> an example.

You	answer		thou	Be

If a command has two simple subjects or predicates, diagram it as shown in these examples.

<u>You</u> and <u>Ben</u> <u>stay</u> here.   <u>Trust</u> and <u>obey</u>.

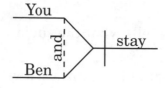

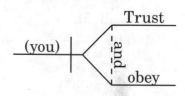

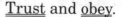

Remember that words like **please, never,** and **always** are not nouns or verbs. They are not part of the skeleton.

Always <u>tell</u> the truth.

Diagram the skeletons of these sentences at the board.
1. Never hand in careless work.
2. Always do your best in school.
3. Rejoice and sing praises.
4. Be a good example.
5. You and Betsy dust the furniture.

> Written Practice >

Diagram the skeletons of these commands.
1. Find the answers in your book.
2. Please hold the door for me.
3. Study to the glory of God.
4. Rejoice evermore.
5. You and Daniel feed the calves.
6. Bless your enemies.
7. Be ye kind one to another.
8. Hate the evil.
9. Always love the good.
10. Honor and obey your parents.

>Review and Practice>

A. Diagram the skeletons of these statements, questions, and commands.
   1. Get up early in the morning.
   2. Go out and watch insects.
   3. Have you counted the body parts of an insect?
   4. Its body has three parts.
   5. What are they called?
   6. Learn them.
   7. An insect has no bones.
   8. Its body has a hard outer covering.

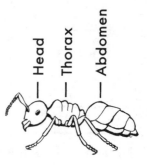

B. Read each group of words. If it needs a subject, write **S.** If it needs a predicate, write **P.** If it is a phrase and needs both a subject and a predicate, write **B.**
   1. Katydids and crickets.
   2. Have two wings.
   3. In the summer.
   4. Squeaked and droned all night.
   5. During the night.
   6. At the moon.

23. Exclamations: Sentences That Show Strong Feeling

Any sentence that expresses strong feeling is an **exclamation.** A statement, a question, or a command is an exclamation if it expresses strong feeling.

What a terrible noise it made! (statement)
What does this mean! (question)
Watch that little girl! (command)

Exclamations may have special word order. If the exclamation is a statement, the skeleton may come at the end of the sentence.

How great <u>God</u> <u>is</u>!

When a question or a command is an exclamation, the word order stays the same.

What <u>have</u> <u>you</u> <u>done</u>!

(<u>you</u>) <u>Bring</u> a bucket!

An exclamation begins with a capital letter and ends with an exclamation mark.

Remember: A sentence that shows strong feeling is an exclamation. It may be a statement, a question, or a command. An exclamation begins with a capital letter and ends with an exclamation mark (!).

 Oral Drill

A. Tell what kind of sentence each one is. Tell what punctuation should be used after each one.
  1. The heavens declare the glory of God
  2. Can you count the stars
  3. Count your blessings one by one
  4. Thank the Lord for His wonderful gifts to the children of men

   5. Who can understand his errors
   6. Where have we not seen the hand of God

B. Which sentences in Part A could be used as exclamations? What end punctuation would they have then?

Written Practice

A. If these sentences were not exclamations, what kind of sentence would they be? Write **statement, question,** or **command** for each.
   1. Look at that beautiful sunset!
   2. How shall we tell all that God has done!
   3. Sing unto the Lord a new song!
   4. Trust in the Lord with all thine heart!
   5. Who is so great a God as our God!

B. These sentences may be a little harder. Write whether each one is a **statement,** a **question,** or a **command.** Give the correct end punctuation.

   Examples: a. Who are all these people
          b. The leaves are falling
          c. Watch your step

   Answers: a. question ?
          b. statement .
          c. command .

1. Be careful of whom you speak, to whom you speak, and how, and when, and where
2. They talk most who have the least to say
3. Never put off until tomorrow what you can do today
4. Did you think to pray this morning
5. My help cometh from the Lord, which made heaven and earth
6. It takes but few words to tell the truth
7. Do not say everything you know, but know everything you say.

C. Write three exclamations that you might say when your grandmother gives you a special gift.

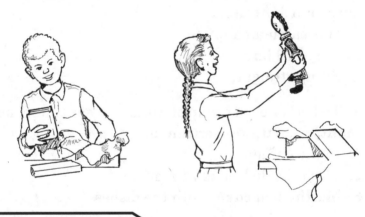

> Review and Practice >

Diagram the sentence skeletons.
1. Father emptied and washed the buckets.
2. Were you helping?
3. Come with us.

24. Review of Sentences

> Oral Drill

A. Give the answers.
1. What is a noun?
2. Give some examples of nouns.
3. What is a verb?
4. Give some examples of verbs.
5. What is a pronoun?
6. Give some examples of pronouns.

B. Tell whether each group of words is a **subject,** a **predicate,** or a **sentence.**
1. Has eaten an apple.
2. A big red bird.
3. Sit up straight.

C. Tell whether each group of words is a **sentence,** a **fragment,** or a **run-on sentence.**
1. In the garden.
2. Wash the dishes, dry them too.
3. Martha helped me with the dishes.

D. Tell where to divide each sentence between the complete subject and the complete predicate. Also give the simple subject and the simple predicate of each sentence.
1. The children were playing.
2. Answer correctly.
3. Jason worked swiftly.
4. A beautiful swan is swimming around the pond.

E. Give the verb phrase in each sentence.
1. Abraham had prayed for his nephew Lot.
2. The people of Sodom were doing many evil things.
3. Lot's family was living in the wicked city.
4. Only Lot and his daughters were rescued from Sodom.
5. Lot's wife was looking back.

> Written Practice >

A. Write **nouns, pronouns,** or **verbs** for each definition or group of examples.
1. They name persons, places, and things.
2. They take the place of nouns.
3. They show action or being.
4. he, she, it, they
5. am, is, are, was
6. run, jump, play
7. father, school, desk, pencils

B. Write whether each group of words is a **subject,** a **predicate,** or a **sentence.**
1. Has seen a bird.
2. My finger hurts.
3. This old blue book.
4. Help!
5. Please pass the bread.

C. Write **S** for sentence, **F** for sentence fragment, and **RO** for run-on sentence.
1. Pick the beans, pull the onions.
2. Sit up.
3. Singing at the top of their voices.

4. All night too.
5. I want to clean the kitchen today.
6. Will you help me?
7. Can you sweep can you dust?
8. The children are making cookies.

D. Diagram the skeletons of the following statements, questions, and commands.
1. The water boiled rapidly.
2. My mother worked and sang.
3. Have you ever seen an eclipse?
4. The birds were chirping merrily.
5. Follow the path of Jesus.
6. Did the daffodils bloom early?

E. Copy the verb phrase in each sentence.
1. Abraham was sitting in the doorway.
2. Some visitors were coming to his tent.
3. They were bringing a message to Abraham.
4. Sarah had prepared a meal.
5. She was listening inside the tent.

---

25. Writing Sentences of Different Lengths

In Lesson 20 you learned that short, choppy sentences do not make good writing. However, it is also not good to write sentences that are too long. Our writing needs to have a proper balance, with some sentences that are short and some that are longer.

Paragraph with short, choppy sentences:

It is winter. There is snow on the ground. I enjoy thinking about gardens. I like to imagine all kinds of lovely flowers. I can almost see their bright colors. I can almost smell their fragrant perfumes.

Paragraph with one long sentence:

In winter when snow is on the ground, I enjoy thinking about gardens and about all kinds of lovely flowers, and imagining their bright colors and their fragrant perfumes.

Paragraph with sentences of different lengths:

In winter when snow is on the ground, I enjoy thinking about gardens. I like to imagine all kinds of lovely flowers. I can almost see their bright colors and smell their fragrant perfumes.

Remember: Do not use too many short sentences or too many long sentences in your writing. Write sentences of different lengths.

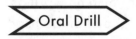

Oral Drill

Tell which of the following paragraphs is better. Tell what is wrong with the other one.

1.   One of the most interesting parks in the world is Yellowstone National Park in the states of Wyoming, Idaho, and Montana. This park is famous for its geysers that shoot columns of hot water and steam into the air. Yellowstone Park has over two hundred of these. Some of the small geysers spout water only four or five feet into the air, but the larger ones throw water as high as two hundred feet. There are also hot springs, which do not shoot water into the air. These can be used for cooking food. Wouldn't you like to visit this park?

PhotoDisc

2.   One of the most interesting parks in the world is Yellowstone National Park, which is in the states of Wyoming, Idaho, and Montana and is famous for its geysers that shoot columns of hot water and steam into the air. Yellowstone Park has over two hundred of these, and some of the small geysers spout water only four or five feet into the air, but the larger ones throw water as high as two hundred feet. There are also hot springs. They do not shoot water into the air. They can be used for cooking food. You would probably enjoy a visit to this park.

Written Practice

A. Rewrite this paragraph so that the sentences have different lengths. Combine some of the short sentences, and divide the long sentence.

> The black bear is the smallest of the North American bears. It is the most common of the North American bears. It is called the "clown of the woods." It is called that because of the funny things some black bears do. They sometimes stand on their heads. They sometimes dance. They sometimes fall over and over. Black bears will seldom attack a person, but they are dangerous if they are wounded or teased or are trying to protect their babies.

B. Write a paragraph of your own about Elijah. Begin by writing a complete sentence to answer each of the following questions. (See 1 Kings 17:5–16.) Then join or divide your sentences so that your paragraph has sentences of different lengths.
   1. How was Elijah fed at the brook Cherith?
   2. Why did he leave Cherith?
   3. Where did he go?
   4. Whom did he see there?
   5. What was she doing?
   6. What did Elijah ask her to make?
   7. What did he promise?

Review and Practice

Write the correct word for each blank.
   1. Good writers —— with their eyes and —— with their ears.

2. A paragraph tells about only one ———.

3. You should ——— the first line of a paragraph.

4. You must ——— your mouth in order to speak clearly.

5. When you write, some of your sentences should be ———, and some should be ———.

---

26. Chapter 2 Review

A. Give the subject pronouns.

B. Tell whether each sentence is a **statement,** a **question,** or a **command.** Also give the correct end punctuation for each sentence.

1. Did Adam and Eve sin
2. God sent a Saviour
3. Honor your parents
4. Did it rain again last night
5. Look at that huge bear
6. Studying English is helpful
7. Do your best

C. Which sentence in Part B would probably be said with strong feeling? What end punctuation should be used to show the strong feeling?

D. On the chalkboard, diagram the skeletons of sentences 1–5 in Part B.

Written Practice

A. For each sentence, write **S, Q,** or **C** for statement, question, or command. Write **E** for one sentence that is probably an exclamation. Also write the correct end punctuation for each sentence.

1. Hannah was praying in the temple
2. Had Samuel heard God's voice
3. Look at the lovely rainbow
4. Bob and his dog are standing in the yard
5. The old man saw us and waved his hat
6. Bring the picnic basket
7. Where are we eating
8. You and Mary sit under the tree

B. Diagram the skeletons of the sentences in Part A. Watch for verb phrases and compound parts.

C. Make one sentence from each set of short, choppy sentences.

1. Eugene fed the calves. Eugene watered the calves.
2. Betty helped Mother bake cookies. Joanna helped Mother bake cookies.
3. The cow is black and white. The cow eats grass. The cow eats hay.

D. Rewrite each long sentence as two shorter sentences.

1. All the other men were afraid of Goliath, but David was not afraid, and he trusted God to help him fight the giant.
2. David put a stone into his sling and hurled it at the giant, and the stone hit Goliath in the forehead, and he fell to the ground.

Parts of Speech

A noun is the name of anything,
As **school** or **garden, hoop** or **swing.**
Adjectives tell the kind of noun,
As **great, small, pretty, white,** or **brown.**
Three little words we often see
Are articles: **a, an,** and **the.**
Instead of nouns the pronouns stand:
Her head, **his** face, **your** arm, **my** hand.
Verbs tell of something being done,
As **read, write, spell, sing, jump,** or **run.**
How things are done the adverbs tell,
As **slowly, quickly, ill,** or **well.**
They also tell us where or when,
As **here** and **there,** or **now** and **then.**
A preposition stands before
A noun, as **in** or **through** a door.
Conjunctions join the words together,
As men **and** women, wind **or** weather.
The interjection shows surprise,
As, **Oh,** how pretty! **Ah,** how wise!

—*Author unknown*

Chapter 3
Nouns

Nouns name.

Persons

Places

Things

grandmother

church

plant

rabbit

carpenter

zoo

book

boy

park

hammer

27. What Is a Noun?

Every word in a sentence has a certain work to do. Nouns have the work of naming persons, places, and things. A noun is a **part of speech.** There are eight parts of speech in all.

A noun is a word that names a person, place, or thing. Suppose someone said to you, "Went to." These words do not express a complete thought. They do not make sense, because they do not tell about a noun.

In order to understand this thought, you need to know who went. You would also want to know the place where he went. When someone says to you, "**Harry** went to **church**," you can understand the thought. The nouns help the sentence to express a complete thought. **Harry** names the person who went, and **church** names the place where he went.

Some nouns name persons. The words **man, stranger, doctor, brother, Ralph, Mr. Jones,** and **fireman** are nouns that name persons.

Some nouns name places. The words **corner, town, church, France,** and **London** are nouns that name places.

Some nouns name things. The words **cat, cloth, hand, apple, money, Bible, word,** and **plants** are nouns that name things.

Remember: A noun is a word that names a person, place, or thing.

A. Give several nouns for each of the following persons, places, and things.

Persons	**Places**	**Things**
1. workers	4. states	8. animals
2. friends	5. countries	9. tools
3. family	6. towns	10. foods
members	7. oceans	11. plants
		12. furniture

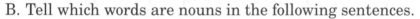

B. Tell which words are nouns in the following sentences.
1. The children went to the zoo in a bus.
2. The pencil fell off the desk.
3. The teacher read a book.

C. In each sentence of Part B above, tell which noun is the simple subject.

> Written Practice

A. Write the definition of a noun. See the "Remember" box.

B. Copy all the nouns in each sentence.
1. Fish swim in the lake.
2. The nurse gave roses to the girl.
3. The children sing at church.
4. Abel offered a sacrifice to the Lord.
5. The Bible teaches about God.

6. The river is full of water.
7. Brother Clyde preached at church.
8. My big, friendly dog is named Rex.
9. Joanna lives in the state of Maryland.
10. Joel is from the country of Canada.
11. My cousins are John, Joe, and Jerry.
12. Their brother drives a truck for a dairy in Altoona.
13. We love our friends.
14. Your grandmother likes petunias.
15. My grandfather planted many trees.

C. In your answers for Part B, underline each noun that is the subject of the sentence.

D. Write a paragraph telling about some things you might show a friend who came to visit your community from another state. Underline all the nouns in your paragraph.

> **Review and Practice**

Diagram the skeletons of the following sentences. Remember that not all nouns are subjects! Put only the simple subject and the simple predicate on each diagram.
1. Brother John taught school yesterday.
2. Is Sister Julia teaching the children?

28. Common Nouns and Proper Nouns

Nouns may be common or proper. A **common noun** names a person, place, or thing without referring to a certain one. It does not name a specific person, place, or thing. A **proper noun** does name a specific person, place, or thing.

Common nouns	Proper nouns
boy	John
dog	Rex
state	Ohio

Proper nouns are always capitalized. Study the following examples of proper nouns.

a. Names of persons:
Calvin Shirk, Brother Amos Martin, Gloria Ashburn

b. Names of places:
  (1) countries or states—Greece, Russia, Spain, Ohio, Missouri, Nevada
  (2) cities and towns—Philadelphia, Pennytown, Canton
  (3) continents—Africa, Europe, North America, Asia, Australia
  (4) oceans and seas—Atlantic Ocean, Pacific Ocean, Indian Ocean, Red Sea

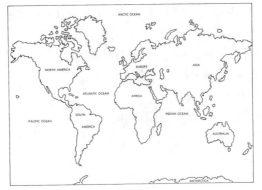

(5) rivers and lakes—Mississippi River, Delaware River, Lake Huron

(6) mountains and deserts—Rocky Mountains, Gobi Desert, Black Hills

(7) parks and buildings—Everglades National Park, Sharon Christian School, Akron Hospital

c. Names of things:

(1) Holidays—Thanksgiving, Easter

(2) Other calendar items—Sunday, Monday, March, July

Remember: Nouns may be common or proper. A proper noun names a specific person, place, or thing. A proper noun must be capitalized.

> Oral Drill

A. Give a proper noun for each common noun.

1. girl
3. teacher
5. woman
7. state

2. town
4. country
6. ocean
8. store

B. Find the nouns in these sentences. Tell which are common nouns and which are proper nouns.

1. Egypt is found on the continent of Africa.
2. The king of Egypt was called Pharaoh.
3. Western Egypt is in the Sahara.
4. The Nile River is the longest river in the world.
5. The mouth of the Nile empties into the Mediterranean Sea.

EGYPT

SAHARA DESERT

C. Tell which words need to be capitalized.
1. william penn, from england, founded the city of philadelphia.
2. Many people came to pennsylvania for freedom of worship.
3. Missionaries have gone to asia, australia, and africa.

> Written Practice >

A. Write a proper noun for each common noun.
1. boy   4. country   7. river
2. minister   5. city   8. building
3. girl   6. continent

B. Copy the nouns in each sentence. Underline all the proper nouns.
1. The Jordan River and the Dead Sea are in Israel.
2. The land of Israel is also called Palestine.
3. Palestine received its name from the Philistines.
4. Many stories of the Bible happened in Palestine.

C. In each sentence, find all the words that need to be capitalized, and write them correctly.

Example: brother amos and brother john plan to visit at milton, vermont.

Answer: Brother Amos, Brother John, Milton, Vermont

1. balboa was an explorer from spain.
2. He discovered the pacific ocean, which is the largest ocean in the world.
3. The other oceans are the atlantic ocean, the indian ocean, and the arctic ocean.

    4. The greatest river in the world is the amazon river.

    5. This river was discovered by explorers from portugal.

    6. The largest river in north america is the mississippi river.

D. Write definitions for the following terms. See the "Remember" boxes.

    1. noun   2. proper noun

E. Write a paragraph about yourself, answering the following questions. Circle all the proper nouns in your paragraph. Underline all the common nouns.

    1. What is your full name?

    2. What is your address?

    3. What is your father's full name?

    4. What are the names of your brothers?

    5. What are the names of your sisters?

    6. What is the name of your church?

---

29. Compound Nouns and Noun Phrases

Sometimes two words are written together as a single noun. Such a noun is a **compound noun.**

Some compound nouns are written as one word: clothesline, stovepipe, bookrack. It is easier to say **clothesline** or **stovepipe** than to say "a line for clothes" or "a pipe for a stove."

Some compound nouns are written as separate words: post office, spark plug, blue jay, fire engine.

Check a good dictionary when you are not sure how a compound noun should be spelled.

You learned about **noun phrases** in Chapter 1. Remember that a noun phrase is two or more words. Sometimes it even has abbreviations and initials.

Because a noun phrase is a proper noun, all the important words are capitalized.

George Washington Carver
John the Baptist

Titles used with the names in noun phrases must be capitalized.

Mr. Clark   **Miss** White
Mrs. Peters   **Dr.** Ronald North
Brother Steven   **Sister** May

Initials in noun phrases must also be capitalized.

Linda **A.** Smith   **C. F.** Pringle
I. J. Jones   Melvin **R.** Weaver

> **Oral Drill**

A. Say the simple subject of each sentence.
   1. Dr. J. L. Smith looked at my throat.
   2. The Civil War began in 1861.
   3. The post office is not open today.

B. Give a compound noun for each phrase.

1. a line for clothes
2. a pin for hair
3. a rack for hats

C. Tell which words are nouns. Tell which nouns should be capitalized.

1. The children saw lake erie on a trip with their family.
2. gerald and alma are attending laurel mennonite school.
3. The jordan river is a winding river.
4. f. d. roosevelt was the president before harry s. truman.

> Written Practice >

A. Copy the simple subject of each sentence. If it is a compound noun or a noun phrase, be sure to copy the whole noun.

Example: Brother Henry Martin is our minister.
Answer: Brother Henry Martin

1. George Washington Carver was a famous scientist.
2. A blue jay was calling outside my window.
3. The mail plane is not flying this week.

B. Write a compound noun for each phrase.

1. a case for books
2. a room to store things
3. a plane that flies in the air

C. Copy all the nouns in each sentence. Capitalize all the proper nouns.

1. moses led the israelites through the red sea and into the wilderness.

2. The sailors threw jonah into the sea.
3. How did jesus help the disciples on the sea of galilee?
4. The alps are mountains in switzerland.

Review and Practice

A. Write the numbers of the groups of words that are complete sentences.
   1. One house was built on a rock.
   2. The other house on the sand.
   3. The house on the sand fell.
   4. Remained standing on the rock.

B. Write **statement, question,** or **command** for each sentence.
   1. Close the door when you leave.
   2. Have you finished your work?
   3. Jesus is the Son of God.

Challenge Exercise

Use a good dictionary to find whether each compound noun is written as one word or as two separate words. Write the nouns correctly.

   Example: blue bird (Is it blue bird or bluebird?)
   Answer: bluebird

1. high school   4. chain saw
2. money bag   5. note book
3. air plane   6. court house

30. Learning About Poetry

Poetry is a special form of writing that is pleasing to the ear. Good poetry uses descriptive words, and it usually has rhyme and rhythm too. The rhyme, rhythm, and descriptive words of a poem work together to stir the feelings of the reader.

Poetry is written differently than other kinds of writing. Usually a certain rhyme and rhythm pattern is followed. Each line begins with a capital letter, and the poem is divided into stanzas rather than paragraphs.

Poets often use descriptive words that form pictures in our minds. Notice the descriptive words and phrases in this poem. Instead of saying **soft, warm fur,** the poet says, "Her coat is so warm."

I Like Little Pussy

I like little Pussy, her coat is so warm;
And if I don't hurt her, she'll do me no harm.
So I'll not pull her tail nor drive her away,
But Pussy and I very gently will play.

She shall sit by my side, and I'll give her some food;
And she'll love me because I am gentle and good.
I'll pat little Pussy, and then she will purr
And thus show her thanks for my kindness to her.

I'll not pinch her ears nor tread on her paws,
Lest I should provoke her to use her sharp claws.
I never will vex her nor make her displeased,
For Pussy can't bear to be worried or teased.

—Jane Taylor

> **Remember:** Poetry is a special form of writing that is pleasing to the ear. When you write poetry, remember to capitalize the first word of each line.

Answer these questions about the poem in the lesson.
1. What descriptive words does the poet use to speak of **chasing the cat away**?
2. What does the poet say the cat is doing when she purrs?
3. What does the poet say instead of "**step** on her paws"?
4. What words does the poet use instead of **upset**?
5. What word means "can't **stand**" something?
6. What does **worried** mean in the last stanza?
7. Which words in this poem rhyme or almost rhyme?
8. What feelings does this poem give you?

> ## Written Practice

A. Copy the poem. Use capital letters correctly.

My Gift

what can I give Him,
   poor as I am?
if I were a shepherd,
   i'd give Him a lamb;
if I were a wise man,
   i would do my part;
but what can I give Him?
i'll give Him my heart.

—*Christina Rossetti*

B. Write a four-line poem about the seasons, the flowers, or the first snow. Try to make at least two lines rhyme.

> ## Review and Practice

Write the correct word for each blank.

1. A paragraph must tell about only ——— topic.
2. The ——— sentence tells what the paragraph is about.
3. Do not use too many ———, choppy sentences in your writing.

Interesting Nouns

One fowl is a **goose,** and two are called **geese;**
Yet the plural of **moose** should never be **meese.**
You may find a lone **mouse** or a whole nest of **mice;**
Then why can't the plural of **house** be made **hice?**
We speak of a **brother** and also of **brethren;**
But though we say **mother,** we never say **methren.**
So nouns and their plurals, it's easy to see,
Make an interesting study—I think you'll agree.

—*Source unknown*

31. Singular Nouns and Plural Nouns

A **singular noun** is a noun that names just one person, place, or thing. **Singular** comes from **single,** which means **one.** A **plural noun** names more than one person, place, or thing.

The plural form of most nouns is made by adding **s** to the singular form.

bird—birds   flower—flowers

The plural form of nouns that end with **s, ch, sh,** or **x** is made by adding **es.**

1. The **bus** goes past the **church.**
   The **buses** go past the **churches.**

2. The **glass** is with the **dish.**
   The **glasses** are with the **dishes.**

3. The **box** is in the **bush.**
   The **boxes** are in the **bushes.**

These nouns are made plural by adding **es** because just adding **s** makes them hard to pronounce.

Remember: Plural nouns name more than one person, place, or thing. The plural form of most nouns is made by adding **s** or **es** to the singular form.

> Oral Drill

A. Tell how to spell the plural form.
   1. name   3. dish
   2. boy   4. box

B. Read each sentence, changing the singular nouns to their plural forms.
   1. The waitress dropped the dish.
   2. The bush caused a rash.

> Written Practice >

A. Write the plural form of each noun.
   1. Bible   4. patch   7. moss   10. fox
   2. star   5. dish   8. dress   11. lunch
   3. field   6. horse   9. watch   12. tax

B. Rewrite the following sentences. Change each singular noun to a plural noun. Change other words to make your sentences sound right.

   Example: A brush is in the box.
   Answer: Brushes are in the boxes.

   1. A robin built a nest in that tree.
   2. A rabbit was nibbling in the garden.
   3. His answer is on his paper.

C. Write sentences of your own, using the plural forms of the following words.
   1. church   4. latch
   2. Bible   5. box
   3. boy   6. class

Review and Practice

A. Copy all the nouns in each sentence. Capitalize all the proper nouns.
   1. On october 12, 1492, christopher columbus discovered america.
   2. The largest country in the world is russia.

B. Diagram the skeleton of each sentence.
   1. Father plowed the garden.
   2. Have the boys planted the seeds?
   3. The family enjoyed the fresh vegetables.

---

32. More Plural Nouns

The plural form of most nouns is made by adding **s** or **es** to the singular form. But sometimes other spelling changes must also be made.

To form the plural of a noun that ends with **y** after a consonant, change the **y** to **i** and add **es.**

    cherry—cherries
    baby—babies
    fly—flies

For the plural form of a noun that ends with **y** after a vowel, add only **s.**

    monkey—monkeys
    boy—boys
    tray—trays

To form the plural of most nouns that end with **f** or **fe,** change the **f** to **v** and add **es.**

> leaf—leaves   knife—knives   calf—calves

For some nouns ending with **f** or **fe,** the **f** is not changed to **v.** Here are some examples.

> chief—chiefs   safe—safes   roof—roofs

The plural form of most nouns ending with **o** after a consonant is made by adding **es.**

> tomato—tomatoes
> mosquito—mosquitoes

There are exceptions to this rule. The plural form of musical terms like the following do not end with **es.**

> soprano—sopranos
> piano—pianos
> alto—altos

Check the dictionary whenever you are not sure about the spelling of a plural noun. If no plural form is shown, the plural form is made in the usual way by adding **s** or **es.**

Oral Drill

A. Tell how to spell the plural form.

1. echo	3. knife	5. key	7. alto
2. toy	4. liberty	6. wife	8. way

B. Tell how to spell the singular form.

1. taxes	3. berries	5. loaves
2. days	4. tables	6. potatoes

C. Change all the singular nouns to plural nouns.

1. The Bible is on the shelf.

2. A rabbit was hopping in the field.

> Written Practice >

A. Copy these singular nouns. After each one, write its plural form.

1. knife	3. piano	5. sheaf	7. roof
2. half	4. day	6. wolf	8. tomato

B. Copy these plural nouns. After each one, write its singular form.

1. potatoes	3. wives	5. loaves
2. gulfs	4. puppies	6. monkeys

C. Rewrite these sentences, changing all the singular nouns to plural nouns. Underline the plural nouns.

1. The soprano should sing louder.

2. The knife is in the box.

3. The monkey had a banana.

4. The puppy barked and heard the echo from the mountain.

D. Write sentences that use the plural forms of the following words. Use the pictures below for ideas.

1. tomato   2. calf   3. boy   4. puppy

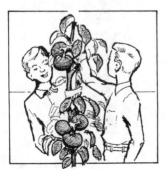 

> Review and Practice >

A. Rewrite each sentence, replacing **thing** or **things** with
   a suitable noun. Underline the nouns you use.

> **Example:** The thing on the front thing had a thing
>   in it.
> **Answer:** The <u>tire</u> on the front <u>wheel</u> had a <u>nail</u> in
>   it.

1. In cold weather I wear things on my hands and a thing
   on my head.
2. I used a thing to eat the soup from a thing on the
   table.
3. After I wrote the thing, I bought a thing at the post
   office and pasted it on the thing.
4. The carpenter used a thing to drive a thing into the
   thing.
5. A large thing with dark green things grew in front of
   our thing.

B. Write the correct words to fill in the blanks.
   1. A ——— is a word that names a person, place, or thing.
   2. A ——— ——— names a specific person, place, or thing.
   3. A ——— ——— names more than one person, place, or
      thing.

33. Irregular Plural Nouns

Some plural nouns are formed in unusual ways. They are called irregular because they are not spelled in the regular way.

There are seven nouns whose plural form is made by changing the vowel.

mouse—mice   tooth—teeth
louse—lice   goose—geese
man—men   foot—feet
woman—women

Three nouns have plural forms that end with **en** or **ren.**

ox—oxen   brother—brethren
child—children

Brethren is an old plural form. Today we usually say **brothers** instead of **brethren.**

A few nouns have no spelling change at all. The plural form is the same as the singular form.

deer   sheep   salmon   trout

A dictionary will help you if you are not sure how to spell a plural noun. Use it when you are in doubt.

> Oral Drill >

A. Look up these words in a classroom dictionary to see how their plural forms are shown.
   1. ox   3. deer   5. class
   2. salmon   4. louse

B. Change all the singular words to their plural forms.

1. The foot of the sheep was hurt.
2. A tomato and a potato were in the basket.

C. Tell how to correct the following sentences.
1. The childs fed five sheeps at the pond.
2. The mans and womans were trying to get rid of the mouses.
3. We cannot find those sly foxs in the woodes.
4. The farmer had sheeps, gooses, and oxes.

> **Written Practice** >

A. Rewrite these sentences, changing all the singular nouns to plural nouns. Underline the plural nouns.
1. The child caught a trout in the creek.
2. The goose and the sheep went to the market in a wagon pulled by an ox.
3. The mouse was running across the beam.

B. Find each incorrect word, and write it correctly.
1. Four deers are in the alfalfa field.
2. The foots of geeses are webbed.
3. The childs caught salmons and trouts.
4. The boy broke two tooths.
5. The boies and girls liked to watch monkies and chimpanzees at the zoo.

C. Write sentences of your own, using five of the irregular plural nouns that you studied in this lesson. (You may use more than one in the same sentence.) Underline the plural nouns.

> **Review and Practice**

A. Find the proper nouns, and write them correctly.

1. dog
2. shep
3. town
4. harrisburg

5. country
6. man
7. germany
8. monday

B. Diagram the skeletons of these sentences.

1. Wash and dry the dishes.
2. Set the table.
3. Are you coming soon?
4. Mary and John are leaving.

C. Correct these run-on sentences by adding proper capitalization and punctuation.

1. The Rhine River is an important river in Europe, the Danube River is large too.
2. Comb your hair eat your breakfast.
3. John ran into the store, Mary held the horse.

Turbo Photo

34. Topic Sentences and Titles

You have learned that a paragraph is a group of sentences that tell about one topic. Each paragraph has a topic sentence, which tells what the rest of the paragraph is about. Usually the topic sentence comes first in a paragraph.

A topic sentence must give a main idea. It must not give details of the paragraph. It only tells what the whole paragraph is about. The topic sentence should be written in an interesting way so that the reader will want to read the whole paragraph.

A title also tells what a paragraph or story is about. A title should give a clue about the topic of the paragraph or story. It should be written in an interesting way, too, so that the reader will want to read the paragraph or story.

Look at this paragraph. Read the title and the topic sentence. Do they make you want to read more?

Writing in the Snow

A patch of fresh snow can be just like a page of writing. On a hike yesterday my father helped me to read the snow writing. Some of it told us that a big jack rabbit had crossed our path a few minutes before we arrived there. Another snow sentence told the story of a prairie chicken scratching for food in a spot where the snow was not drifted. One big blot on the white page told the story of a field mouse that had been caught and carried off by an owl or hawk. My father and I wrote in the snow too, but our story was not as interesting as the animals' stories.

> **Remember:** A topic sentence must give the main idea of a paragraph. A title should give an interesting clue about the topic so that the reader will want to read the paragraph or story.

> **Oral Drill**

A. The following paragraph needs a title and a topic sentence. Read it and choose the best ones from those given below. Tell what is wrong with the others.

> He has eight arms, which he can wrap around his enemy. Each arm is dotted with suction cups. The octopus can hang on, pull the enemy underwater, and drown him. But usually the octopus would rather hide than fight. So when he is in danger, he may shoot out a dark liquid that spreads like a cloud around him. Then the octopus disappears into a deep hole or hides behind an underwater bush until the danger is past.

1. Titles

   a. The Octopus
   b. The Eight-armed Ink Shooter
   c. The Disappearing Act
2. Topic Sentences
   a. The octopus is in the mollusk family.
   b. The octopus is an interesting creature.
   c. The octopus has unusual ways of protecting himself.

B. Tell which sentence in each pair would make a better topic sentence, and why.

1. a. I have a baby brother who is eighteen months old.
   b. My eighteen-month-old brother can get into more trouble than anyone else I know.
2. a. My classmates help to make school a truly enjoyable place.
   b. There are nineteen students in our class.

C. Which title in each pair is more interesting? Why?
1. a. I Am a Drop of Water
   b. The Water Cycle
2. a. One Hundred Dollars
   b. If I Had One Hundred Dollars

D. Give a good title for the following paragraph.

> The Dutch build dikes around their land to keep out the sea. The dikes are like huge walls made mostly of sand and stones. They may be as high as sixty feet and wide enough for roads to be built on them. Some even have trees and buildings on them. From the top of a dike, you can see down into the chimneys of the houses below! The fish in the water on one side are higher than the birds in the air on the other side! The dikes help to make the Netherlands a truly fascinating land to visit.

> Written Practice

A. Write the letter of the best title and topic sentence for the paragraph below.

> A leaping snake three feet long can leap three feet through the air. Once a man was working in a jungle in Belize. Suddenly a leaping snake lunged at the man

and bit him through the boot. The man quickly jumped into a jeep and drove to the hospital. There he received medicine that saved his life.

1. Titles
    a. A Day in the Jungle
    b. Dangerous Snakes in the Jungle
    c. The Danger of Leaping Snakes
2. Topic sentences
    a. Many kinds of poisonous snakes live in the jungle.
    b. The leaping snake is a poisonous snake of the jungle.
    c. A jungle has many wild animals that can bring swift danger to people.

B. For each pair, write the letter of the topic sentence that is better. Also write why it is better.
1. a. If I had a whole day to do as I pleased, I would do one thing I have always wanted to do.
    b. If I had a whole day to do as I pleased, I would read a good book.
2. a. Last week many things happened at home.
    b. Last week some unusual things happened in our family.
3. a. Get some nails and boards.
    b. Making a birdhouse is an interesting project.

C. Write the letter of the better title in each pair. Also write why it is better.
1. a. My First Airplane Ride
    b. A Ride in the Air
2. a. A Person I Know
    b. An Interesting Person

D. Write a good topic sentence for the following paragraph.

Reclaiming Land From the Sea

_____

_____

First, the Dutch build a dike in the water around the
piece of land they want to reclaim. Then they pump the
water out of the enclosed area into the sea. They must
dig canals and set up pumps to drain the new land. The
salt from the seawater must be scraped off, and then
the land must rest five years before it can be used. The
farmers fertilize the land, and finally they can plant
crops. But the farmers must always keep a close watch
on the dikes, or the sea may come back in!

_____

35. Unity and Order

Every paragraph must have one main idea, which is given
in the topic sentence. All the other sentences develop the
topic sentence by explaining it or adding more information.
When all the sentences work together in this way, we say
the paragraph has **unity.**

The sentences in a paragraph must also be written in
a proper **order.** One kind of order is the order of time. A
paragraph that tells a story should say things in the order
in which they happened. A paragraph that explains how
to do something should tell what to do first, second, and

so on. Time order helps to make paragraphs clear and understandable.

Another kind of order is the order of importance. Paragraphs that give reasons for something may begin with the most important reason and end with the least important reason. Or they may give the least important reason first and the most important one last. Another way to follow the order of importance is to start with the least interesting fact and build up to the one that is most interesting.

When you write a paragraph, be sure to keep to the topic. Do not include any sentence that does not add to the topic sentence. Also write in a good order so that your paragraph makes sense. Paragraphs that have unity and order are easy to read and understand.

> **Remember:** The sentences in a paragraph should have unity and order. Two kinds of order are the order of time and the order of importance.

Oral Drill

Answer these questions about the paragraphs on the next page.

1. Is each paragraph written in the **order of time** or the **order of importance**?
2. Which paragraph tells a story?
3. Which paragraph explains how to do something?
4. Which paragraph gives reasons?
5. What is the topic sentence of each paragraph?

The *Titanic*

In 1912 a huge ship named the *Titanic* was built. People thought this ship was unsinkable. One man said that even God could not sink her. This ship had special watertight compartments to keep her from sinking. Only a few life belts and lifeboats were put on her because people thought these were not needed. But the *Titanic* struck an iceberg on her first voyage. Before many people knew there was danger, she was filling up with water and leaning sharply to one side. The *Titanic* sank on April 15, 1912, and sixteen hundred people went down with her.

Why Jesus Came

Jesus came into the world for several reasons. He came to comfort the sad and heal the sick. He came to teach people how they should live. He came to help men know God better. Above all, Jesus came to bring salvation so that all people may have eternal life.

Preparing Conch

Conch is a seafood that is served in various ways. You first need to go out into the ocean and find at least five shells with live conch in them. Punch little holes in each shell, and tie the shells together. Store them in the water near the shore where you can find them later. If you tie fewer than five together, they will walk away!

When you are ready to eat conch, get your shells and punch a large hole in each one. Use a knife to separate the snail from its shell. Pull the snail out of the hole you just made. Then clean the snail, and beat the meat with a wooden mallet until it is soft. Eat it raw or cook it the way you like it best.

Written Practice

A. Arrange these sentences in good order to make a proper paragraph. Leave out two sentences that do not belong. The first sentence is the topic sentence.

1. One day ten lepers cried out to Jesus for help.
2. Jesus asked, "Were not ten cleansed? But where are the nine?"
3. Leprosy was an incurable disease.
4. As they went, their leprosy disappeared!
5. But Jesus did not go to meet them.
6. Only one man had remembered to give thanks, and he was a Samaritan.
7. We should be thankful for all our blessings.
8. Instead, He told them to go and show themselves to the priests.
9. One of the men came back, fell down at Jesus' feet, and thanked Him.

B. Write a paragraph explaining how to do one of the following things. Start with a good topic sentence, and write in the order of time.

1. How to plant a row of beans.
2. How to clean a room.

3. How to fry an egg.
4. How to measure and saw a board.

> Review and Practice >

Write the words that belong in these blanks.
1. The —— line of each paragraph is indented.
2. Short, choppy sentences should be —— to make longer sentences.
3. Run-on sentences should be —— into shorter sentences.
4. Each line of a poem begins with a —— letter.

36. Chapter 3 Review

> Oral Drill >

A. Give the correct words to complete these sentences.
1. A —— names a person, place, or thing.
2. A —— noun names a specific person, place, or thing.
3. A —— noun does not name a specific person, place, or thing.
4. A —— noun names only one.
5. A —— noun names more than one.
6. A noun like **doorbell** is a (compound noun, noun phrase).
7. A noun like **Simon Peter** is a (compound noun, noun phrase).

B. Diagram the skeletons at the chalkboard.
1. Please work faster.
2. Were John and Eileen biking all morning?
3. My grandmother will come tomorrow.
4. The post office will deliver your letter.

> Written Practice >

A. Rewrite these sentences. Add correct capitalization and punctuation.
1. paris, france, is a famous city in europe
2. the barn is on fire
3. was george washington the first president of the united states
4. king charles ruled in england
5. come to visit us the last sunday in may
6. shall we visit the rocky mountains, lake louise, or yellowstone national park

7. my dentist is j. n. kaiser
8. the amazon river is a great river in south america
9. the indian ocean is near india

B. Write the plural form of each noun.

1. box	7. fox	13. salmon
2. match	8. alto	14. goose
3. dish	9. wife	15. man
4. paper	10. loaf	16. donkey
5. class	11. lady	17. roof
6. horse	12. sheep	18. potato

C. Diagram the sentence skeletons.

1. Please help us.
2. My brother and sister left yesterday.
3. Did you hear the blue jay?
4. The mail plane will go out tomorrow.

D. Fill in the blanks.

1. The ——— sentence tells what the paragraph is about.
2. A paragraph must speak about ——— topic only.
3. Paragraphs must have ——— and ——— so that the reader can understand them.
4. Paragraphs may be written in the order of ——— or the order of ———.

E. Copy this poem correctly.

To the Fireflies
i see you moving through the sky
like little lanterns passing by.
i watch you flit down in the grass
and flash a signal as you pass.
you make me think that I must be
a light to those who look at me.

—*Edith Witmer*

F. Write the following sentences in good paragraph form. Put the sentences in proper order. Leave out one sentence that does not belong. Divide sentences that are too long, and join sentences that are too choppy.

1. Carol studied the mirror carefully.
2. At last she decided that it must be a shiny piece of tin behind some glass.

3. She could not understand what was on the back side to make it so shiny.

4. She said to her friend, "I know how to make a mirror.

5. All you do is take a piece of glass.

6. Put some tin behind it.

7. You have a mirror."

8. Later she decided to try it just to make sure it would work, but it did not make a mirror after all, and she had to go back and tell her friend she was wrong.

9. Once before she had to tell someone she was wrong.

10. It would have been much better if she had tried it first to make sure it would work, and Carol learned that it is not wise to give directions about things we do not know ourselves.

G. Copy the best title for the paragraph above.

How to Make a Mirror

A Lesson From a Mirror

Why Mirrors Are Shiny

Winter Night

Blow, wind, **blow!**
Drift the **flying** snow!
Send it **twirling, whirling** overhead!
There**'s** a bedroom in a tree
Where, snug as snug **can be**,
The fluffy squirrel **nests** his cozy bed.

Shriek, wind, **shriek!**
Make the branches **creak!**
Battle with the boughs till break of day!
In a snow cave warm and tight,
Through the icy winter night,
The rabbit **sleeps** the peaceful hours away.

Call, wind, **call**,
In entry and in hall,
Straight from the mountain white and wild!
Softly **purrs** the pussy cat
On her little fluffy mat,
And near her **nestles** close her furry child.

Scold, wind, **scold**,
So bitter and so bold!
Shake the windows with your tap, tap, tap!
There with half-shut dreamy eyes,
The little drowsy baby **lies**,
Cuddled closely in his mother's lap.

—*Mary F. Butts*

All the verb forms in this poem are in bold print.
Notice how descriptive they are. Verbs are needed to
make our language interesting!

Chapter 4

Verbs

Verbs show action or being.

Action

Being

run

jump

sing

study

The boy is ill.

They are here.

I am happy.

37. Action Verbs

A **verb** is a part of speech. We could not speak without verbs. Most verbs are words that show action.

Verbs can show different kinds of action. They can show physical action or mental action. Words like **jump, run, swim,** and **cry** show physical action. Words like **think, study, read,** and **memorize** show mental action.

Action verbs can also show ownership or possession. The words **have, has,** and **had** show that someone owns or possesses something.

> John **has** a coat.
> Leopards **have** spots.

The word **has** shows that John owns a coat. The verb **have** shows that leopards possess spots.

Every sentence must have a verb. A sentence cannot have a complete thought without a verb. You learned in Chapter 1 that the simple predicate is a verb. The simple predicate is often called the verb in a sentence.

Remember that sometimes two verbs are joined together by **and** to make a compound predicate. You studied compound predicates in Chapter 1.

Mary **sewed** and **ironed.**

Remember: Most verbs are words that show action.

 Oral Drill

A. Give the following verbs.
 1. Five that show physical action.
 2. Five that show mental action.
 3. Three action verbs that show ownership.

B. Give the verbs in these sentences. Tell whether each verb shows **physical** action, **mental** action, or **ownership.**
 1. My dog jumped over that fence.
 2. Memorize this chapter of the Bible.
 3. Jesus healed many sick people.
 4. Jesus loves everyone.
 5. God placed the sun, moon, and stars in the sky.
 6. We have many blessings.
 7. Jane worked hard.
 8. I thought hard and remembered the answer.
 9. Brown ducks quacked and waddled around the lake.
 10. The red squirrel cracked a nut and ate it.

> **Written Practice** >

A. Copy the verbs in these sentences. After each verb, write **P, M,** or **O** to tell whether it shows physical action, mental action, or ownership.
  1. Few roses bloom without thorns.
  2. The men dug ditches.
  3. God filled the ditches with water.
  4. In the beginning God created the heaven and the earth.
  5. All creation praises His Name.
  6. We thank Him for His wonderful works.
  7. Jerry has a cold.

B. List the following verbs.
  1. Five that show physical action.
  2. Five that show mental action.
  3. Three action verbs that show ownership.

C. Copy and complete this sentence: **Most verbs are words that...**

D. Write two sentences that use verbs showing physical action. Look at the picture below for ideas.

E. Write a sentence of your own, using a verb that shows mental action.

> Review and Practice >

A. Copy the simple subject and the simple predicate of each sentence, and draw a dividing line between them. Underline the simple subject with one line, and the simple predicate (the verb) with two lines.
   1. The white swan swam gracefully.
   2. Grievous words stir up anger.
   3. God does all things well.
   4. Fools hate wisdom and understanding.
   5. Easy paths lead downward.
   6. Six woolly sheep grazed in the meadow.
   7. Mary had mumps.

B. Match the parts of speech to their definitions.
   1. A word that stands for a noun.   a. noun
   2. A word that names a person, place,   b. verb
      or thing.   c. pronoun
   3. A word that shows action or being.

C. In each sentence, find all the words that need capital letters, and write them correctly.
   1. does brother john live in canada?
   2. the mississippi river flows through the united states.
   3. the bethel christian school visited the zoo last friday.

38. The Verb *Be*

You have learned that most verbs show action. But there is one verb that does not show action. It is the verb **be.** The verbs in these sentences are forms of **be.**

> **Be** patient.
> God **is** love.
> The flowers **are** pretty.

The verb **be** has eight forms in all. The following sentences give examples of how the eight forms are used.

I **am** at school.   They **were** upstairs.
She **is** at home.   He will **be** at church.
You **are** here.   We have **been** there.
He **was** away.   Are you **being** quiet?

Which forms of **be** would you use in these sentences?

> My brother (be) at work.
> Yesterday we (be) reading about Joseph.

Remember: A verb is a word that shows action or being. The eight forms of **be** are **am, is, are, was, were, be, been,** and **being.**

Oral Drill

A. Give the correct form of each **be** in bold print.
1. It **be** the early bird that catches the worm.
2. "I **be** now ready to be offered, and the time of my departure **be** at hand."
3. Some things **be** easier said than done.

4. "Ye **be** my friends, if ye do whatsoever I command you."

5. James and John **be** disciples of Jesus.

6. Peter **be** a disciple too.

B. Tell which words are forms of **be.**

> The people were tired and hungry. They had been following Jesus to hear Him preach. Philip said, "There is not enough money to buy bread."
>
> One boy thought, "I am willing to share my lunch." In it there were five loaves and two fishes.
>
> Andrew asked, "What are they among so many?"
>
> Jesus gave thanks. Then He gave the food to the disciples to pass among the hungry people. There was more than enough food for everyone. There were twelve baskets left over.
>
> Many people were being blessed because one boy was willing to share what he had.

> **Written Practice**

A. Write the correct form of each **be** in bold print.

1. The Lord **be** my shepherd.

2. We **be** thankful for God's many gifts.

3. The children **be** singing a new song.

4. I **be** here before.

5. I **be** thankful now.

6. The children of Israel **be** in the wilderness forty years.

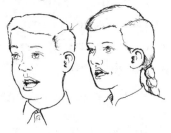

B. Write the definition of a verb.

C. List all the forms of the verb **be.**

D. Use three forms of **be** in sentences of your own.

> **Review and Practice**

A. Copy the verbs in these sentences. After each verb, write **A** or **B** to tell whether it shows action or being.
   1. I am the light of the world.
   2. The Gospel is a message of joy.
   3. We know about it through the Bible.
   4. The dolls are in the girls' room.
   5. God loves His people.
   6. Who feeds the birds?

B. Copy the nouns in these sentences. Capitalize all the proper nouns.
   1. dennis ran to the orchard.
   2. columbus sailed across the atlantic ocean.
   3. mount everest is the highest mountain in the world.
   4. conrad and james were in the barn.

---

39. Helping Verbs and Verb Phrases

A group of words working together as one verb is a **verb phrase.** A verb phrase is made up of a **main verb** and one or more **helping verbs.** In this sentence, the verb phrase is in bold print.

We **had been eating** breakfast.

In the sentence above, the main verb is **eating.** The helping verbs are **had** and **been.**

The main verb in a verb phrase is always the last word. The main verb may show action or being.

Action: had been **eating**
Being: may have **been**

Learn these helping verbs.

1. Forms of **be** can be helping verbs or main verbs.

   Helping verbs: **am** seen, **is** held, **are** kept, **was** told, **were** sent, will **be** won, has **been** sold, was **being** put
   Main verbs: Sue **is** here. She **was** absent.

2. Forms of **have** can be helping verbs or main verbs.

   Helping verbs: **have** walked, **has** run, **had** driven
   Main verbs: I **have** a dog. Bob **has** a rabbit.

3. Forms of **do** can be helping verbs or main verbs.

   Helping verbs: **do** care, **does** need, **did** listen
   Main verbs: We **do** our best. Kay **did** her work.

4. Some verbs can be helping verbs but not main verbs. One set is the three forms of **may: may, might,** and **must.** Three other sets come in pairs: **can—could, shall—should,** and **will—would.**

   may leave, **might** fall, **must** obey
   can help, **could** work
   shall write, **should** answer
   will think, **would** know

Remember: A group of words working together as one verb is a verb phrase. The last word in a verb phrase is the main verb. A main verb can be an action verb or a form of **be.**

▷ Oral Drill ▷

Give the verb phrases in these sentences. Tell which is the main verb in each phrase.

1. Some snow has fallen.
2. My Lord can supply all my needs.
3. We did read the story of Noah's ark.
4. You may be picking peas tomorrow.
5. The men will be mining coal today.
6. We will help you.

▷ Written Practice ▷

A. Copy each verb phrase, and underline the main verb.

> **Example:** The children will be helping Mother.
> **Answer:** will be <u>helping</u>

1. Francis has taken his crayons home.
2. God had sent His Son.
3. I will praise the Lord.
4. We have been sewing dresses.
5. Mother will cook potatoes for supper.
6. They are playing the same games every day.

B. Follow the directions. Try to answer from memory.
   1. Write the definition of a verb.
   2. List the following groups of helping verbs.
      a. Eight forms of **be.**
      b. Three forms of **have.**
      c. Three forms of **do.**
      d. Three forms of **may.**
      e. Three pairs of other helping verbs that cannot be main verbs.

C. Use these as helping verbs in sentences of your own.

1. been   3. does   5. can
2. have   4. may   6. will

> Review and Practice >

A. Diagram the skeletons of the following sentences.
   1. You will be walking with us.
   2. Mervin and Steven swept the floor and washed the windows in the barn.
   3. Have they done a good job?
   4. Sing heartily unto the Lord.

B. Copy all the verbs in the following sentences. Watch for compound predicates.
   1. Paul and Silas sang and prayed in prison.
   2. The jailer believed and rejoiced.
   3. He washed their wounds and set food before them.
   4. Carol saw the children and waved to them.
   5. The boys mowed and raked the yard.

---

40. Developing Paragraphs by Giving Examples

Remember that a paragraph is a group of sentences that develop a single topic. The topic sentence usually comes first, and it tells what the paragraph is about. The other sentences add more information to develop the topic.

Paragraphs can be developed in different ways. One way is by giving examples. In the following paragraph, the topic is the special tools that birds have to get their food. Can you find four examples of special tools?

God gave birds special tools to get their food. Wood warblers have long, thin beaks for spearing up insects from among leaves on the ground. Swifts and swallows have wide mouths surrounded by bristles that help them catch flying insects. Sparrows, finches, and buntings have feet that are specially made to scratch for seeds. A sparrow can hop up and down and scratch with both feet at once! Cardinals and blue jays have short, stout bills for cracking hard seeds. "Behold the fowls of the air: for they sow not, neither do they reap, nor gather into barns; yet your heavenly Father feedeth them" (Matthew 6:26).

Remember: One way of developing paragraphs is by giving examples.

> Oral Drill >

Read this paragraph. Then answer the questions that follow it.

The right kind of dog makes an excellent pet, but dogs serve people in many other ways as well. Dogs are used to guard property. They can learn to herd sheep or cattle. Some dogs serve as eyes for blind people, and some learn to pull carts. Other dogs hunt small game, and still others search for lawbreakers or lost children. Every dog should be immunized against rabies. With their remarkable sense of smell, dogs can find illegal drugs and hidden explosives. Because dogs are useful in so many ways, they are among the most valuable animals that work for people.

1. Which is the topic sentence?
2. This paragraph also has a summarizing sentence. A summarizing sentence comes at the end of a paragraph, and it restates the main idea in other words. Which is the summarizing sentence?
3. This paragraph is developed by seven examples of how dogs are useful to people. What are these examples?
4. Which sentence does not belong in the paragraph?
5. Does the paragraph have a good variety of sentences?

> **Written Practice**

Choose one sentence from the list below and on the next page, and use it as a topic sentence. Write a paragraph that develops the topic by giving examples. Your paragraph should have from five to eight sentences.

1. Our food comes from many places, far and near.
2. There are many jobs around the house that children can do.

3. We have many kinds of weather in our part of the country.
4. An orderly life includes many small habits.

> **Review and Practice**

1. What do we call spoken English?
2. A paragraph has (unity, order) when all the sentences tell about one topic.
3. Sentences in a paragraph may come in the order of ——— or the order of ———.
4. What are two things that a title should do?

41. Verbs Show Tense

Tense means **time.** Verbs show tense. Verbs can show present tense, past tense, and future tense.

Present tense verbs tell about things happening right now. We say they are happening in the present. Sometimes a verb in the present tense ends with **s.**

I **work** now.
He **walks** to school.
They **wash** their hands.

Past tense verbs tell about things that happened before this time. We say they happened in the past. The past tense of most verbs ends with **ed.**

I **worked** yesterday.
He **walked** to school.
They **washed** the dishes.

Future tense verbs tell about things that have not happened yet but will happen sometime later. We say they will happen in the future. The words **shall** and **will** are used as helping verbs to show future tense.

I **shall do** my work tomorrow.
He **will walk** to school.
They **will wash** the windows.

Here is a chart showing four verbs in all three tenses.

Present	Past	Future
look	looked	will look
talk	talked	will talk
enjoy	enjoyed	will enjoy
decide	decided	will decide

Remember: Tense means **time.** Verbs can show present tense, past tense, and future tense.

A. Give the missing tenses. The first one is done for you.

Present	Past	Future
1. promise	promised	will promise
2. ——	stayed	—— ——
3. bloom	——	—— ——
4. ——	——	will wash
5. ——	studied	—— ——

B. Say each verb or verb phrase, and tell whether it is in **present, past,** or **future** tense.

1. We see many kinds of birds in our woods.
2. We shall see them too.
3. You will study plants soon.
4. Pioneer children feared wolves.
5. Men chopped down many trees.
6. Trust in the Lord.
7. Pray to Him.

C. Change the following sentences to future tense.

1. The boys know the answer.
2. We rake the leaves.

> Written Practice >

A. Copy the chart, and fill in the missing tenses. The first one is done for you.

Present	Past	Future
1. help	helped	will help
2. climb	————	———— ————
3. touch	————	———— ————
4. ————	filled	———— ————
5. comb	————	———— ————
6. ————	————	will learn
7. show	————	———— ————

B. Copy the verb or verb phrase in each sentence. Write whether each one is in **present, past,** or **future** tense.

> **Examples:**   a. We painted the wall.
> b. I will learn my lessons.
> **Answers:**   a. painted—past
> b. will learn—future

1. A woodpecker drilled these holes.
2. Wolves travel in packs.
3. Last year we studied flowers.
4. Jesus loves me.
5. Jesus will come again.
6. We will trust in Him.

C. Rewrite each sentence, making the changes given in the directions.

1. Change the verb to future tense. Use the helping verb **will.** Underline the verb phrase.
   a. Dennis finishes his work.
   b. Wanda bakes cookies.
   c. The children laugh.

2. Change the verb to future tense. Use the helping verb **shall.** Underline the verb phrase.
   a. I wait here.
   b. We know the answer.
   c. I walk slowly.

D. Write the correct word for each blank.
   1. A verb is a word that shows —— or ——.
   2. **Tense** means ——.
   3. Verbs can show —— tense, —— tense, and ——
      tense.

E. Write three sentences of your own. In the first sentence, use a present tense verb. In the second sentence, use a past tense verb. In the third sentence, use a future tense verb.

---

42. Agreement of Subjects and Verbs

Many verbs in the present tense end with **s.** We may call this the **s form** of the verb. Study the following examples.

Wrong	**Right**
Jesus am the Truth.	Jesus **is** the Truth.
He do love us.	He **does** love us.
God have great power.	God **has** great power.
He watch over us.	He **watches** over us.

Verbs in the **s** form are used with all singular subjects except **I** and **you.** Singular subjects are subjects that name only one person, place, or thing.

> The dog **buries** the bone. (not **bury**)
> Alice **has** a letter. (not **have**)
> She **writes** to Mary. (not **write**)
> I **like** springtime. (not **likes**)
> You **mow** the lawn. (not **mows**)

If the subject is singular and is not **I** or **you,** be sure to use the **s** form of the verb. Do not use the **s** form if the subject is plural.

Be sure to spell the **s** form correctly. For many verbs, simply add **s.**

> jump—jumps   run—runs
> sing—sings   read—reads

Add **es** to verbs that end with **s, sh, ch,** or **x.**

> bless—blesses   catch—catches
> wish—wishes   mix—mixes

If a verb ends with **y** after a consonant, change the **y** to **i** and add **es.** Simply add **s** if the **y** comes after a vowel.

> study—studies   pray—prays
> carry—carries   enjoy—enjoys

Remember: Verbs in the **s** form go with all singular subjects except **I** and **you.** A singular subject names only one person, place, or thing.

▷ Oral Drill ▷

A. Tell which is the correct verb form.
1. Charles (come, comes) into the store.
2. We (has, have) the book.
3. John (carry, carries) the basket.
4. Mary (find, finds) a coin.
5. The boys (feed, feeds) the cows.
6. He (do, does) the work.
7. You (is, are) a good helper.
8. I (is, am, are) glad.

B. In each sentence, change the subject to **My father.**
1. I fly to Canada.   2. I lay bricks.

▷ Written Practice ▷

A. Copy the correct verb to go with each subject.
1. She (has, have) my bucket.
2. You (has, have) my coat.
3. Jane (do, does) the cleaning.
4. They (help, helps) us.
5. Mary (do, does) like to sing.
6. The students (sing, sings) beautiful songs.

B. In each sentence, change the subject to **My brother.**
Change the verb to make it agree with the new subject.
Underline the verb in your new sentence.

   Example: We study the poem.
   Answer: My brother studies the poem.

1. We catch chickens.
2. We plow the garden.

3. They crush the boxes.
4. The boys climb the ladder.

Review and Practice

A. Copy the verbs in these sentences. Be ready to tell in class what kind of verb each one is: **action, being,** or **helping.** (Some are two kinds.)

1. We have bananas.
2. They are delicious.
3. The children were memorizing a psalm.
4. Study your lesson well.
5. We might be going soon.
6. Can I carry this heavy box?

B. Write the correct words to fill in the blanks.
1. A verb is a word that shows —— or ——.
2. A verb —— is a group of verbs working together.
3. —— means **time.**
4. Verbs can show —— tense, —— tense, and —— tense.
5. The **s** form of a verb may be used only with a —— subject.

C. Write the plural form of each noun.

1. apple	4. berry	7. potato
2. church	5. key	8. alto
3. fox	6. calf	9. ox

43. Past Forms of Regular Verbs

Remember that past tense verbs tell about things that happened before this time. We say they happened in the past. They tell about something already done or finished.

The past form of **regular verbs** is formed by adding **ed** to the present form.

want—wanted   listen—listened

For some verbs, a spelling change must be made when **ed** is added. Study the following rules.

1. If a verb ends with **e,** drop the **e** before adding **ed.**

   like—liked   promise—promised

2. If a verb ends with **y** after a consonant, change the **y** to **i** before adding **ed.** If the **y** comes after a vowel, simply add **ed.** (This rule is much like the one for adding **s** or **es.**)

   study—studied   pray—prayed
   carry—carried   enjoy—enjoyed

3. If a verb ends with one consonant after a short vowel, double the last consonant before adding **ed.**

   rub—rubbed   tip—tipped

Past forms that end with **ed** may be used with or without the helping verbs **have, has,** and **had.**

I **looked** under the bed for my shoes.
I **have looked** under the bed for my shoes.

Ruth **dropped** the bag
   of groceries.
Ruth **has dropped** the
   bag of groceries.

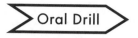

Oral Drill

A. Spell the correct past form of each verb.

1. pat	3. love	5. trade	7. hike
2. try	4. trip	6. hoe	8. plow

B. Change each sentence so that the verb is a past form.

1. They dip the candles in wax.
2. We hike on that mountain.
3. We promise to be there.
4. He trims the hedge.
5. I brush the horse's back.
6. She answers the questions.
7. They hurry back to their seats.

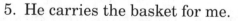

Written Practice

A. Write the correct past forms of these verbs.

1. rake	3. rub	5. wash	7. touch
2. sound	4. carry	6. bury	8. decide

B. Rewrite these sentences to tell about the past. Underline the verbs in your new sentences.

Example: We work hard.
Answer: We <u>worked</u> hard.

1. We fill the holes.
2. You fold your paper.
3. She stays here.
4. They climb the bank.
5. He carries the basket for me.
6. We study our Sunday school lessons.

> **Review and Practice** >

A. Copy the verb phrases in these sentences. Underline the main verb in each phrase.
  1. Cain had worked in the fields.
  2. Abel had been tending sheep.
  3. Cain was bringing the fruit of the ground.
  4. Abel was obeying God.
  5. God was pleased with Abel.
  6. Then Abel was killed by Cain.
  7. Cain would be punished for his sin.

B. Copy the verb or verb phrase in each sentence. Write **present, past,** or **future** after each one to tell which tense it is.
  1. Saul looked for his father's donkeys.
  2. A servant went with him.
  3. Ask the man of God.
  4. Samuel spoke to Saul.
  5. You will be king.
  6. Saul prophesied.

---

44. Developing Paragraphs by Using Steps

In Lesson 40 you learned that giving examples is one way of developing paragraphs. Another way to develop them is by using steps. The steps may come in the order in which things happened (the order of time). Then the writer may use words such as **then, soon, next, later, immediately,** and **afterward** to help the reader understand the time order.

A paragraph may also use steps to describe something. For example, you can write a paragraph describing a flower by telling about its parts step by step. You might start with the top of the flower and move down, or you may begin at the roots and go up.

The following paragraph gives a step-by-step description of plants. Notice how it begins with the roots and ends with the upper parts.

> Most plants have certain main parts that are easy to recognize. Out of sight underground are the roots. The large roots divide into smaller branches, and together they anchor the plant in the earth. Above the roots, the stem grows like a central supporting tower. The stem usually divides into branches that have leaves, flowers, and seeds. And in every seed, by the marvelous power of God, there is a pattern for producing another plant of the very same kind.

Remember: Paragraphs can be developed by using steps. The steps may come in the order of time, or they may describe the parts step by step.

 Oral Drill

Answer these questions about the paragraph in the lesson.

1. What is the paragraph about?
2. What is the topic sentence?

3. Does the paragraph develop the topic sentence by giving a time order or by describing the parts in order?

4. In what order are the parts named?

5. What would happen if the paragraph first described the stem, then the leaves and flowers, then the roots, and then the seeds?

> Written Practice

A. Write the following sentences in paragraph form and in correct time order. The first sentence is the topic sentence.

1. There was once an ungodly farmer who was scoffing at his Christian neighbor.

2. Now he had more corn in his cribs than ever before.

3. He said that he had plowed and harrowed his cornfield on Sunday.

4. The Christian thought awhile.

5. He had planted the seed on Sunday, cultivated the corn on Sunday, and harvested the crop on Sunday.

6. "I can only say," he finally replied, "that the Lord does not settle all His accounts in October."

7. What could the Christian neighbor say about that?

B. Write the topic sentence of the following paragraph. Does the paragraph develop the topic **by giving a time order** or **by describing the parts in order**?

The camel is a large, awkward, stiff-legged, goose-necked, humpbacked, shaggy animal. It has a divided upper lip like a rabbit's, and a dull, sad expression on its small face. Overhanging eyelids and eyelashes protect its bulging eyes from the fierce sun. Horny pads on its chest and knees protect it from the sand when it kneels. Because God made the camel in this way, it is well suited for life in the desert.

45. Past Forms of Irregular Verbs

The past forms of some verbs do not end with **ed.** Verbs with such past forms are **irregular verbs.**

The girls **sweep** the floor.
Mother **swept** the kitchen.

The verbs in the following sentences are not correct. They do not sound right, do they?

The boys sweeped the basement.
I sayed the answer loudly and clearly.
I holded the rope at recess.
Marcia setted the table.

A dictionary will help you when you are not sure how to spell the past form of a verb. If it does not show a past form, spell it in the regular way by adding **ed.** Do not be afraid to use the dictionary!

Study these irregular verb forms. The past forms in this list do not change when the helping verbs **have, has,** and **had** are used.

Present	Past form without helper	Past form with helper
bring	brought	(have) brought
burst	burst	(has) burst
feel	felt	(had) felt
hold	held	(have) held
lay	laid	(has) laid
lead	led	(had) led
leave	left	(have) left
lose	lost	(has) lost
pay	paid	(had) paid
say	said	(have) said
send	sent	(has) sent
set	set	(had) set
sit	sat	(have) sat
swing	swung	(has) swung
think	thought	(had) thought
weep	wept	(have) wept
win	won	(has) won
wring	wrung	(had) wrung

> Oral Drill

A. Spell the past form of each verb correctly.

| 1. win | 3. lose | 5. pay | 7. set |
| 2. sit | 4. burst | 6. say | 8. swing |

B. Change each sentence so that it tells about the past.

1. We leave early for school.
2. The stove feels hot.
3. The Good Shepherd leads
   His sheep.
4. I think hard at school.
5. The washerwoman wrings
   out the clothes.
6. The children swing on the rope.
7. Father pays the bills.
8. A widow picks up sticks.
9. God sends a prophet to her house.
10. God blesses her.

> **Written Practice**

A. Write the past form of each verb correctly.

| 1. build | 3. lay | 5. send | 7. think |
| 2. weep | 4. set | 6. leave | 8. lead |

B. Rewrite these sentences, using the past form of each verb.
Underline the verbs in your new sentences.
1. The boys win the game.
2. The girls lose.
3. Karen sets the dishes on the table.
4. The children sit on the grass to eat lunch.
5. The balloons burst in the heat.
6. The students say their memory verses in the morning.

C. Use each of these words in sentences of your own.

| 1. swing | 2. swung | 3. lose | 4. lost |

> **Review and Practice**

Write the correct word for each blank.

1. A verb is a word that shows —— or ——.
2. A verb —— is a group of verbs working together.
3. —— means **time.**
4. Verbs can show —— tense, —— tense, and —— tense.
5. The **s** form of a verb must go with a —— subject.
6. The past form of regular verbs is made by adding the suffix ——.
7. Verbs whose past forms are not made by adding **ed** are —— verbs.

---

46. More About Irregular Verbs

You have learned that verbs whose past forms do not end with **ed** are irregular verbs. The verbs **come** and **go** are two irregular verbs. For the past tense, we do not say "comed" or "goed." Instead we say **came** and **went.**

> **Present tense**—People **come** into the store.
> **Past tense**—People **came** into the store.
>
> **Present tense**—I **go** for more nails.
> **Past tense**—I **went** for more nails.

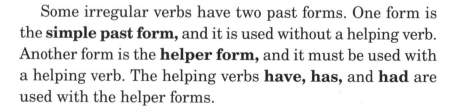

Some irregular verbs have two past forms. One form is the **simple past form,** and it is used without a helping verb. Another form is the **helper form,** and it must be used with a helping verb. The helping verbs **have, has,** and **had** are used with the helper forms.

Present form—I **see** a deer.
Simple past form—I **saw** a deer.
Helper form—I have **seen** a deer.

Study these examples of verbs whose past forms are made in irregular ways.

Present	Simple past	Helper form
come	came	(have) come
go	went	(has) gone
give	gave	(had) given
see	saw	(have) seen
eat	ate	(has) eaten
do	did	(had) done
sing	sang	(have) sung
ring	rang	(has) rung
know	knew	(had) known
break	broke	(have) broken
grow	grew	(has) grown
tear	tore	(had) torn
write	wrote	(have) written
wear	wore	(has) worn

Check a dictionary when you are not sure how to spell the past form of a verb.

Spell the simple past form and the helper form of each verb in the following list. For numbers 1 and 2, look in a dictionary to see how the past forms are shown.

Present	Simple past	Helper form
1. draw	———	(have) ———
2. ride	———	(has) ———
3. wear	———	(had) ———
4. know	———	(have) ———
5. eat	———	(has) ———
6. see	———	(had) ———
7. do	———	(have) ———
8. ring	———	(has) ———
9. go	———	(had) ———
10. tear	———	(have) ———
11. are	———	(have) ———

> Written Practice

A. Copy the verb in each sentence. After the verb, write the simple past form and the helper form with the helping verb **have.**

> **Example:** Most farmers eat a hearty breakfast.
> **Answer:**   eat, ate, have eaten

1. The horses come down the road.
2. We go to school early.
3. Beth and Faye do their lessons well.
4. They know where to find the answers.
5. We wear gloves in cold weather.
6. The bells ring clearly.
7. These rocks break easily.
8. The girls tear the rags into strips.
9. Some plants grow rapidly.
10. We see the goodness of God.
11. Keith and Kevin write neatly.
12. The people give cheerfully.

B. Write each of the following verbs in sentences of your own.

1. sing   3. sung   5. saw
2. sang   4. see   6. seen

> Review and Practice >

A. Diagram the sentence skeletons.
   1. Sandra will feed her dog.
   2. Please close the windows.
   3. Brian and Timothy washed and waxed the car.
   4. Did you hear the birds?

B. Copy each sentence. Use capital letters and punctuation correctly.
   1. john quincy adams was the sixth president of the united states
   2. the arabian desert is along the red sea
   3. were you in school on monday

---

47. Past Forms That Need Helpers

Some past forms of verbs always need helping verbs. The past forms that end with an **n** or **un** sound are usually the ones that need a helper. We use the helping verbs **have, has,** and **had** with such verbs.

Wrong	**Right**
I seen a robin.	I **have seen** a robin.
He broken the dish.	He **has broken** the dish.
They begun the work.	They **had begun** the work.

The simple past forms of verbs must not be used with the helping verbs **have, has,** and **had.**

Wrong	Right
He has broke the dish.	He **broke** the dish.
	He **has broken** the dish.
I have ate my lunch.	I **ate** my lunch.
	I **have eaten** my lunch.
I had wrote a letter.	I **wrote** a letter.
	I **had written** a letter.

In most sentences with a verb phrase, the simple subject comes first and then the whole verb phrase. But in a question, the helping verb comes first. The simple subject is written between the helping verb and the main verb.

You **have eaten** your dinner.
Have you **eaten** your dinner?

She **has drunk** the milk.
Has she **drunk** the milk?

Study this chart. Notice that all the helper forms have an **n** or **un** sound.

Present	Simple past	Helper form
see	saw	(have) seen
do	did	(have) done
sing	sang	(have) sung
ring	rang	(have) rung
grow	grew	(have) grown
speak	spoke	(have) spoken
ride	rode	(have) ridden
drink	drank	(have) drunk

Remember: A past form that has an n or un sound usually needs the helping verb have, has, or had.

Oral Drill

A. Say **yes** or **no** to tell whether each verb form must be used with a helping verb.

1. saw	5. spoke	9. blew
2. seen	6. ridden	10. taken
3. rang	7. done	11. swam
4. sung	8. rung	12. went

B. Tell how to correct the wrong verb forms in these sentences.

1. My cousins have went on a trip.
2. The ducks have swam all around the pond.
3. Alta has spoke well.
4. The children swang on the vines in the tree.
5. Had you knew the answer?
6. Who taken my place?
7. It had began to rain.
8. Elijah run before Ahab's chariot.
9. Mother sung while she worked.
10. The ship sunk to the bottom of the ocean.
11. It had sank there long ago.
12. Have you rode your new bike?
13. Have you began your next lesson?
14. I already done it.

> **Written Practice** >

A. Choose the correct verb form for each sentence. If it is a helper form, write the helping verb with it.

> **Examples:**   a.   I (rang, rung) the bell.
>   b.   I have (rang, rung) the bell.
> **Answers:**   a.   rang
>   b.   have rung

1. The men have (saw, seen) the fire.
2. I (saw, seen) a deer.
3. Mark (saw, seen) a bear last week.
4. Sue (came, come) home yesterday.
5. She had (went, gone) to visit Aunt May.
6. She (went, gone) on the train.
7. Paul had (did, done) his work well.
8. He (did, done) all he was told to do.
9. Have you (gave, given) the money to Mother?
10. Patty (gave, given) me this.

B. Copy each sentence, leaving out the unnecessary helping verb.

1. The telephone had rang.
2. We have sang this carol.
3. We have wrote a letter.
4. John had went home.
5. Henry and Frank have came along.
6. Marlin has rang the bell.
7. Becky has broke the vase.
8. The baby has ate her porridge.

> Review and Practice >

A. Write the plural form of each noun.
1. bus   3. sheep   5. child
2. box   4. city   6. day

B. Copy each verb below. After the verb, write the simple past form and the helper form with the helping verb **have.**

   Example: break, broke, have broken

1. come   3. sing   5. know
2. see   4. write   6. wear

---

48. Writing Directions

To develop a paragraph in steps, you may tell things in the order they happened. You may also describe something by naming the parts step by step. Another way of developing a paragraph in steps is to write directions in the order in which things should be done. This kind of paragraph explains how to do something step by step.

When we write a paragraph to tell how to do something, we need to write the steps in the order of time. We begin by telling which step should be done first. Then we tell which step is second, third, and so on.

Do not begin every sentence in your paragraph with the words **then** or **and then.** Use words like **first, second, third, later, next,** and **finally** so that the reader can easily understand the directions.

It is also important to give directions accurately. One wrong measurement or ingredient in a recipe can make the food unfit to eat. One wrong or missing sentence in giving directions can cause much trouble and misunderstanding. Never try to tell someone how to do something unless you know how to do it yourself.

Follow these rules for giving directions.

1. Be sure to know your subject. Know all the important details, such as the name of each part you mention.

2. Make your directions short, but tell accurately the best way to do what you are describing.

3. Use exact words and give each step in the right order to make your directions clear.

4. Use a variety of words to begin your sentences.

Remember: A paragraph that tells how to do something should be developed by using steps. The steps should come in the order in which they are to be done.

> Oral Drill >

Tell which of these paragraphs is properly developed by using steps. Tell how to improve the poor paragraph.

1.   Making a Crystal Garden

Begin by laying three or four pieces of freshly washed coal in a bowl. Mix together 6 tablespoons water, 6 tablespoons salt, 6 tablespoons liquid laundry bluing, and 1 tablespoon ammonia. Pour this mixture over the coal. For a more colorful garden, put a few drops of food coloring on the coal. Then set your garden in the sunlight or some other warm, dry place, and in a few hours it will begin to grow. To keep it growing, mix more liquid and carefully pour it into the bottom of the bowl. Give your garden to someone who needs love and cheer.

2.   Making a Crystal Garden

Get some water, salt, and bluing. Put these things on a few pieces of coal. Put the coal in a dish. Use any color of dish you like. I think maybe you are supposed to put some vinegar on it too. Set it in a window on the north side of the house where it will be in the sunlight. Soon it will begin to grow. Keep your garden growing by adding more liquid. Give it away. Add more color to it if you like.

> **Written Practice**

A. Make a list of steps that tell how to do something. You may choose one of the following tasks. Be sure the steps are in the correct order, telling what should be first, second, and so on.
1. Washing dishes.
2. Cleaning a room.
3. Cleaning a fish aquarium.

4. Getting a garden ready for planting.
5. Packing a lunch for school.
6. Frying an egg.
7. Painting a doghouse.
8. Mowing a lawn.

B. Use your list for Part A to write a paragraph giving a set of directions. Follow the rules for making your paragraph clear and interesting. Write five to ten sentences.

---

49. Chapter 4 Review

 Oral Drill

A. Define a verb.

B. Give the two action verbs in each sentence. Tell whether each verb shows **physical** action, **mental** action, or **ownership.**
   1. I thought hard and wrote the answer.
   2. I rode my bike after I studied my lesson.
   3. I had that coat before I got this one.

C. Say the verbs. Tell whether each one shows **action** or **being.**
   1. Is your cold better?
   2. Drink more juice.
   3. Work in the morning.
   4. Are those your boots?

D. Choose the correct words in parentheses.
1. Bruce (do, does) his work well.
2. The little girl (sing, sings) well.
3. She (drank, drunk) all her milk.
4. Marvin and Nicholas (work, works) in the field.
5. Has Mother (took, taken) the clothes off the line?
6. The bell (rang, rung) loudly.
7. Sarah had (ran, run) out to the garage.
8. We (sang, sung) while we worked.
9. The ship (sank, sunk) in the Atlantic Ocean.

> Written Practice >

A. Copy each verb phrase, and underline the main verb.
1. We have been picking cherries.
2. Will you be freezing them?
3. We have canned many cherries.
4. Next winter we can be eating them.

B. Copy the verbs. After each one, write **present, past,** or
future.
1. We eat lunch at twelve o'clock.
2. You grew an inch this past year!
3. How much will you grow this year?

C. Write the present, past, and future tenses of each verb.
Use **will** for the helping verb in future tense.

Present	**Past**	**Future**
1. carry	——	—— ——
2. ——	learned	—— ——
3. ——	——	will know
4. ——	did	—— ——
5. ——	saw	—— ——
6. ——	came	—— ——
7. go	——	—— ——
8. eat	——	—— ——

D. Write the correct words in parentheses.
   1. The horses (run, runs) down the lane.
   2. Timothy (study, studies) hard.
   3. Joshua and Jonathan (help, helps) their father.
   4. Who (took, taken) the books off the table?
   5. School (began, begun) early this morning.
   6. The teacher has (rang, rung) the bell.
   7. Judy (ran, run) to the house as fast as she could.
   8. Have you (sang, sung) today?
   9. The ship had (sank, sunk) long ago.

E. Copy each verb below. After the verb, write the simple past form and helper form with the helping verb **has.**

Example: go, went, has gone

1. come
2. do
3. see
4. give
5. eat
6. sing
7. know
8. have
9. break

F. Write the definitions.
1. A paragraph is . . .
2. A topic sentence is . . .

G. Use the paragraph below to do the following exercises.
1. Copy the topic sentence.
2. Write the letter that tells how the topic sentence is developed.
   a. By telling things in the order they happened.
   b. By giving steps in the order they should be done.
   c. By describing something step by step.
   d. By giving examples.
3. Write the first three words of the sentence that does not belong.

Railroads provide different kinds of transportation. One important kind is passenger service. Passenger trains may carry people from city to city or from one part of a city to another part. Airplanes are faster than trains. Railroads also provide freight service. Freight trains haul coal, grain, lumber, machinery, and other products. Some trains provide piggyback service. They can haul many truck trailers on flatcars for less money than it would cost to drive them all separately on the highway.

Building Correctly

Building correctly includes many things:
Right motives, good planning, and fresh zeal that clings
To old proven methods, materials, and tools;
For building correctly means minding good rules.

Right motives for building all center in one—
Obedience to parents, and not just for fun;
Because parents send us to school, understand,
They want us to keep our instructor's command.

Good planning is needful for order and rest;
It helps us be punctual and work at our best.
Write down your assignments and then plan with care;
For worthy assignments, we need to prepare.

Fresh zeal is created by motives of right;
Obedience to parents should be our delight.
Good planning will also give zeal to press on
And bring to completion the work we've begun.

Zeal surely needs anchors, not wings for a flight;
It needs to be anchored in things that are right.
Attach all your energy fast to this rule:
"Obey well your parents, especially in school."

Chapter 5
Using Verbs Correctly

A WISE SON
MAKETH A
GLAD FATHER
Proverbs 10:1

is—are	their—they're	set—sit
was—were	your—you're	let—leave
doesn't—don't	raise—rise	can—may
its—it's	lay—lie	teach—learn

50. Action Verbs With Direct Objects

Sometimes an action verb is followed by a **direct object.** A direct object is a noun or pronoun that receives the action of the verb.

To find a direct object, first find the skeleton of the sentence (the simple subject and the simple predicate). Then ask **whom** or **what** after the skeleton.

Robert planted a tree.

Robert is the simple subject, and **planted** is the simple predicate. Robert planted what? Robert planted a **tree.** **Tree** is the direct object.

Robert was not planted, but the **tree** was planted. So we say that **tree** receives the action of **planted.** A direct object always receives action. Only action verbs can have direct objects.

On a sentence diagram, a direct object is written on the base line after the skeleton. A straight line separates the direct object from the verb. This line does not go through the base line, but rests on it.

Robert planted a tree.

| Robert | planted | tree |

> **Remember:** A direct object is a noun or pronoun that receives the action of a verb. Only action verbs can have direct objects. To find a direct object, say the sentence skeleton and then ask **whom** or **what** after it.

 Oral Drill

A. Find the direct object in each sentence by saying the skeleton and then asking **whom** or **what** after it.
1. The little cat can catch the bird.
2. God sends the rain.
3. Has Charles raised the window?
4. We thank the Lord.
5. Robert's red hen laid two eggs yesterday.
6. Did Alta pay Mrs. Brown for the butter?
7. Mr. Brown built a pen for his rabbits.
8. The warm sun melted the snow.

B. On the chalkboard, diagram the skeletons and direct objects of the sentences in Part A.

 Written Practice

A. Diagram the skeletons and direct objects of these sentences.
1. Father was laying bricks.
2. My mother will bake cookies.
3. Does the cat catch the mice?
4. Bring more water.
5. Our neighbor is raising peanuts.

6. A soft answer turneth away wrath.
7. Jesus healed the sick people.
8. Did the girls sing the new song here?
9. God sent a whale.
10. The whale swallowed Jonah.
11. Jonah preached a message to Nineveh.
12. God spared Nineveh.
13. Was Janice helping Mother this morning?
14. Lightning struck our big apple tree.
15. The strong wind carried the thick smoke.

B. Write the definition of a verb.

C. Write two sentences with direct objects. Use the following
   pictures to help you.

Review and Practice

A. Write the following sentences correctly.
   1. Dale hurried out and run down the road.
   2. They has had a lot of trouble lately.
   3. I had wrote Martha a letter.
   4. I seen her in church yesterday.

B. Copy the verbs in these sentences. After each verb, write **P, M,** or **O** to tell whether it shows physical action, mental action, or ownership.

1. The children have English books on their desks.
2. They study their lessons diligently.
3. Many fish swim in the pond.
4. Squirrels scold and chatter in the trees.
5. The Canada geese had a nest by the pond.

---

51. Action Verbs Without Direct Objects

In Lesson 50 you learned that a direct object is a noun or pronoun that receives the action of a verb. A direct object answers the question **whom** or **what** after a verb. But some sentences do not have a word that receives the action. Such a sentence does not have a direct object.

To see whether a sentence has a direct object, find the skeleton and then ask **whom** or **what** after it. If no word answers this question, the sentence does not have a direct object.

Look at the following sentences.

The children went to bed.
They slept soundly.

For the first sentence above, ask, "Children went what?" **To bed** does not tell **what** they went but **where** they went. So **bed** does not receive the action of the verb, and it is not the direct object. No other word tells **whom** or **what** they went, either. So this sentence does not have a direct object.

For the second sentence, ask, "They slept what?" **Soundly** does not tell **what** they slept but **how** they slept. So s**oundly** does not receive the action of the verb, and it is not the direct object. No other word tells **whom** or **what** they slept, either. So this sentence does not have a direct object.

Do not think that a sentence has a direct object just because some words follow the verb. A sentence has a direct object only if there is a noun or a pronoun that receives the action of the verb.

Remember: Not every action verb is followed by a direct object.

> Oral Drill

A. In each sentence, give the simple subject, the simple predicate, and the direct object if there is one.

1. Birds live in many places.
2. Canaries sing lively, cheerful songs.
3. Bobwhites live in fields and woods.
4. They eat many seeds.
5. Is Sister Betty asking another question?
6. A wrathful man stirreth up strife.
7. Set the alarm clock.
8. I can pay William.
9. The priests would blow the trumpets.
10. The people marched around Jericho.
11. The walls fell down flat.
12. God's people took Jericho.

B. On the chalkboard, diagram the skeletons and direct objects of the sentences in Part A.

> **Written Practice**

A. Diagram the simple subjects and the simple predicates. Also diagram all the direct objects.
1. The children may eat the oranges.
2. They have stopped the train.
3. Is Gerald counting the boards?
4. Lift your end higher.
5. Float the logs down the canal.
6. We shall dig here.
7. A talebearer revealeth secrets.
8. The men went down to Ai.
9. The enemies chased the Israelites.
10. Joshua tore his clothes.
11. He fell on his face before God.
12. Achan had stolen some things.
13. The people stoned Achan.
14. Then the men conquered Ai.

B. Copy the correct words.
1. A direct object follows a verb that shows (action, being).
2. A direct object (performs, receives) action.

Review and Practice

A. Write the correct word for each blank.
   1. A —— names a person, place, or thing.
   2. A —— shows action or being.
   3. A —— takes the place of a noun.

B. Write the correct letter for each definition.
   1. It shows strong feeling.
   2. It tells you to do something.   a. statement
   3. It gives a fact.   b. question
   4. It asks for information.   c. command
   5. The subject **you** is understood.   d. exclamation
   6. It can be a statement, question,
      or command.

C. Write the past form of each verb.
   1. win   2. lay   3. weep   4. think

Challenge Exercise

Some action verbs cannot have direct objects. They cannot have a noun to receive the action. For example, we can **come** inside or **go** outside, but it is not possible to **come** or **go** any person, place, or thing.

Copy the verbs below. If the verb can have a receiver of the action, write a direct object of your own after it. If the verb cannot have a direct object, write **none** after it.

   Examples: a. read   b. fall
   Answers: a. read, book   b. fall, none

   1. draw   4. lie   7. sleep
   2. sit   5. write   8. rise
   3. drop   6. collect   9. catch

52. Nouns After the Verb *Be*

The verb **be** does not show action. So the eight forms of **be** cannot have direct objects. But sometimes a noun does follow a form of **be.** Look at this sentence.

My sister is a teacher.

In the sentence above, the noun **teacher** follows **is. Teacher** is a **predicate noun** in this sentence. A predicate noun is a noun in the predicate that names the same person, place, or thing as the subject. In other words, it renames the subject.

In the sentence **My sister is a teacher, sister** is the subject and **teacher** is a predicate noun that renames the subject. **Teacher** names the same person as **sister.**

In a sentence with a predicate noun, the verb **be** is like an equal sign. It says that something in the predicate is the same as something in the subject.

My sister is a teacher.
    sister is teacher
    sister = teacher

Those birds are bluebirds.
    birds are bluebirds
    birds = bluebirds

To find a predicate noun, first find the sentence skeleton. (The verb will be a form of **be.**) Then ask, "What noun in the predicate names the same person, place, or thing as the subject? What noun in the predicate equals the simple subject?" In the two examples above, **teacher** equals **sister,** and **bluebirds** equals **birds.**

Predicate nouns are diagramed on the base line after the skeleton. A slanted line is placed between the verb and the predicate noun. The line leans toward the subject to show that the predicate noun is renaming the subject.

Those birds are bluebirds.

birds | are \ bluebirds

Remember: A predicate noun is a noun in the predicate that renames the subject. A predicate noun follows a form of **be.**

> Oral Drill >

A. Tell whether each sentence has a **direct object** or a **predicate noun.** The verb will help you to decide.
   1. Anita called my friend.
   2. Anita is my friend.
   3. My cousin is a girl.
   4. My cousin saw a girl.
   5. Jesus was a man.
   6. Jesus helped a man.

B. Diagram the skeletons and predicate nouns at the chalk-board.
   1. My father is my teacher.
   2. Those flowers are pansies.
   3. Jesus is my best friend.
   4. David was a shepherd.
   5. The disciples were followers of Jesus.

> **Written Practice** >

A. Write **DO** or **PN** to tell whether each sentence has a direct object or a predicate noun. The verb will help you to decide.

1. Howard saw my brother.
2. Howard is my brother.
3. My sister will be the new teacher.
4. My sister met the new teacher.
5. Grandfather Miller was a plumber.
6. Grandfather called a plumber.
7. David killed a giant.
8. Goliath was a giant.

B. Diagram the simple subject, simple predicate, and predicate noun in each sentence.

1. Mary is my friend.
2. Charles is my brother.
3. This building was a schoolhouse.
4. The largest birds are ostriches.
5. A smile is sunshine to the heart.

C. Write a sentence about each picture. Use a predicate noun in each sentence.

> **Review and Practice**

A. Copy all the verbs in these sentences. Underline the helping verbs.
1. God loves all people.
2. Have you written your lesson neatly?
3. Jerry has been finishing his work on time.

B. Copy the correct verb to go with each subject.
1. Many children (run, runs) at recess time.
2. Sometimes they (play, plays) tag.
3. John (run, runs) like a deer.
4. Susan (jump, jumps) rope quite well.
5. I (has, have) heard that story before.
6. You (is, are) welcome.

53. Using *Raise* and *Rise*

Some verbs are very much alike, yet they have different meanings. We need to be careful how we use them.

The verb **raise** means **to make something go up or grow up.**

> Please **raise** the window.
> Uncle William **raises** turkeys.
> The students are **raising** their hands.

The verb rise means to get up or go up.

> We **rise** early in the morning.

The sun **rises** in the east.
My kite is **rising** into the air.

Raise takes a direct object. A noun or a pronoun must tell **what** is raised. In the following sentences, the words in bold print tell what is raised.

> The boys raise **calves.**
> Father is raising the **window.**
> Mother raises **petunias.**
> Ralph raises his **hand.**

The verb **rise** never takes a direct object. It is not possible to **rise** anything. All the words after **rise** answer questions like **when** or **where** something rises.

> The ocean tides **rise** twice a day.
> The sun **rises** in the east.
> The old dog is **rising** to greet us.

Remember: The verb **raise** means **to make something go up or grow up.** The verb **rise** means **to get up or go up.**

Oral Drill

A. Tell which verb is correct. If you use a form of **raise,** tell what the direct object is.
  1. Rhoda (raises, rises) her hand.
  2. The smoke (raises, rises) in a steady column.
  3. We (raise, rise) potatoes on our farm.
  4. The geese are (raising, rising) swiftly into the air.
  5. The dust (raises, rises) from the dry road.

B. Tell whether to use **raise** or **rise** in each blank. Then change each sentence, using the **ing** form and the **s** form. You will need to change some other words to make the sentences sound right.

> **Example:** The children —— their Bibles to sing that song.
>
> **Answer:** raise
> The children are raising their Bibles to sing that song.
> The child raises his Bible to sing that song.

1. The boys —— their hands.
2. The children —— to say their verses.
3. The balloons —— into the air.
4. Those people —— plenty of potatoes.

> **Written Practice**

A. Write the correct form of **raise** or **rise**. If you use a form of **raise**, also write the direct object.
1. —— your hand before you answer.
2. The boys are —— rabbits to sell.
3. The sun always —— in the east.
4. We —— much corn every year.
5. The steam is —— from the kettle.
6. When do you usually —— in the morning?
7. You may —— that question tomorrow.

B. Write the correct verb. Write the direct object when you use a form of **raise**.
1. In the evening the moon (raises, rises).

2. Bread (raises, rises).
3. The yeast (raises, rises) the bread.
4. On a rainy day, fish (raise, rise) to the surface.
5. Our spirits (raise, rise) when we hear good news.
6. The good news (raises, rises) our spirits.
7. High mountains (raise, rise) in the distance.
8. Steam was (raising, rising) the lid of the kettle.
9. The creek (raises, rises) on a rainy day.

> Review and Practice >

In each sentence, diagram the skeleton and the direct object or predicate noun.
1. The Bible has many books.
2. The Bible is a book.
3. Those animals are sheep.
4. The farmer raises sheep.

---

54. Using *Lay* and *Lie*

Do chickens **lay** or **lie** eggs? Should you **lay** or **lie** down to rest? Did the teacher **lay** or **lie** a book on the desk? In this lesson you will learn the meanings and correct usage of **lay** and **lie.**

The verb **lay** means **to put or place something.**

Lay the book on the table.
The man **lays** bricks.
The hens are **laying** eggs.

The verb **lie** means **to rest or recline.**

> **Lie** down until you feel better.
> The dog **lies** under the steps.
> The cat is **lying** on the windowsill.

Lay takes a direct object that tells **what** is laid. In the following sentences, the direct objects are in bold print.

> Lay the **book** on the table.
> Father lays his **hat** on the shelf.
> The chickens are laying **eggs.**

Lie never takes a direct object because we cannot **lie** anything. In the following sentences, the words after the forms of **lie** tell **where.**

> Fallen leaves **lie** on the ground.
> Thick dust **lies** beside the road.
> Ronald is **lying** in the grass.

Remember: The verb **lay** means **to put or place something.** The verb **lie** means **to rest or recline.**

A. Tell which verb is correct. If you use a form of **lay,** also give the direct object.
1. The brown hen always (lays, lies) brown eggs.
2. Grandma (lays, lies) in bed much of the time.
3. My father (lays, lies) bricks at work.
4. Workers are (laying, lying) linoleum on the floor.
5. I will (lay, lie) down and rest.

6. (Lay, Lie) your papers on the teacher's desk.
7. One paper (lays, lies) on the floor.
8. The dog is (laying, lying) in the kennel.
9. The baby (lays, lies) down for a nap every day.

B. Tell whether to use **lay** or **lie** in each blank. Then change each sentence, using the **ing** form and the **s** form. You will need to change some other words to make the sentences sound right.

> **Example:** The rakes ——— in the lane.
>
> **Answer:** lie
>   The rakes are **lying** in the lane.
>   The rake **lies** in the lane.

1. Chickens ——— eggs.
2. Two cats ——— in the sun.
3. My books ——— on the table.
4. The men ——— blocks.

Written Practice

A. Write the correct verbs. If you use a form of **lay,** also write the direct object.
1. The men (lay, lie) new carpet.
2. During the night the children (lay, lie) in their beds.
3. The hoe is (laying, lying) in the garden.
4. Frank (lays, lies) his coat on the sofa.
5. The village (lays, lies) in a narrow valley.
6. (Lay, Lie) a good foundation.
7. (Lay, Lie) down here to rest.

B. Write **R** for right and **W** for wrong.
 1. Carl **lays** down on the sofa.
 2. Your coat is **laying** on the ground.
 3. The workmen will **lay** a new carpet for us.
 4. Joan carefully **lies** the baby in the crib.
 5. The bluebird **lays** an egg in her nest.
 6. Rachel **lies** down to rest.

> Review and Practice

A. Copy all the nouns. Capitalize the proper nouns.
 1. When will brother harold return from mexico?
 2. sam is the oldest boy in the family.
 3. The columbia river empties into the pacific ocean.

B. In each sentence, diagram the skeleton and the direct object or predicate noun.
 1. Jacob was the son of Isaac.
 2. Jacob had twelve sons.
 3. Ahab fought the king of Syria.
 4. Ahab was the king of Israel.

55. Taking Notes for a Report

A report is several paragraphs that give information about a particular topic. Writing a good report requires that you gather facts. You need to observe carefully and listen closely. You also need to read what others have written because it is impossible to observe everything by yourself. A good writer must be a good reader.

The first step in writing a report is to decide what your topic will be. Then look that topic up in an encyclopedia or other reference book. But you must not copy whole sentences and paragraphs from a reference book. Copying someone else's writing and using it as your own is not honest. It is a form of stealing.

Taking notes from what others have written is different. It is not wrong to get ideas from others. The wrong is done when you copy their sentences. So copy only **key words** that give main ideas, and use the ideas to write your own sentences. That is how to take notes.

Notes are usually short sentences and phrases that are written quickly. When you take notes, do not worry about writing complete sentences or making them of different lengths. You can take care of those things when you are actually writing the report.

Suppose you want to write about reptiles, and you read this sentence in a reference book.

> Reptiles have backbones, their skin is dry and scaly, and they breathe with lungs.

How could you take notes from this information?

This sentence tells about the **backbones, skin,** and **lungs** of reptiles. These are the key words. So your notes may look like this.

Reptiles
have backbones
have dry, scaly skin
breathe with lungs

All the main ideas are there, but the sentence was not copied. When you write your report, you can put these ideas in different sentences wherever they seem to fit best. Then the report will be completely your own because you did the writing.

Take notes from several different books if possible. Then the report will be all the more your own, and it will also be more interesting and informative. Put all your notes in one list, and arrange your list in a proper order. It may be the order of time or importance, or it may be a step-by-step description of different parts.

Then write your report. Proofread it, correct the mistakes, and rewrite it as neatly as you can.

Remember: To take notes, copy only key words that give main ideas. Write them in short sentences and phrases of your own.

Read the following information. Find the key words, and tell what notes you would write.

> Reptiles are cold-blooded animals. This means that a reptile cannot keep its body warm from the inside as we do. It must seek air with a comfortable temperature, or bask in the sunshine.

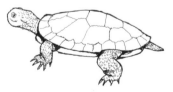 

> Written Practice >

A. Write some notes for a report on the topic **Bobwhites.**
Use the information in the following paragraph. Your list
should have three or more main ideas.

> Bobwhites are small plump birds with brown and
> white feathers. They get their name from their clear call,
> which sounds like "Bob-white!" The bobwhite is a kind of
> quail. Its favorite food is weed seeds, and it also eats
> many harmful insects.

B. Write a set of notes for a report with some interesting
facts about reptiles. Use the information given in the
lesson. Check an encyclopedia or other reference book for
more information.

Arrange your notes in the order of importance or in
a way that describes reptiles step by step. Then write a
report that has ten to fifteen sentences. Proofread your
report, and rewrite it neatly.

> Review and Practice >

Write the correct word for each blank.
1. The —— sentence tells what a paragraph is about.
2. Indent the —— line of a paragraph.
3. Each —— in poetry begins with a capital letter.
4. Paragraphs may be written in the order of —— or
   the order of ——.

56. Using *Set* and *Sit*

Do toys **set** or **sit** on the floor? Do students **set** or **sit** in their seats? Do Mother's helpers **set** or **sit** the table? In this lesson you will study the correct usage of **set** and **sit**.

Set means **to put or place something.**

The children **set** the vase on the windowsill.
Irene **sets** the roses on my desk.
The girls are **setting** the table.

Sit means **to rest or be seated.**

You may **sit** here.
Joseph **sits** in his seat to study.
The old cat was **sitting** on the fence post.

Set takes a direct object.

Set the **table.**
Mary sets her **books** on this desk.
Julia is setting the **table.**

Sit never takes a direct object.

I **sit** by the fire.
My cat **sits** with me.
My little sister is **sitting** beside me.

Remember: Set means to put or place something. Sit means to rest or be seated.

A. Tell which verb is correct. If you choose **set,** also give the direct object.

1. The old cabins (set, sit) close to the road.
2. The boys (set, sit) tables under the trees.
3. They (set, sit) benches beside the tables.
4. The mothers (set, sit) in chairs.
5. These tools (set, sit) on the shelf every day.
6. We (set, sit) them where they belong.

B. Change each sentence in Part A, using the **ing** form and the **s** form of **set** and **sit**. You will need to change some other words to make the sentences sound right.

> Written Practice

A. Write the correct verb. Copy all the direct objects.
    1. Please (set, sit) the table for dinner.
    2. May I (set, sit) beside you?
    3. Yes, you may (set, sit) here.
    4. Please (set, sit) that vase in the center of the table.
    5. A large rock (sets, sits) in the road.
    6. A little boy was (setting, sitting) on it.
    7. Father's car (sets, sits) under the tree.
    8. Please (set, sit) the chest here.

B. Choose one of the following verb forms for each blank: **set, sets, setting, sit, sits, sitting.** If you write a form of **set,** also copy the direct object.
    1. We ——— around the table for family devotions.
    2. I am ——— beside my brother.
    3. Let's ——— the new chair in the living room.
    4. We are ——— the kettle on the stove.
    5. Grandfather often ——— in this chair.

Review and Practice

A. In each sentence, diagram the skeleton and the direct object or predicate noun.
  1. Peter and John were fishermen.
  2. Jesus called four fishermen.
  3. Luke was a physician.
  4. Dorcas made garments for others.

B. Choose the correct verbs. Also copy the direct objects.
  1. Jesus said that He would (raise, rise) from the dead.
  2. Did Elisha (raise, rise) the Shunammite woman's son?
  3. The wounded man was (laying, lying) beside the road, but the Levite did not help him.
  4. Didn't the Good Samaritan (set, sit) the man on his own beast?

C. Copy each wrong word. Write the correct word beside it.
  1. We were setting beside the creek.
  2. Kevin was laying in the shade.
  3. The moon was raising over the valley.
  4. Your coat is laying on the grass.
  5. The poor dog sets there all day.
  6. They build the house last year.
  7. The children have swang on the swing many times.

57. Using *Let* and *Leave*

Look at the following sentences. Do you know which ones are correct?

Let the children come along.
Leave the children come along.

Let the dog at home.
Leave the dog at home.

In this lesson you will study the meanings and correct usage of **let** and **leave.**

Let means **to allow or permit.** Notice how the present form, the **s** form, and the **ing** form are used below.

I **let** the cows go into the meadow.
My parents **let** me plant a garden.
Our teacher **lets** us give oral book reports.
Mother **lets** me play when the work is finished.
Mark is **letting** the chickens go outside.
He is **letting** the ducks go too.

Leave means **to go away or allow to remain behind.** The sentences below use the present form, the **s** form, and the **ing** form.

The Millers **leave** promptly for church.
The children usually **leave** their coats here.
Our neighbor **leaves** home every morning.
Paul always **leaves** his hat on the rack.
We are **leaving** the dog behind.
Anna is **leaving** the cat with Grandmother.

The verb **let** is usually used with another verb form. **Leave** is not used in this way.

Father often **lets** me **hold** the horses.
John **lets** Jerry **help** with the plowing.

Remember: Let means **to allow or permit. Leave** means **to go away or allow to remain behind.**

> Oral Drill >

A. Choose the correct verb.
   1. I sometimes (let, leave) Edward help me with my work.
   2. Tomorrow David will (let, leave) for Guatemala.
   3. Please (let, leave) me use the hammer.
   4. We will (let, leave) the boat at Plymouth.
   5. Carol (lets, leaves) us read her books.

B. Which sentences in Part A have two verb forms?

C. Change the verbs in the following sentences to the **ing** form. Use the helping verbs **is** or **are.**
   1. Mother lets the children eat early.
   2. Bob and Mary leave together.
   3. Marlin lets the calf run.
   4. We leave the cup at the spring.

D. Tell how to correct the following sentences.
   1. Do not leave the goats eat the flowers.
   2. I see it, but I will let it there.
   3. Will you please leave me use your telephone?
   4. The baby is leaving the cat eat his cookie.
   5. The teacher does not leave us read storybooks until our work is finished.

> Written Practice >

Write the correct verbs. If you choose a form of **let,** also write the other verb form.
1. Mother does not (let, leave) us at home alone.
2. (Let, Leave) me help you with those boxes.
3. God said to Pharaoh, "(Let, Leave) my people go."
4. Martin (lets, leaves) the cows come into the barn every evening.
5. We will (let, leave) early in the morning.
6. Marjorie (lets, leaves) me wear her dress.
7. My cousin was (letting, leaving) me ride his bicycle.
8. (Let, Leave) the book on my desk.

> Review and Practice >

A. Write the correct verbs. Copy all the direct objects.
1. Paul was (setting, sitting) on the porch.
2. The moon was (raising, rising) above the trees.
3. The book (lays, lies) on the porch.
4. We (set, sit) our lunch boxes on the shelf.
5. If you are tired, (lay, lie) down and rest.
6. Please (lay, lie) the paper on the table.
7. (Raise, Rise) your hands high.
8. Ruth will go away and (let, leave) the dog here.
9. Did you (let, leave) your book at home?

B. Write the plural form of each noun.

1. house	3. boy	5. child	7. trio
2. trout	4. tooth	6. leaf	8. country

58. Contractions

Contractions are words made from two words combined into one word, with one or more letters left out. An apostrophe shows where letters are missing.

are not   aren't

The contraction **aren't** is made from the two words **are** and **not.** The apostrophe shows where the letter **o** is missing.

Many contractions are made from common verbs combined with **not.** The verbs are usually forms of **be** or other helping verbs.

isn't, aren't, wasn't, weren't, didn't, haven't, hasn't, hadn't, couldn't, shouldn't, won't, can't

The contractions **can't** and **won't** are unusual. **Can not** has two **n**'s, but **can't** has only one. The spelling **won't** comes from the two old words **woll not.** Today we no longer use **woll not,** but we do use **won't.**

Some contractions are made by combining pronouns with forms of **be.**

you're, he's, she's, it's, we're, they're

Some contractions are made by combining pronouns with other helping verbs.

I have—I've	she has—she's
you have—you've	they had—they'd
I will—I'll	he will—he'll
you will—you'll	they will—they'll
I would—I'd	we would—we'd
she would—she'd	who would—who'd

Some contractions can mean one of two things. **He's** may mean **he is** or **he has**. **We'd** may mean **we had** or **we would**.

Some people use the contraction **ain't** for the words **am not, are not,** or **is not;** but this is not proper English. Never use **ain't** in speaking or writing.

> Oral Drill >

A. Say the words that were used to make these contractions. Tell what letters are missing.

1. I'm	6. you're	11. we'll
2. you'd	7. they've	12. isn't
3. hasn't	8. we're	13. he'd
4. didn't	9. they'll	14. can't
5. I've	10. wouldn't	15. it's

B. Tell how to correct the following sentences.
1. I'm afraid I wo'nt get there in time.
2. What will happen if yo'ure late?
3. I ain't sure what will happen.
4. Its not time to go in yet.
5. Theyr'e going in anyway.

> Written Practice >

A. Write contractions for the following phrases. Use the apostrophe correctly.

1. is not	5. are not	9. we have
2. I had	6. he has	10. he would
3. it is	7. you are	11. you will
4. I am	8. will not	12. she is

B. Copy each sentence, and correct the contraction mistakes.
  1. I would'nt like that kind of work.
  2. I ain't sure how to do it.
  3. Theyre not sure when to come.
  4. Eve should'nt have eaten the fruit.
  5. Its not raining yet.
  6. It probably wo'nt rain soon either.
  7. Youre wishing it would rain.
  8. Wer'e needing rain badly.

C. Write sentences of your own, using contractions for the following pairs of words:
  are not, I am, he has, it is.

Review and Practice

A. For each meaning, write the letter of the correct word or words.

    a. sentence   d. simple subject
    b. subject   e. simple predicate
    c. predicate

  1. The verb in a sentence.
  2. Group of words that express a complete thought.
  3. Sentence part that tells who or what the sentence is about.
  4. The main noun in a sentence.
  5. Sentence part that tells what the subject does or is.

B. Diagram the skeletons, direct objects, and predicate nouns.
  1. Quietly the owls swoop down.
  2. They snatch little animals away in an instant.
  3. Young owls are hungry birds.
  4. They must be fed every fifteen minutes.

59. Using *Don't* and *Doesn't*

The words **don't** and **doesn't** are contractions. **Don't** is made from the phrase **do not,** and **doesn't** is made from the phrase **does not.**

Does goes with a singular subject. So we should also use **doesn't** with a singular subject.

> The child **does** his work well.
> He **doesn't** work too slowly.

Do goes with a plural subject. So we should also use **don't** with a plural subject.

> The children **do** the work.
> They **don't** waste time.

Use **do** or **don't** with the subject pronouns **I** and **you.**

> I **do** want to learn.
> I **don't** know everything.

> You **do** your work well.
> You **don't** waste time.

You should not say:

> I does want to learn.
> I doesn't know everything.

> You does your work well.
> You doesn't waste time.

Be sure to use the right contraction. If you are not sure whether to say **don't** or **doesn't,** use **do** or **does** alone in the sentence. Try this test with the following sentence.

> John (do or does?) know the answer.

Does fits in the sentence, so **doesn't** is also correct. It would not be correct to say, "John don't know the answer."

When a sentence has a compound subject, use a verb that goes with a plural subject.

Wrong: Mary and Martha does the dishes.

Mary and Martha doesn't complain.

Right: John and Mary **do** the chores fast.

John and Mary **don't** lose time.

A. For each sentence, tell which would fit, **do** or **does.** Then tell whether **don't** or **doesn't** would fit.

1. You —— speak clearly.
2. Jane —— have a cold.
3. You and I —— belong in this class.

4. It —— look as if it will rain.

B. Tell which is the right contraction, **don't** or **doesn't.**

1. He ——.
2. She ——.
3. You ——.
4. We ——.
5. I ——.
6. It ——.
7. They ——.
8. Mary ——.
9. Jonathan ——.
10. The boys ——.
11. Isaac and Mahlon ——.
12. Rachel and Rebecca ——.

C. The verb in each sentence is wrong. Read the sentences correctly.

1. This boy don't pay attention.
2. Now he don't understand the lesson.
3. Brother Melvin don't work on Sunday.

4. He don't take an order on Sunday either.

5. The corn don't look as if it's growing well.

6. If it don't rain soon, we'll have a poor harvest.

7. At the North Pole, the sun don't set during the summer.

8. The sun don't rise during the winter there.

9. The Bible don't say when the world will end.

10. Father don't think it is far away.

> Written Practice >

A. Copy each sentence, and fill in the blank with **do** or **does.**
Then write the sentence again, and use **don't** or **doesn't.**
Underline the words you use.

> **Example:** I —— like dogs.
> **Answer:**   I <u>do</u> like dogs.
>   I <u>don't</u> like dogs.

1. Robert and Ernest —— know you.

2. John —— know we are here.

3. You —— like to pick peas.

4. It —— matter what you write.

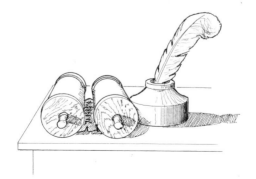

B. Write the correct contraction.

1. John (don't, doesn't) feel well today.
2. Brian and Daryl (don't, doesn't) know we are coming.
3. Aaron and Adam (don't, doesn't) waste much time.
4. Mary (don't, doesn't) know how to knit.
5. Larry (don't, doesn't) know the song.
6. Jerry (don't, doesn't) come to our school.
7. The children (don't, doesn't) need to help with the mowing today.
8. It (don't, doesn't) help to cry over spilled milk.
9. Ruth and Mary (don't, doesn't) know the way.
10. (Don't, Doesn't) corn grow in Alaska?
11. The teacher (don't, doesn't) have the book.
12. Many people (don't, doesn't) know about God.

> Review and Practice >

Copy the chart, and fill in the missing tenses. The first one is done for you.

Present	**Past**	**Future**
1. study	studied	will study
2. open	———	——— ———
3. ———	———	will pray
4. stop	———	——— ———
5. hurry	———	——— ———
6. ———	———	will fade

60. Using *Can, May, Teach,* and *Learn*

Use the verbs **can, may, teach,** and **learn** correctly.
Study the meaning of each word.

Can means **to be able.**

> I **can** speak German.
> I **can** lift a feed bag.

May means **to be permitted.**

> Samuel **may** unlock the door.
> Karen **may** read her storybook now.

When you ask your mother if you **may** get a cookie, you
are asking for permission. But when you ask her if you
can get a cookie, you are asking if you are able to get one.
Mother might say, "Yes, I'm sure you **can** get a cookie. I
know you are healthy and can walk that far. But I will not
give you permission to get a cookie right now. You **may** not
have one."

Teach means **to give knowledge.**

> Sister Miriam **taught** us the multiplication tables.
> Mother **taught** me a new song.

$$12 \times 9 = 108$$

Learn means **to get knowledge.**

> I **learned** the multiplication tables to the twelves.
> Susan is **learning** how to ride a bicycle.

$$12 \times 5 = 60 \qquad 12 \times 12 = 144 \qquad 12 \times 2 = 24 \qquad 12 \times 6 = 72$$

When other people help us by telling us facts or showing
us how to do something, they are **teaching** us. But in order
to **learn** something, we must apply ourselves. No one can
learn us anything.

Remember: **Can** means **to be able**. **May** means **to be per-mitted**. **Teach** means **to give knowledge**. **Learn** means **to get knowledge**.

Tell how to correct the following sentences.
1. Can I go outside now?
2. Can I get a drink at recess?
3. Father learned me how to build a birdhouse.
4. My brother learned me to ride a bike.

> Written Practice

For each sentence, write **can** or **may** or the correct form of **teach** or **learn.**

1. Mother, —— we take our crayons to school?
2. —— you draw a good picture of a horse?
3. We are —— to paint in art class.
4. The apostle Paul had —— to be content even in prison.
5. —— you sing the new song very well?
6. My sister —— me a new poem.
7. I have —— the whole poem by memory.
8. Jesus sat down and —— the people.
9. The people —— many good things from Him.
10. By reading the Bible, we can —— how God wants us to live.
11. Yes, boys, you —— go skating if you are careful.

> **Review and Practice**

A. Use a form of each verb in a sentence of your own.

1. set	3. raise	5. lay	7. let
2. sit	4. rise	6. lie	8. leave

B. Copy the verb or verb phrase in each sentence. After it write **A** for action or **B** for being.

1. Carl opened the door.
2. Mother is a good cook.
3. Brother Miller is leaving for Canada.
4. Did you help Grandfather?
5. Mordecai was a Jew.
6. Mother raises pretty flowers.

C. Diagram the skeleton and any direct object or predicate noun in each sentence of Part B.

---

61. Writing a Book Report

A book report tells what a book is about. If it is well written, a book report may help other people decide to read a certain book.

To write a book report, first choose a book and get it approved by your teacher or parents. Read the whole book before you begin writing your report.

A book report often has three paragraphs. The first paragraph should include the following information.

1. The title of the book. The title should be under-lined.
2. The name of the author (the person who wrote the book).
3. The copyright date of the book.
4. Where the book can be found.

The second paragraph should give this information.
1. The main characters. Is the story about just one person or about a family?
2. Whether the story is true.
3. The setting. In what country did it happen? Did the main characters live in a city or in the country? Did the story happen recently or long ago?
4. The main problem. What trouble or difficulty does the person or family need to deal with?

The third paragraph should tell what you think is the most interesting part of the book. Tell enough to interest others in reading it, but do not tell how everything turned out. One good way to end is with a sentence like this: Read the book to find out what happened next. Then sign your name at the end of the book report.

When you write a book report, first make a list of main ideas you want to cover. Do not copy sentences from the book, but write in your own words. Remember to use a variety of sentence patterns and descriptive words.

Make your book report brief. Do not write more than ten sentences in any paragraph. You do not need to tell about everything that happened in the book.

> **Remember:** A book report should give enough information to be interesting, but it should be brief.

> Oral Drill >

Read the following book report. Then answer the questions that follow it.

The Fisherman's Daughter was written by Mary Zook. The story was rewritten from an old source and has no copyright. You can buy the book from Rod and Staff Publishers at Crockett, Kentucky. We also have a copy in our school library.

In this book Gatty Miller works hard to bring cheer and comfort to her sister, Elsie. Elsie is ill and cannot get out of bed. Gatty and her family live near the sea. Her father and brothers are fishermen. They often face fearful storms. Elsie encourages Gatty and the rest of the family by her faith and trust in God.

The part I like best is where Gatty found herself in some dark cellars. She had followed her brother's stray rabbit into the dark holes. While she was down there, she heard voices. Some evil men were making plans to rob a house nearby. How did Gatty get out again? What did she do about it? How did all this work together for good? How did it help her sick sister Elsie? Read this story to find out.

                                                    Wendy Rhodes

1. What information is given in the first paragraph?
2. How is the setting explained in the second paragraph? What is the main problem?
3. How does the third paragraph help to stir your interest in the book?
4. What is the signature at the end of the report?

Written Practice

Write a report on a book you have read recently. Follow the directions in the lesson.

Review and Practice

1. A good writer must —— closely and —— carefully.
2. Avoid short, —— sentences in your writing.
3. —— is a special kind of writing that is pleasing to the ear.
4. You should never —— someone else's writing and use it as your own.

62. Choral Reading

Choral reading refers to reading something together. This is like singing together. Reciting something together by memory is much the same as choral reading.

For good choral reading, the group needs to stay together. Doing so requires a leader, either your teacher or a classmate. No one person should speak louder than the rest.

Do not speak in a singsong voice, but read with proper expression. A good reader changes the pitch and tone of his voice to bring out the meaning. Sometimes his voice will be soft and low. At other times he may read louder. Sometimes his voice may sound sad. At other times he may sound happy and gay.

Pronounce words correctly and watch punctuation marks as you read. Pause briefly at each comma. In poetry, do not pause at the end of a line unless it is punctuated. At a period let your voice pitch drop, and pause a little longer than at a comma.

Remember: In choral reading, stay together and use good expression. Pronounce every word clearly.

Oral Drill

A. Read this sentence aloud several times. Each time emphasize a different word by saying that word more forcefully.
See how the meaning of the sentence changes. Read the
questions about the sentence. Notice how emphasizing a
different word answers a different question.

Harold gave my brother a new book.

1. **Who** gave my brother a new book?
2. Did Harold **lend** my brother a new book?
3. Did Harold give **his** brother a new book?
4. Did Harold give my **sister** a new book?
5. Did Harold give my brother an **old** book?
6. **What** did Harold give my brother?

B. Read these sentences chorally, emphasizing a different
word each time. Discuss the differences in meaning. Be
sure to stay together as a group, and emphasize the same
words.
1. Maria bought two cats.
2. All the boys have doughnuts.
3. Today we know all the answers.

C. Read this poem together chorally. Do not read in a sing-song manner. Emphasize the words in bold print.

The Violet

Down in a **green** and **shady** bed,
    A **modest** violet grew.
Its stalk was **bent;** it **hung** its head
    As if to hide from view.
And yet it was a **lovely** flower—
    Its colors **bright** and **fair!**
It might have graced a lovely **bower**
    Instead of hiding **there.**
But **there** it was, **content** to bloom
    In modest tints arrayed,
And there diffuse its **sweet** perfume
    Within the silent shade.
Then let **me** to the valley go
    This **pretty flower** to see,
That I may also learn to grow
    In **sweet** humility.

—*Jane Taylor*

> Review and Practice

A. Write the correct words for these sentences.
1. Spoken English is called ——— ———.
2. When taking notes, copy only key ——— that give main ———.
3. Before you write a book report, ——— the whole book.
4. A book report (should, should not) tell how the story turned out.

B. Diagram the skeletons, direct objects, and predicate nouns.
   1. Our neighbor is a doctor.
   2. Our neighbor called the doctor.
   3. Paul encouraged the believers.
   4. Paul was a believer.

---

63.   Chapter 5 Review

 Oral Drill

A. Define a verb.

B. Give the correct words.
   1. A direct object follows a verb of (action, being).
   2. A predicate noun follows a verb of (action, being).
   3. A (direct object, predicate noun) receives action.
   4. A (direct object, predicate noun) renames the subject.
   5. To find a direct object, say the skeleton and then ask —— or —— after it.

C. Do the following things.
   1. Say the eight forms of the verb **be.**
   2. List fifteen other helping verbs.

> Written Practice

A. Diagram the skeletons, direct objects, and predicate nouns for each sentence.

1. The children ate cookies.
2. My mother is a good cook.
3. We will sit here.
4. He leadeth me beside the
   still waters.
5. My father is a carpenter.
6. Can you catch the ball?
'7. My favorite pets are kittens.

B. Choose and write the correct verb form for each sentence.
   In numbers 1–6, write the direct object if there is one.
   1. (Raise, Rise) your hand if you know the answer.
   2. The sun always (raises, rises) in the east.
   3. The chickens (lay, lie) eggs.
   4. The little children must (lay, lie) down and rest.
   5. My car is (setting, sitting) in the drive.
   6. Please (set, sit) this vase on the windowsill.
   7. Do not (let, leave) the sheep go out through the gate.
   8. Mother (lets, leaves) us play in the water.
   9. Father (lets, leaves) his hat on the shelf.

C. Answer these questions.
   1. Why should you not copy from a reference book?
   2. How should you take notes?
   3. What should you do before you begin writing a book
      report?

D. Take notes from the following information. Write the
   heading **Ants,** and list four main ideas under it.

   Ants are insects that live in colonies. A queen lays
   the eggs. Workers care for the larvae and pupae of the
   colony. Workers also gather food for the colony.

E. Choose and write the correct words.
1. (Its, It's) time to leave.
2. (Its, It's) nest is in this tree.
3. Tell me when (their, they're) coming.
4. (Their, They're) house is white.
5. (Your, You're) paper is written neatly.
6. (Your, You're) working hard.
7. We (don't, doesn't) understand all about God's love.
8. Mary (isn't, ain't) ready to go.
9. She (don't, doesn't) watch the clock.
10. This paragraph (don't, doesn't) have the answer.

F. Write contractions for the following phrases. Use apostrophes correctly.
1. is not   4. it is   7. we have
2. can not   5. he has   8. I had
3. will not   6. you are   9. he would

G. For each sentence, write **can** or **may** or the correct form of **teach** or **learn.**
1. —— we take our books home?
2. —— you jump this high?
3. My sister is —— me a new song.
4. I —— to sew last summer.
5. Paul —— the people at Athens.
6. They —— that their gods were false.

H. Rewrite the following sentences in paragraph form, giving the steps in correct order. Use this topic sentence: **Writing a book report is not hard if you follow some simple steps.**

1. In the second paragraph, name the main characters of the story and give the setting.
2. First, choose a good book and get it approved by your parents or teacher.
3. In the third paragraph, tell about the most interesting part of the book.
4. Read the whole book, and take some notes on it.
5. Last of all, sign your name at the end of the book report.
6. In the first paragraph of your report, write the title of the book, the name of the author, the copyright date, and where the book can be found.

I. Write **true** or **false** for each sentence.
1. For good choral reading, you need a leader.
2. The best way to have proper expression in choral reading is to make sure the group is large enough.
3. You should pause briefly at each comma.
4. You should let your voice pitch drop at a period and pause a little longer than at a comma.
5. In choral reading, you should try to keep ahead of the rest of the group.
6. Watch punctuation marks carefully in choral reading.

A Lesson on Possessive Pronouns

Oh, let us now study possessive pronouns;
Let's turn on **our** smiles and get rid of **our** frowns.
Consider this poem; just make up **your** mind:
How many possessives in here can you find?
The lesson is simple; it's really not hard—
Imagine we're eating in **your** own back yard.

Don't selfishly say that "This food is all **mine,**
I'll eat it myself right here under the pine."
Far better 'twould be if you'd say "It is **ours.**
We'll eat it together here 'mong all the flowers.
We've sandwiches, cookies, and ripe golden pears.
Here's **yours, his,** and **hers;** in the basket is **theirs.**"

Do not forget Mother; share some of **your** lunch,
And give **my** small brother a cracker to munch.
The songbirds are lifting **their** voices today,
All nature is adding glad song to **our** day.
God's bountiful blessings extend to us each;
Now thank Him for giving the blessing of speech!

—Mary Jane

Chapter 6
Pronouns

Pronouns stand for nouns.			
		Pronouns for Speaker	**Pronouns for Person Spoken To**	**Pronouns for Other Person or Thing**

		Pronouns for Speaker	Pronouns for Person Spoken To	Pronouns for Other Person or Thing
Subject Pronouns	Singular	I	you	he, she, it
	Plural	we	you	they
Object Pronouns	Singular	me	you	him, her, it
	Plural	us	you	them
Possessive Pronouns	Singular	my, mine	your, yours	his, her, hers, its
	Plural	our, ours	your, yours	their, theirs

her

it

he

them

mine

64. Pronouns Stand for Nouns

You have learned that nouns and verbs are parts of speech. In all, the English language has eight parts of speech. A **pronoun** is another part of speech. A pronoun is a word that takes the place of a noun.

David was a shepherd.
He cared for his father's sheep.

When you are learning something new, someone needs to explain it to you carefully. But it is not necessary to have it explained every time you do it. This would be a waste of time, and you would get tired of hearing the same instructions over and over.

It is the same way with using nouns and pronouns. We need to use nouns to tell who or what is being talked about. But after this information is known, hearing the noun over and over again would be tiresome and unnecessary. We are glad that pronouns can take the place of nouns.

Read the following story. Notice how tiresome it becomes when nouns are repeated where pronouns should be used.

1
Fanny Crosby was born on March 24, 1820. **Fanny's**

home was a place of much Bible reading and prayer.

2   3
Fanny did not remember **Fanny's** father, because

4   5
Fanny's father died before **Fanny** was a year old.

6
When Fanny was born, **Fanny** could see; but when

7   8
Fanny was six weeks old, **Fanny** got a cold that

9
affected **Fanny's** eyes. Since the family doctor was

gone at the time, another doctor was called. This

10
doctor put something on **Fanny's** eyes that was harm-

11   12
ful and caused **Fanny** to lose most of **Fanny's** sight.

13
For a few years, **Fanny** could see a bright light, but

14
later **Fanny** was completely blind.

15   16
Fanny did not feel sorry for **Fanny's** self. **Fanny** was

17
content to accept what God allowed in **Fanny's** life.

Remember: A pronoun is a word that takes the place of a noun.

 Oral Drill

A. Look at the pronouns on the chart at the beginning of this chapter. Tell which pronouns could take the place of the words in bold print in the story about Fanny Crosby.

B. In the following sentences, tell which words are pronouns. Then tell which noun each pronoun stands for.
1. Jesus is like a shepherd. He cares for His sheep.
2. The children loved Jesus. Their mothers brought them to be blessed by Him.
3. Joel has a little puppy. He is kind to it.
4. Mary played with her doll. She sang songs to it.

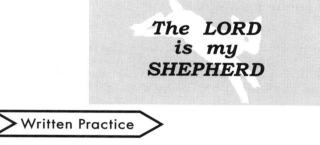

The LORD
is my
SHEPHERD

> Written Practice >

A. Write suitable pronouns for the words in bold print.

Saul began preaching in Damascus. (1) **Saul** taught the people in the synagogues. Many Jews who listened to (2) **Saul** became believers. But the rulers were not happy with Saul's teaching. So (3) **the rulers** placed guards at each gate and ordered (4) **the guards** to kill (5) **Saul.**

But the believers hid Saul until night came. Then (6) **the believers** took (7) **Saul** to a building on top of the city wall. Saul climbed into a large basket. (8) **Saul's** friends lowered (9) **the basket** with (10) **Saul** inside. Saul got away safely.

B. Copy the two pronouns in sentence **b** of each pair. Write the noun in sentence **a** that each pronoun stands for.

Example: a. Saul saw a bright light.

b. It was so bright that he became blind.

Answer: It—light, he—Saul

1. a. God spoke to Ananias about Saul.
   b. He told Ananias to visit him.
2. a. Ananias laid his hands on Saul.
   b. Saul received his sight, and he was baptized.
3. a. Barnabas was kind to Saul.
   b. He helped him to make Christian friends.
4. a. Dorcas showed love to the poor people.
   b. She made clothes for many of them.

C. Write the definition of a pronoun.

> Review and Practice >

A. Write these sentences correctly.
   1. does the atlantic ocean separate europe and north america
   2. henry has written a report about king solomon
   3. mr. r. l. yoder has been living in pennsylvania

B. Copy the verb phrases from the sentences in Part A.

C. Write the correct verbs.
   1. Please don't (set, sit) your books on my lunch.
   2. Dan sometimes (lays, lies) blocks with Father.
   3. The sun is (raising, rising) over the ocean.
   4. My cousin was (letting, leaving) me ride his bicycle.
   5. It (don't, doesn't) make much difference to me.
   6. (Can, May) I try to (teach, learn) Benny his verse?

65. Subject Pronouns

We need to choose pronouns according to the way they are used in sentences. When a pronoun is the subject of a sentence, we must choose a **subject pronoun.** The subject pronouns are as follows:

I, you, he, she, it, we, they

These sentences show how the subject pronouns are used.

> **She** wrote many songs.
> **He** wrote the music.

Sometimes we use a pronoun with a noun or another pronoun in a compound subject. In that case, we should choose the same pronoun that we would use if the pronoun stood alone. Look at these sentences. Do you know which pronoun to use in the second one?

> Moses was called by God.
> (He, Him) and Aaron led the Israelites.

Because we would say **He led,** we should also say **He and Aaron led.** We should not say **Him and Aaron led,** because we would not say **Him led.**

Remember: The subject pronouns are **I, you, he, she, it, we,** and **they.**

> Oral Drill

A. Say the subject pronouns in these sentences.
  1. God created the world. He made the plants and animals.

2. God made man in His own image.
3. The serpent talked to Eve. She listened to it.
4. Adam and Eve sinned. They ate the forbidden fruit.
5. Goliath was a giant. He boasted against God.
6. David slung a stone. It struck Goliath in the forehead.
7. We love God because He first loved us.
8. Rhoda and I sang a new song together.
9. The puppies followed James and me.

B. Some pronouns in these sentences are used incorrectly.
Give subject pronouns to take their place.
1. Her and me will go.
2. Him and them will stay here.
3. John and us learned a new song.
4. You and him should sing it at home.

C. Replace the words in bold print with subject pronouns.
1. John and **Joe** are making a birdhouse.
2. Did **Mother** call?
3. **Mary** and Martha are sewing new dresses.
4. Father and **the boys** dug the ditch.

D. Tell which are the correct pronouns.
1. Jane and (I, me) like cats.
2. (They, Them) and their sisters took flowers to Grandmother.
3. (She, Her) and (I, me) worked quietly.
4. (They, Them) are Jerry's papers.
5. Maggie and (she, her) folded the clothes.

> **Written Practice**

A. Copy the subject pronouns.
   1. You and he must wait.
   2. She and I have found the answer.
   3. He that covereth his sins shall not prosper.
   4. A woman that feareth the Lord, she shall be praised.
   5. Eat honey, for it is good.
   6. They that be wise shall shine as the brightness of the firmament.

B. Copy each pronoun that is used incorrectly, and write a subject pronoun to take its place.
   1. John and him will clean the shop.
   2. Mabel and us will be there.
   3. Her and me will come together.

C. Write subject pronouns that could replace the words in bold print.
   1. **Tom** and **Mary** are pulling weeds.
   2. **The boys** will help.
   3. Did **Anita** call?

D. Copy the correct pronouns in parentheses.
   1. Grandmother and (they, them) will come by train.
   2. (They, Them) and (we, us) plan to go and meet them.
   3. (They, Them) are mine.
   4. They and (we, us) were playing a new game.
   5. Katie and (I, me) gave the clothes to Rhoda.
   6. Ron and (we, us) stopped to pet the dog.

7. Dorcas and (she, her) helped to scrub the floor.

8. Paul and (he, him) chased the cows in.

E. Write all the subject pronouns.

> Review and Practice >

A. Write the part of speech that completes each sentence.
   1. A ——— names a person, place, or thing.
   2. A ——— shows action or being.
   3. A ——— takes the place of a noun.

B. Diagram the skeletons, direct objects, and predicate nouns.
   1. Please close the door.
   2. Is your father a carpenter?
   3. Bill and Joe are good workers.
   4. Elaine and Joy brought their books and papers.

> Challenge Exercise >

Copy all the subject pronouns in Luke 2:1–10. (There are eight in all.) Beside each pronoun, write the noun for which it stands.

---

66. Object Pronouns

You have learned that pronouns must be chosen according to their use in sentences. If we use a pronoun for the subject, we must choose a subject pronoun. But if we use a pronoun for an object, we must choose an **object pronoun.** The object pronouns are as follows:

me, you, him, her, it, us, them

The pronouns **you** and **it** do not have two forms as the other pronouns do. When they are used as object pronouns, they have the same form as when they are used as subject pronouns.

Object pronouns can be used as direct objects. Remember that a direct object receives the action of a verb.

> Jesus loves **me.**
> Frank saw **you.**
> Carol helped **him.**
> Mother took **her** along

Object pronouns are also used after **prepositions.** A preposition is a little word like **to, in, from, with, for,** and **after.** The noun or pronoun after a preposition is the **object of the preposition.** You will learn more about prepositions in Chapter 10.

> The card is not <u>for</u> **me.**
> It is <u>for</u> **her.**
> Read the story <u>to</u> **them.**

Remember: The object pronouns are **me, you, him, her, it, us,** and **them.** They can be used as direct objects or after prepositions like **to, in, from, with, for,** and **after.**

A. Find each object pronoun in these sentences. Tell if it is the **direct object** or the **object of a preposition.**
  1. John saw me.
  2. We shall go after them.
  3. Harold will get it.
  4. She came with him.
  5. God so loved us that He sent the Saviour.
  6. Please give the books to her.

B. Tell which pronoun is correct.
  1. The boys saw (they, them).
  2. Shirley took us with (she, her).
  3. God is good to (we, us).
  4. The kitten ran away from (I, me).
  5. The flowers were for (she, her).

A. Copy all the object pronouns in these sentences. ~~After each pronoun, write~~ **DO** ~~for direct object or~~ **OP** ~~for object of a preposition.~~
  1. David took us with him.
  2. I gave it to her.
  3. We are waiting for him.
  4. God has been good to me.
  5. I will give thanks to Him.
  6. The boys brought them for us.
  7. The man with him showed a map to them.
  8. They brought it for us.

B. Copy the correct pronouns in parentheses. Some answers
   are subject pronouns, and some are object pronouns.
   1. (We, Us) waited for (she, her).
   2. Jane and Judy saw (he, him).
   3. (He, Him) and Eva came with (she, her).
   4. The gift is from (I, me).
   5. We visited (they, them).
   6. (They, Them) came for (I, me).
   7. Bernice and (I, me) helped (she, her).
   8. Jesus is a friend to (I, me).

> Review and Practice >

A. Do the following exercises.
   1. Write the definition of a pronoun.
   2. List the subject pronouns.
   3. List the object pronouns.

B. Write **S** for sentence, **F** for fragment, and **RO** for run-on
   sentence.
   1. The black kitten is mine the white one is yours.
   2. Cuddly and playful kittens.
   3. Do you like kittens?
   4. Keep this kitten, take care of it.

C. Copy the verbs in these sentences. Write **action** or **being**
   after each one.
   1. Consider the lilies of the field.
   2. The flowers are beautiful.
   3. God made all things well.

67. Pronouns in the Predicate

You have learned that some nouns in the predicate rename the subject. They are called predicate nouns. The following sentence has a predicate noun.

My aunt is a **teacher.**

In this sentence, **teacher** is a predicate noun because it names the same person as the subject **aunt.**

Sometimes a pronoun takes the place of a predicate noun. Then it is called a **predicate pronoun.** The following sentences have predicate pronouns.

Our teacher is **she.**   Their leader was **he.**

A pronoun that takes the place of a predicate noun must be one of the subject pronouns (I, you, he, she, it, we, they). This is because the predicate pronoun names the same person or thing as the subject. Really, if the predicate pronoun and the subject are exchanged, the sentence means the same. Notice how the following sentences mean the same as the ones above.

She is our teacher.   He was their leader.

These sentences show why predicate pronouns have the same form as the pronouns used for subjects.

Pronouns that rename the subject never come after action verbs. They follow forms of the verb **be.** The forms of **be** are **am, is, are, was, were, be, been,** and **being.**

Do you remember how to diagram predicate nouns? Pronouns that rename the subject are diagramed in the same way. Study this example.

Our teacher is she.   teacher | is \ she

> **Remember:** Pronouns that take the place of predicate nouns must be subject pronouns.

A. Tell whether the verb in each sentence shows **action** or **being.** Give the pronouns, and tell whether each one is a **direct object** or a **predicate pronoun.**

1. Ann visited her.
2. The priest was he.
3. Mary helped us.
4. The visitors were they.
5. Was that person you?
6. The queen was she.

B. On the board, diagram the nouns, verbs, and pronouns in the sentences of Part A. Write **A** above the action verbs and **B** above the forms of **be.** Label the direct objects **DO** and the predicate pronouns **PP.**

C. Tell how to correct the mistakes in these sentences.

1. She saw I.
2. The prince was him.
3. We met they.
4. Who told he?
5. I know she.
6. The pupils were them.

Written Practice

A. Write the correct pronouns.

1. The president is (he, him).
2. We helped (they, them).
3. Did Mother find (she, her)?
4. The newcomers are (they, them).
5. Peter knows (he, him).
6. My cousin is (she, her).
7. God will never forget (I, me).
8. The missionary was (he, him).

B. Diagram the nouns, verbs, and pronouns in sentences 1–5 of Part A. Write **A** above the action verbs and **B** above the forms of **be.** Label the direct objects **DO** and the predicate pronouns **PP.**

C. Write sentences of your own according to the following directions.
   1. Write a sentence with a form of **be** and a pronoun that renames the subject.
   2. Write a sentence with an action verb and a direct object that is a pronoun.

Review and Practice

A. Copy and complete this chart.

Present	Past	Future
1. help	——	will ——
2. hop	——	will ——
3. ——	burst	will ——
4. ——	——	will sit

B. Write words to fill in the blanks.
   1. A pronoun is a word that takes the place of a ——.
   2. **I, you, he, she, it, we,** and **they** are —— pronouns.
   3. **Me, you, him, her, it, us,** and **them** are —— pronouns.

Challenge Exercise

Write all the subject and object pronouns from the story of Dorcas in Acts 9:36–41. Write the noun that each pronoun stands for.

68. Writing a Story From a Picture

Artists use their brushes to paint beautiful pictures. Many paintings show interesting happenings and suggest a story.

Writing a good story is like painting a picture. An artist uses the proper tools: good brushes and paint. A writer also has tools: descriptive words, variety in sentences, and orderly paragraphs.

A painting loses its beauty if it shows too many details. Too many details make it look cluttered. In the same way, too many details can clutter up a story and make it unpleasant to read. A story, like a painting, must include enough details to make it interesting but not so many that it becomes cluttered.

You have learned that a sentence should be left out of a paragraph if it does not tell about the topic sentence. Writing a story is much the same as writing a paragraph. If a sentence gives details that do not help to tell the story, that sentence must be left out.

Remember: Include enough details in your story to make it interesting. Leave out any details that do not help to tell the story.

Discuss the picture. Answer the following questions about it.

1. What would you name each child?
2. What are the children preparing to do?
3. To whom do you suppose they are writing?
4. What preparations have they made?
5. With what kind of pen will they write the letter?
6. Why are they dressed in such unusual clothes?
7. What accident has happened?
8. What must be done before they can go on with the letter writing?
9. What do you suppose they will write about?
10. What do you think the children are saying to each other?

> **Written Practice** >

Write a story about the picture. Follow these directions.
1. List the important ideas you will tell about. You may get ideas from the questions in Oral Drill, but you do not need to answer all the questions.
2. Make sure your ideas are in the right order. Then write your story. Remember to use descriptive words and variety in your sentences. Do not make the story too long.
3. Proofread your story, and correct the mistakes. Then rewrite the story, and add a good title.

> **Review and Practice** >

Read this paragraph, and do the exercises below.

> The president receives from two to four thousand letters from children each week. He cannot answer them all, so volunteers read them. They usually reply with a booklet or newsletter that answers the questions asked. The volunteers give the president only a sampling of the letters. The president himself answers some of them. In order to receive an answer from the president, the writer must ask something that only the president can answer. I like to get letters.

1. Choose and write the best title for the paragraph.
   a. The President's Volunteers
   b. Writing to the President
2. Write the topic sentence of the paragraph.
3. Write the sentence that should be left out of the paragraph.

69. Using the Correct Pronoun

Use a subject pronoun for the subject of a sentence. Be especially careful when the sentence has a compound subject.

John and **I** took a hike.
Nancy and **she** went along.

Also use a subject pronoun to take the place of a predicate noun. Do not use an object pronoun for this.

The captain was **he.** (not **him**)
The fourth graders are **they.** (not **them**)

Use object pronouns for direct objects. Direct objects receive the action of action verbs.

My brother helped **me.**
Mother took **them** along.

Use object pronouns for the objects of prepositions. Remember that prepositions are little words like **to, in, from, with, for,** and **after.**

The card is for **her.** (not **she**)

Remember: Be sure to use subject pronouns and object pronouns correctly.

> Oral Drill >

A. Tell which pronoun is correct. Tell whether the pronoun is used as a **subject**, a **direct object**, a **predicate pronoun,** or the **object of a preposition.**

1. Arnold and (I, me) like dogs.
2. The dogs like (we, us) too.
3. The leader was (he, him).
4. (He, Him) and his sisters took a picnic lunch.
5. Mother told a story to (we, us).
6. (She, her) and (I, me) listened quietly.
7. John and (they, them) came by bus.
8. Mother made lemonade for (they, them).
9. (They, Them) and (we, us) plan to leave.
10. The travelers were (they, them).

B. Tell how to correct each sentence, and why it should be corrected.

> **Example:** Martha and her were helping Mother.
> **Answer:**   Martha and she were helping Mother.
> **She** is a subject.

1. William and me got tadpoles out of the pond.
2. Janet and him put them into a glass bowl.
3. Him and her fed them every day.
4. Soon them grew legs and became frogs!
5. Father bought a magnet for we.
6. Him and me let Lily play with it.
7. God loves we all.
8. Them and us should be thankful for God's love.

> **Written Practice** >

Copy the correct pronouns. After each pronoun, write **S** if it is a subject, **DO** if it is a direct object, **PP** if it is a predicate pronoun, or **OP** if it is the object of a preposition.

1. Mark and (he, him) will feed the cows.
2. Jane and (I, me) want to leave soon.
3. We told the story to (they, them).
4. They paid (she, her) for the eggs.
5. (He, Him) and (I, me) have finished.
6. The visitors from Chicago are (they, them).
7. Give the paper to (he, him).
8. Please show the picture to (we, us).
9. That boy is (he, him).
10. A letter came for (I, me).
11. This note is for (he, him).
12. The package is for (she, her).
13. The girl in the car is (she, her).
14. (They, Them) brought a book for (we, us).
15. Gail and (she, her) will tell the story.
16. Write a letter to (she, her).

> **Review and Practice** >

A. Copy the predicate nouns from these sentences. Then write a pronoun that could take the place of each one.
1. The visitors are Mexicans.
2. The teacher is Brother Thomas.
3. My cousin is Sandra.

B. Diagram the skeletons and any direct objects or predicate
   nouns.

1. The sun rises early.
2. John raised the window.
3. Is John your brother?
4. Set the vase on the table.
5. Sit in this chair.
6. These books are old dictionaries.
7. Lay this book on the table.
8. The cows are lying in the shade.

---

70. Possessive Pronouns

You have studied two groups of pronouns—the subject
pronouns and the object pronouns. Today you will study
a third group, the **possessive pronouns.** The possessive
pronouns are as follows:

**my, mine, your, yours, his, her, hers, its,
our, ours, their, theirs**

Possessive pronouns show possession (ownership). They
are pronouns because they take the place of possessive nouns.
Look at the possessive pronouns in these sentences.

Mary's sister is here.
Her sister is here.

The raccoon's home was in a tree.
Its home was in a tree.

The possessive pronouns **my, mine, your,** and **yours** stand for the name of the speaker or the person spoken to.

> **My** hope is in God.
> **Your** trust will be rewarded.

Never write possessive pronouns with apostrophes. The following words are contractions, not possessive pronouns.

> **It's** means **it is.**
> **You're** means **you are.**
> **They're** means **they are.**

Remember: The possessive pronouns show ownership. They never need an apostrophe.

 Oral Drill

A. Tell whether **its** or **it's** is correct for each blank. Remember that **it's** means **it is.**
   1. ———— better to be alone than in bad company.
   2. ———— better to become bent from hard work than to become crooked from avoiding it.
   3. The Bible is God's Word.
      ———— lessons are valuable.
   4. ———— the early bird that catches the worm.
   5. The bird flew to ———— nest.
   6. That is a cardinal. ———— feathers are red.

B. Tell which word is correct. Remember that the words with apostrophes are contractions.
1. (Your, You're) house is our first stop.
2. (Your, You're) early today.
3. (Their, They're) children are not at home.
4. (Their, They're) at Bible school tonight.

> Written Practice

Choose and write the correct words.
1. (Its, It's) not time to go yet.
2. You have a pony! (Its, It's) ready to ride.
3. (Its, It's) saddle is in the barn.
4. (Its, It's) not hungry right now.
5. (Your, You're) going to take a ride.
6. (Your, You're) feet go in here.
7. (Their, They're) barn is small.
8. (Their, They're) planning to move soon.
9. (Its, It's) too small for them.
10. (Your, You're) welcome to see it.

> Review and Practice

A. Copy the two pronouns in each sentence. Write **S** after subject pronouns, **O** after object pronouns, and **P** after possessive pronouns.
1. Merle and I will go with them.
2. She gave the sandwich to him.
3. Mary and I will help you.
4. Our visitors were they.
5. They will come to your house.
6. She was not with us.
7. We have a card for you.

8. This book is yours and not mine.
9. She must have theirs.
10. Jesus loves me; this I know.

B. Choose the correct pronouns. ~~After each answer, write S~~ ~~for subject or~~ **OP** ~~for object of a preposition~~.
1. Paul and (I, me) will drive the tractors.
2. Aunt Martha sent a book to (we, us).
3. It was a present from (she, her).
4. Sarah and (I, me) can hardly wait to read it.
5. Carol and (she, her) have a puppy.
6. The girls gave the puppy to (he, him).

C. Choose the correct pronouns. ~~Write~~ **DO** ~~after direct~~ ~~objects and~~ **PP** ~~after predicate pronouns~~.

1. The new workers are (they, them).
2. We will help (they, them) with the job.
3. The bees stung (she, her).
4. My grandfather is (he, him).
5. Will we visit (he, him) today?

D. Write **S** for each statement, **Q** for each question, and **C** for each command. Write the correct end punctuation for each sentence.
1. Please help us pod these peas
2. We have much work to do today
3. May I help you
4. Study hard
5. Will we soon finish

E. Copy sentences 1 and 2 of Part D, but write them as exclamations. Use the correct end punctuation.

71. Plural Pronouns

You have learned that a plural noun names more than one person, place, or thing. A **plural pronoun** also refers to more than one person, place, or thing. These are the plural pronouns.

**we, you, they, us, them,
our, ours, your, yours, their, theirs**

A plural pronoun can take the place of a plural noun. It can also take the place of two or more nouns or other pronouns. Study the following examples.

The children want to go outside.
They want to go outside.

You and Martha may go out to play.
You may go out to play.

Mary and Martha may go out to play.
They may go out to play.

Please tell the story to **Sue, him, and me.**
Please tell the story to **us.**

Give the book to **Mildred and May.**
Give the book to **them.**

The pronoun **you** can be singular or plural. Never say **yous** or **youns** when speaking to more than one person.

Wrong:
You boys were small when yous were here last.
Right:
You boys were small when **you** were here last.

> **Remember:** Use plural pronouns when speaking about more than one person, place, or thing. The pronoun **you** can be singular or plural.

A. Give plural pronouns to replace the words in bold print.
1. **Paul and I** are here.
2. We are waiting for **William and her.**
3. He and Betty will see Irene and Sandra.
4. Was it you and Father?
5. Would you and Sarah please help Rhoda and me?

B. Tell how to correct the following sentences.
1. Have yous ever seen a swallowtail butterfly?
2. Did youns know that butterflies taste with their feet?
3. Maybe yous have heard about the fish that have taste buds all over their skin.
4. Youns can read many things about insects in this book.
5. God made many interesting creatures for yous to enjoy.

> Written Practice

Write plural pronouns to take the place of the words in bold print.
1. **Rachel and I** went for a walk.
2. I hope **you and Ruth** will go with **Rachel and me**.

3. **Rachel, Ruth, and I** saw some butterflies.
4. **Ruth and I** wanted to catch the butterflies.
5. **The butterflies** flew away
   too fast.
6. God made **the butterflies**
   swift and beautiful.

> Review and Practice

A. Copy the three pronouns in each sentence. Write **S** after
   subject pronouns, **O** after object pronouns, and **P** after
   possessive pronouns.
   1. He sent it with yours.
   2. You put mine with theirs.
   3. She and I went with them.
   4. They will bring ours to you.

B. Write the correct pronouns.
   1. The boy in the picture is (he, him).
   2. A branch hit (she, her).
   3. Nathan and (I, me) were with (she, her).
   4. Mother said (you, yous) may have these oranges.
   5. My sister is (she, her).
   6. Mary gave apples to (they, them).
   7. (He, Him) and (she, her) are twins.
   8. (They, Them) want to play with (we, us).

C. Diagram the skeletons, direct objects, and predicate
   pronouns in these sentences.
   1. Julia told the story to me.
   2. It belongs to you.
   3. The minister is he.
   4. Mary and she helped us.
   5. John and he sang cheerfully.

72. Using Pronouns Correctly

Pronouns must be used correctly and courteously. When you speak about another person and yourself, you should say the other person's name first and **I** or **me** last. This is more courteous than saying **I** or **me** first.

Wrong:

> I and Mary helped Mother.
> I and Karl did the milking.
> Father helped me and him.

Right:

> Mary and I helped Mother.
> Karl and I did the milking.
> Father helped him and me.

The work of a pronoun is to take the place of a noun. So it is not correct to use both the noun and the pronoun together when speaking about someone.

> **Wrong:** Abraham he believed God.
> **Right:**   Abraham believed God.

Remember: When speaking about another person and yourself, say the other person's name first and **I** or **me** last. Do not use both the noun and the pronoun together when speaking about someone.

▷ Oral Drill ▷

Tell how to correct the following sentences.
1. Youns are fast workers.
2. We will come and help yous do your work.
3. Donald he wrote a letter to Samuel.

4. Nancy she ate with me.
5. I and you are here early.
6. Mother is calling me and you.
7. I and Karla are good friends.
8. Mary spoke to me and Karla.
9. We will help yous finish your work.
10. I and Mary don't mind hoeing corn.

> **Written Practice**

Rewrite these sentences correctly.

1. Eve she listened to the serpent.
2. Adam he took some of the fruit from Eve.
3. Yous should learn your verses.
4. I and you finished our work first.
5. Mother helped me and Karla.
6. I and you must clean the chicken house.
7. Mr. Brown gave me and Karl each a dime.
8. Fanny she was a blind girl.
9. Nancy she was with me yesterday.
10. I and Nancy forgot to be quiet.

> **Review and Practice**

A. Choose the correct pronoun. Be ready to tell in class how each pronoun is used.

1. Henry and (I, me) dug the potatoes.
2. The shepherd is (he, him).
3. Tina and (she, her) told (I, me) about it.
4. Father bought a dog for (he, him).
5. If I always tell the truth, people can always believe (I, me).

B. Write pronouns to replace the words in bold print.
   1. Father and **Betty** will send Harold and **the others** some seeds.
   2. We have made a sandbox for **the children.**
   3. **The children** also made something for Alice and **Betty.**
   4. Mother baked a pie for Mark and **Kevin.**
   5. I sent the letter to **Franklin and Elvin.**
   6. The girl at the door is **Nancy.**

C. Do the following exercises.
   1. Write the definition of a pronoun.
   2. List the subject pronouns.
   3. List the object pronouns.

> Challenge Exercise >

Write a paragraph about the children in the picture below. Circle all the pronouns you use. Draw an arrow from each pronoun to the noun that it stands for.

73. *This, That, These,* and *Those*

The words **this, that, these,** and **those** are often used to tell **which** about a noun. But sometimes they tell **which** and also take the place of the noun. Then these words are pronouns.

> **That** tree is tall. (tells which tree)
> **That** is a tall tree. (takes the place of **That tree**)

This and **that** are singular pronouns. They refer to only one person or thing. Use them when speaking about one.

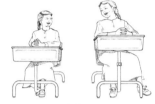

> **This** is a low desk.
> **That** is a higher one.

These and **those** are plural pronouns. They refer to more than one person or thing. Use them when speaking about more than one.

> **These** are our cows.
> **Those** are theirs.

This and **these** refer to persons or things close at hand. **That** and **those** refer to persons or things at a distance.

Do not use **them** where **they, these,** or **those** should be used. **Them** is never correct as the subject of a sentence.

> **Wrong:** Them are the pies Mother made.
> **Right:** **Those** are the pies Mother made.

Do not say **this here, that there, these here,** or **those there. Here** and **there** are unnecessary with **this, that, these,** and **those.**

Remember: Do not use **them** where **they, these,** or **those** should be used. Do not use **here** or **there** with **this, that, these,** and **those.**

Oral Drill

Correct these sentences.
1. This here is a cold room.
2. Them there are rusty.
3. This here is a good song about God's love.
4. We'll get more chairs if these here aren't enough.
5. Them there will do.
6. That is closer than this.
7. Them are high mountains.
8. Them are interesting Bible stories.

Written Practice

A. Rewrite these sentences correctly.
1. These here are delicious apples.
2. Them there are rotten.
3. Do you see that there?
4. It is just like this here.
5. Them are pretty.
6. That there is mine.
7. That is closer to me than this is.
8. Get more boxes if these here aren't enough.

B. Write sentences using the pronouns **this, that, these,** and **those.** Get ideas from this picture.

> Review and Practice >

A. Write words to fill in the blanks.
1. —— nouns always need to be capitalized.
2. The last verb in a verb phrase is always the —— verb.
3. Verbs can show —— tense, —— tense, and ——
tense.
4. The past tense of the verb **leave** is ——.

B. Write these sentences correctly. Some have several mistakes.
1. This here is your's and that there is our's.
2. Me and Alice finished first.
3. Him and Amy did not see me and Ralph.
4. Its cold outside.
5. The hired man is him.
6. The work was easy for me and Mother.
7. Father and them are still working.

74. The Parts and Form of a Friendly Letter

Sometimes we want to talk to a friend who lives far away from us. Maybe we cannot visit our friend, but we can always send a letter. A letter that is written because of friendship is a **friendly letter.**

A friendly letter has five parts: the heading, greeting, body, closing, and signature.

The **heading** of a letter shows the address of the person who wrote the letter and the date it was written. The heading goes in the upper right corner of the letter.

Route 1, Box 21
Hopewell, Virginia 23860
October 23, 20—

182 East Deer Street
Toronto, Ontario M5V 1E9
June 16, 20—

The first line of the heading contains the route number or the street address. A comma is placed after the route number. No comma is placed between a house number and a street name. Every word in the first line of a heading begins with a capital letter.

The second line of a heading shows the name of the city and the state or province. The name of the city is followed by a comma. The Zip Code or postal code follows the name of the state or province. No comma is placed between the name of the state and the Zip Code or between the name of the province and the postal code. Every word in the second line of a heading is capitalized.

The third line of the heading is for the date. A comma is placed between the number of the day and the year.

The **greeting** of a letter begins at the left margin. In a greeting, the first word and any person's name begin with a capital letter. A capital letter is used for a title or abbreviation such as **Dr.** (Doctor), **Mr.** (Mister), **Mrs.** (Mistress), or **Miss.** A period always follows an abbreviation. The greeting of a letter ends with a comma.

Dear Mr. Wright,
My dear sister,
Dear Miss Clark,
Dear friends,

The **body** of a letter is written in paragraphs, following the correct form for sentences and paragraphs.

The **closing** of a letter begins in line with the left edge of the heading. Only the first word in a closing begins with a capital letter. A comma comes at the end.

Very truly yours,
Your friend,

The **signature** is the name of the person who wrote the letter. It begins in line with the closing. Each name and initial in a signature is capitalized, and there is no end punctuation.

Carol Miller
John D. Thomas
Paul Smith
L. M. Baer

Route 2, Box 64
Millersburg, Ohio 44654
June 16, 20—

Dear Ronald,

Our dog, Lassie, had four puppies. They are starting to run around and get into mischief.

Father built a new bird feeder last winter. We enjoyed watching the many birds that came to visit it.

Your friend,
Richard

 Oral Drill

A. Study the model of the friendly letter.
   1. Name the five parts of the letter.
   2. Point out each part of the letter.
   3. What are some words that are capitalized?
   4. What are some punctuation marks that you see?

B. Tell what should be corrected in the following letter.

> 659 applewood drive
> cleveland ohio 44131
> december 19 20—

dear daniel

Yesterday I was at my grandfather's place. He let me help milk the cows. I liked it very much. Did you ever milk cows?

On Wednesday I am going to my grandfather's place again. We are going to cut hay. I wish you could be there too on Wednesday.

> yours truly
> david

Written Practice

Follow these steps to write a friendly letter.
1. Write the heading of a letter at the proper place on a paper. Use your own address and today's date.
2. Write the greeting of a letter at the proper place. Use the name of one of your best friends.
3. Write the body of the letter. Write one paragraph inviting your friend to your house for a visit.
4. Add a closing and signature to your letter.

Review and Practice

Write **true** or **false**.
1. The last sentence of a paragraph always tells what the paragraph is about.
2. You must move your mouth to speak clearly.

3. A good paragraph has some short sentences and some longer sentences.

4. A paragraph should include as many details as possible.

> Challenge Exercise

Write a friendly letter to a child your age whose parents are missionaries. Get the address from your teacher or parents. Then send the letter.

---

75. Addressing an Envelope

When you want to mail a letter, write the receiver's address correctly and neatly in the center of an envelope. A neat, attractive envelope shows good manners and consideration for the mailman.

The return address is the address of the sender, and it belongs in the upper left corner. The sender's name is written

```
Marilyn Foster
Route 1, Box 104
Lakeview, CA 92353
```

```
              LINDA A SMITH
              426 SPRING CREEK ROAD
              PINE VALLEY NY 14872
```

in the first line, and the other lines are the same as the address in the letter heading.

When you write an address on an envelope, be sure to write neatly and correctly so that the letter reaches its destination. In the United States, the postal service wants the receiver's address to be printed with all capital letters and no punctuation.

The receiver's address should be written in about the center of the envelope. It usually contains three lines. The person's name is written in the first line, the street address (or route and box number) in the second line, and the city, state, and Zip Code in the third line.

The post office has made two-letter abbreviations of state names to be used with Zip Codes. Each abbreviation is made up of two capital letters, and no period comes after it. See the following examples. Do you know the abbreviation for your state?

PA—Pennsylvania	KY—Kentucky
MD—Maryland	OH—Ohio
CA—California	NY—New York
VA—Virginia	IL—Illinois

 Oral Drill

A. Tell what the post office abbreviation is for each of the following states.

1. Your state
2. California
3. Virginia
4. New York

B. Tell what state each of the following abbreviations stands for.

1. MD   2. OH   3. IL   4. KY

> Written Practice

A. Write each address correctly, as a receiver's address should be written on an envelope.

from 1. paul m johnson
405 east church rd
forksville VA 23940

sent to 2. martha ann perkins
route 2 box 107
bethel MO 63434

B. Address an envelope correctly for the letter you wrote in Lesson 74.

C. Address an envelope to your school. Use your own address for the return address.

> Review and Practice

1. A paragraph must speak about —— topic only.
2. For good choral reading, you need a ——.
3. You should pause briefly at each ——.
4. Name the five parts of a friendly letter.

NE   MA

HARRISON CHRISTIAN SCHOOL
64784 C.R. 11
GOSHEN, IN 46526

76. Chapter 6 Review

> Oral Drill >

A. Do the following exercises.
    1. Give the definition of a pronoun.
    2. Name the subject pronouns.
    3. Name the object pronouns.

B. Read each sentence, replacing the word or words in bold print with a pronoun.
    1. **Mary and Martha** loved Jesus.
    2. **Jesus** came to help **Mary and Martha** when Lazarus died.
    3. Jesus wants to help **you and me** today.

C. Choose the correct pronoun in each sentence, and say why you chose that one.
    1. Father and (we, us) went to town.
    2. Joel, Mark, and (I, me) bought a calf.
    3. Father helped (we, us) when we loaded it.
    4. It kicked (I, me) once.
    5. The calf is for (we, us).
    6. Joel and (we, us) will raise it.
    7. (He, Him) and Norman went to the cave.
    8. Later we could not find (they, them).
    9. We looked for (they, them) a long time.
    10. Look over there. Those boys are (they, them).

> Written Practice >

A. Copy each verb, and label it **A** for action or **B** for being. Also copy the pronouns, and label them **DO** for direct object or **PP** for predicate pronoun.
   1. The man was he.
   2. Mother helped me.
   3. Father called them.
   4. The cook is she.
   5. Ask them.

B. Diagram the nouns, verbs, and pronouns in the sentences for Part A.

C. Copy the correct pronoun in each sentence.
   1. David and (he, him) were close friends.
   2. Saul became angry with (he, him).
   3. The teacher was (she, her).
   4. Father bought a bicycle for (I, me).
   5. James and (I, me) ride it often.
   6. My father is (he, him).
   7. Mother and (she, her) prepared supper.
   8. Susie told (I, me) about the accident.

D. Write the correct words.
   1. The calf is pushing (its, it's) head through the fence.
   2. Clear the sink. (Its, It's) too full.
   3. Clean the living room. (Its, It's) windows need to be washed.
   4. (Your, You're) going to finish (your, you're) work before I do.
   5. (Their, They're) not very plentiful.
   6. (Their, They're) water supply is low.

E. Write the following sentences correctly.
  1. Them are beautiful violets!
  2. I and Beth would like some.
  3. Beth she likes flowers.
  4. Youns may pick a few.
  5. That there is a really pretty one.
  6. This here is the one I like best.

F. Give the labels for the five parts of this letter.
  1.   San Andros
                             N. Andros Island, Bahamas
                             May 24, 20—
  2. Dear John,
  3.   We went crabbing last night. Do you know how to
     go crabbing? Well, you take a flashlight and go find
     a crab's hole. Listen carefully and you will hear one
     walking. Shine your light around till you see the crab.
     Then grab it just right so that it will not pinch you! Put it
     into your sack. Every now and then, shake the sack to
     keep the crab from crawling out. After you have caught
     several, take them home. Choose a fat one, and have
     your mother make crab and rice to eat.
         I hope you can come and visit us soon here at the
     mission. Then we will give you crab and rice to eat.
  4.   Yours truly,
  5.   Reuben

G. Copy this letter, and correct the mistakes.

760 burnt house road
carlisle PA 17013
june 6 20—

dear reuben

thank you for your letter I hope I can come someday and have crab and rice with you do you like it I think I would enjoy going crabbing too, but I hope you will catch the crabs I'm afraid I'll get pinched! I will be glad to hold the bag

on wednesday we plan to begin building a new barn a large work crew is coming to help I wish you could be here to see it maybe the next time you come home for a visit, it will be finished

sincerely yours
john

H. Write correctly the addresses on this envelope.

miss lorraine weaver
route 1 box 668
pensacola FL 32507

dorothy a sauder
739 lincoln avenue
dongola IL 62926

Praise

For gentle dawn of morning light,
Bright stars that twinkle in the night,
For bursting buds and sprouting plants,
Contented cows and busy ants;

For songs of birds and hum of bees,
And wind that whistles through the trees,
For rippling brook and bubbling spring,
A baby's coo and songs we sing;

For soft, cool grass beneath bare feet,
The clasp of hands when friends we greet,
For warmth of fire on chilly days,
Or shade that hides the sun's fierce rays;

For scent of pine and cedar wood,
Aromas from the cooking food,
For fragrance of the blossoming trees,
And salty odors from the seas;

For taste of vegetables and meat,
Ice cream and cake, which are a treat,
For good, sweet honey made by bees—
Great God, we praise Thee for all these!

In this poem, many descriptive adjectives are used to tell about different things. See how many adjectives you can find.

Chapter 7
Adjectives

Adjectives tell *which*, *whose*, *how many*, and *what kind of*.				
Articles	**Which**	**Whose**	**How Many**	**What Kind Of**
a an the	**Demonstrative Pronouns** this that these those **Numbers of Order** second fifth tenth fifteenth	**Possessive Nouns** girl's Mary's John's cat's men's students' **Possessive Pronouns** my, your his, her its, our their	**Counting Numbers** zero one eight fifty **Indefinite Numbers** few several all much many each every	**Color** red, blue green, tan **Size** huge, tiny wide, tall **Shape** round, square **Sound** harsh, shrill **Taste** sweet, sour **Touch** soft, hard rough, smooth

77. Adjectives

Adjectives are the fourth part of speech that you are studying. Adjectives modify, or add to, nouns and pronouns. They tell **which, whose, how many,** and **what kind of.**

The words **a, an,** and **the** are also adjectives. These little words are called **articles** or **noun markers.**

In the following sentences, look at the adjectives in bold print. What does each adjective tell? Which ones are articles?

> **My little** brother caught **four tiny silver** fish.
> **Israel's first** king was **a tall young** man.
> **Fleecy white** clouds drifted across **the blue** sky.

On a sentence diagram, an adjective is put on a slanted line below the noun it modifies. Adjectives may modify subjects, direct objects, or predicate nouns.

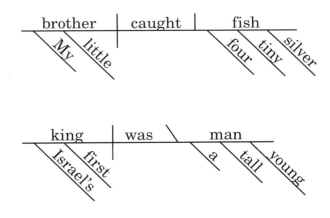

> **Remember:** Adjectives modify nouns and pronouns. An adjective tells **which, whose, how many,** or **what kind of.** The articles **a, an,** and **the** are also adjectives.

Oral Drill

A. Find the **articles** on the chart at the beginning of this chapter. Find the adjectives that tell **which, whose, how many,** and **what kind of.** Give more adjectives of your own for each list.

B. Give some adjectives to describe these things.
1. mountains   3. trees
2. birds

C. Add adjectives to these sentences.
1. Cat caught mouse.   2. Bull watched boys.

D. Diagram these sentences at the chalkboard. (They all have direct objects.) Also tell which heading each adjective would fit under: **article, which, whose, how many, or what kind of.**
1. Two red squirrels were gathering many nuts.
2. The fluffy white snow covered our muddy tracks.
3. A rich young ruler asked an important question.

E. All these sentences have predicate nouns. Diagram them on the chalkboard, and tell which heading each adjective would fit under: **article, which, whose, how many,** or **what kind of.**
1. Jonathan and David were true friends.
2. Judah was Jacob's fourth son.
3. My pet is a lovely white swan.

A. Write five headings on your paper as shown in the following example. Under the correct heading, write each adjective in the sentences below. The adjectives are in bold print.

Example: The six red apples were in **Mary's big** bowl.

Answer:

Article	Which	Whose	How many	What kind of
The		Mary's	six	red, big

1. **That weak, rotten** post broke in **the fierce, cruel** wind.

2. **Their** friends lived in **the first** house on **the old crooked** street.
3. **Our brown** hens lay **many** eggs.
4. **A thankful** heart is **a great** blessing.
5. **Daniel's three** friends would not worship **the king's golden** image.

B. Diagram these sentences. Numbers 6 and 7 have predicate nouns.
1. Several big white hens were cackling.
2. The gray cat watched the lively sparrows.
3. Joe's brown cow was munching the green grass.
4. That mischievous little monkey was swinging.
5. The little boy found a shiny new dime.
6. The fifth girl is my older sister.
7. Mother's chocolate cake was a delicious treat.

C. Write five adjectives that might describe trees or flowers. Do not use names of trees or flowers.

D. Copy these sentences. Add at least three adjectives to each one.
1. Cow drank water.
2. Children were watching clouds.
3. Boy read letter.

> Review and Practice >

Copy each verb. After it write **A** for action or **B** for being.
1. Richard fed the cows.
2. The sunset was beautiful.
3. Paul is my brother.
4. Timothy and Steve wrote several stories.
5. Where were the pencils?
6. The gray squirrel ate a nut.
7. Her white cat ran away.

---

78. Possessive Nouns Used as Adjectives

Some adjectives are made by adding **'s** to nouns. These are **possessive nouns,** but they are used as adjectives because they tell **whose.**

> **Shirley's** answer was correct.
> The **boys'** hats are in **Father's** car.

If a possessive noun refers to only one, it is a singular possessive noun. If it refers to more than one, it is a plural possessive noun.

To make the possessive form of a singular noun, add an apostrophe and **s.**

John's   mother's   horse's   Lois's

To make the possessive form of a plural noun that ends with **s,** add only an apostrophe.

babies'   parents'   disciples'   farmers'

If a plural noun does not end with **s,** make the possessive form by adding an apostrophe and **s.**

children's   deer's   geese's   mice's

Never use an apostrophe to form a plural noun. A plural noun does not show possession. It simply names more than one person, place, or thing.

Wrong: The boy's are riding horse's.
Right: The **boys** are riding **horses.**

Study this chart and the sentences below it.

Singular	Singular Possessive	Plural	Plural Possessive
girl	girl's	girls	girls'
mouse	mouse's	mice	mice's
sheep	sheep's	sheep	sheep's
baby	baby's	babies	babies'

The **baby** is awake.
The **baby's** crib is in this room.

This room is full of **babies.**
The **babies'** cribs are all in this room.

 Oral Drill

A. Tell whether each possessive noun is singular or plural.
   1. **Donna's** answer was not correct.
   2. The **birds'** songs annoyed **David's** cat.
   3. The five **deer's** tracks could be seen in the **farmers'** fields.

B. Change each phrase so that it uses a possessive noun as an adjective. Tell how to spell each possessive noun.

   Example: the doll that belongs to the girl
   Answer: the girl's doll

   1. the purse that belongs to the woman
   2. the coats owned by the women
   3. the bats of the boys
   4. the ball belonging to the boy

C. Tell how to spell the missing words.

Singular	Singular Possessive	Plural	Plural Possessive
1. teacher	——	——	——
2. fox	——	——	——
3. goose	——	——	——
4. child	——	——	——

D. Tell which words need apostrophes.
   1. There are new fences on Brother Andrews land.
   2. The womens coats are on these racks.
   3. The two girls dolls are over there.

> Written Practice >

A. Rewrite each phrase so that it uses a possessive noun as an adjective.
1. the bone belonging to the dog
2. the tail of the mouse
3. the room for the women
4. the dens of the bears

B. Write the missing words.

Singular	Singular Possessive	Plural	Plural Possessive
1. boy	————	————	————
2. church	————	————	————
3. man	————	————	————
4. city	————	————	————
5. wolf	————	————	————
6. woman	————	————	————

C. Find the words that need apostrophes, and write them correctly.
1. Several pupils maps are on the teachers desk.
2. Toms brother is wearing his fathers coat.
3. Harolds red hens lay many large brown eggs.
4. Both boys bats are in the girls coatroom.

> Review and Practice

A. Write the correct verb for each sentence.
   1. (Raise, Rise) to your feet when you shake hands.
   2. Jesus could (raise, rise) the dead back to life.
   3. (Let, Leave) the book on my desk.

B. Write the correct pronouns. Tell how each one is used by writing **DO** for direct object or **OP** for object of a preposition.
   1. You saw (they, them) last night.
   2. Did you and Donna talk to (she, her)?
   3. Will you sit with (I, me) tonight?
   4. Judy welcomed (we, us) warmly.
   5. This card is for (he, him).

C. Write correctly each word that needs a capital letter.
   1. the apostle paul wrote letters to the church in corinth.
   2. he also wrote to the churches in ephesus and philippi.
   3. the ionian sea and the aegean sea are parts of the mediterranean sea.
   4. on monday, august 5, my father went to richmond, virginia.
   5. the missouri river is very low this year.
   6. the city of new orleans was built at the mouth of the mississippi river.

79. Possessive Pronouns Used as Adjectives

Here are the rules that you have learned about possessive nouns.

1. To make the possessive form of a singular noun, add an apostrophe and **s.**

    Silas's coat   horse's hoof   cat's bell

2. To make the possessive form of a plural noun that ends with **s,** add only an apostrophe.

    boys' coats   horses' stalls   cats' dishes

3. To make the possessive form of a plural noun that does not end with **s,** add an apostrophe and **s.**

    four deer's tracks   two geese's feathers

A possessive pronoun takes the place of a possessive noun. A possessive pronoun never needs an apostrophe.

Wrong: your's, her's, it's, our's, their's
Right: yours, hers, its, ours, theirs

Martha's coat is on the hook.
Your coat is over here.
Hers is in the closet.

William's mail came today.
Our mail has not come yet.
Theirs came early.

Do not confuse contractions with possessive pronouns.

It's means **it is.**
You're means **you are.**
They're means **they are.**

Do not use contractions for possessive pronouns.

> **It's** interesting to watch the bluebird build a nest.
> (**It's** means **it is.**)
> **Its** nest is in the new house that Father put up.
> (**Its** is a possessive pronoun.)
> **You're** early this morning!
> (**You're** means **you are.**)
> **Your** pies are ready.
> (**Your** is a possessive pronoun.)

When you see a pronoun with an apostrophe, think of the two words it stands for. Do not use it in a sentence unless it could be replaced by those two words.

Remember: Possessive pronouns do not have apostrophes. Be careful not to confuse contractions with possessive pronouns.

> ## Oral Drill

Choose the correct words in parentheses, and tell whether each one is a **contraction** or a **possessive pronoun.** Tell what each contraction means.

1. (Their, They're) bringing the children here.
2. (Their, They're) house is too small.
3. (Your, You're) coat is out on the playground.
4. (Your, You're) the only one here this morning.
5. (Its, It's) too early to leave.
6. (Its, It's) burrow is under the ground.
7. (Its, It's) good to see you again.

> Written Practice >

A. Copy the correct words in parentheses.
   1. Those toys are the (childrens, children's).
   2. Give the hammer to (Davids, David's) father.
   3. Please feed the (cows, cow's).
   4. These books are (yours, your's) and (Ruths, Ruth's).
   5. The (kittens, kitten's) paw is hurt.
   6. Our (teachers, teacher's) are having a meeting.
   7. The two (dogs, dog's, dogs') were lost.
   8. Both (dogs, dog's, dogs') owners offered a reward for finding the (dogs, dog's).
   9. The blue truck is (Jerrys, Jerry's, Jerrys').
   10. The three (boys, boy's, boys') stories did not agree.

B. Use the following words in sentences of your own.
   1. its   3. your   5. their
   2. it's   4. you're   6. they're

> Review and Practice >

A. Write the missing words.

Singular	Singular Possessive	Plural	Plural Possessive
1. girl	——	——	——
2. box	——	——	——
3. man	——	——	——
4. baby	——	——	——

B. Write words to complete these sentences.
   1. A —— names a person, place, or thing.
   2. A —— shows action or being.

3. A —— takes the place of a noun.

4. An —— describes a noun or a pronoun.

C. Diagram these sentences.

1. My dog bit him.

2. Wilbur's fat steers ate our fresh green beans.

3. Joel's new pet is a lively little puppy.

4. The big shaggy dog was chasing Ronnie's orange cat.

---

80. Giving an Oral Book Report

In Lesson 61 you learned how to write a book report. Today you will learn about book reports that are given orally. An oral book report is interesting to listen to if the one who gives it is well prepared.

First, choose and read a good book. Then take notes on the main facts about the book. These include the title of the book, the name of the author, the copyright date, and where the book can be found. They also include the main characters in the story, the main problem, and the setting—where the story happened and in what time period.

List these points on an index card or a small piece of paper. Do not write everything you plan to say, but only the main points.

Practice giving your report to someone else. Maybe one of your parents, brothers, or sisters will listen to you. Practice in front of a mirror to check your expressions. Use your hands to make meaningful gestures, but do not fidget or move about unnecessarily.

When you give your report, be sure to speak clearly and loudly enough so that everyone can hear you easily. Look at your audience, not at your shoes or the floor. Do not keep your eyes glued to your notes, but refer to them only if you need to. Do not read your report—tell it! Keep a pleasant expression on your face.

Do not tell about everything in the book, but stick to the main points. Then tell about a part that you found especially interesting. Leave your listeners in some suspense so that they will also want to read the book.

Remember: When giving an oral book report, speak clearly and use good expression. Make your report interesting so that your listeners will want to read the book too.

 **Oral Drill**

A. Write down the date on which you are to give your oral book report. Your teacher will tell you this.

B. Listen as your classmates give their book reports. Discuss good points about the reports and also ways in which they could be improved.

Written Practice

A. List the main points of the book on which you will give an oral report. Put the points in order.

B. Practice giving your report to others before it is your turn at school.

C. Give your report in front of the class when your teacher tells you. After you have finished, hand in your notes for your teacher to check.

> Review and Practice

A. Rewrite each phrase so that it uses a possessive noun as an adjective.
   1. the hair belonging to the baby
   2. the tail of the deer
   3. the purses of the women

B. Write the missing words.

Singular	Singular Possessive	Plural	Plural Possessive
1. fox	——	——	——
2. baby	——	——	——
3. father	——	——	——

C. Copy the correct words in parentheses. After each answer, write **C** for contraction or **P** for possessive form. If it is a contraction, also write the two words it stands for.
   1. (Their, They're) having a hymn sing tonight.
   2. All the people have brought (their, they're) books.
   3. (Your, You're) voice is good for soprano.
   4. We hope (your, you're) planning to help us.
   5. (Its, It's) time to start singing.

D. Write the correct words.
1. A good writer must —— closely and —— carefully.
2. Do not write short, —— sentences or sentences that are too ——.
3. Sentences in a paragraph may be written in the order of —— or the order of ——.
4. Name the five parts of a friendly letter.

---

81. Adjectives That Compare

Sometimes adjectives that tell **what kind of** are used to compare things. Many of these adjectives have **forms of comparison.** Following are some examples of adjectives and their forms of comparison.

soft	softer	softest
old	older	oldest
tall	taller	tallest

When only one person or thing is described, use adjectives without **er** or **est.**

This is a **soft** bed.
Abraham became an **old** man.

When two persons or things are compared, use adjectives that end with the suffix **er.** Use the word **more** with many adjectives that have two or more syllables.

This bed is **softer** than that one.

John is **older** than Jerry.

She is usually **more thoughtful** than he is.

Do not add **er** to an adjective and also use **more** with it.

Wrong: This lesson is more harder than that one.

Right: This lesson is **harder** than that one.

When three or more persons or things are compared, use adjectives that end with the suffix **est.** Use **most** with many adjectives of two or more syllables.

This is the **softest** bed of them all.

Jean is the **oldest** girl in her class.

Which man was the **most considerate** of his neighbor?

Do not add **est** to an adjective and also use **most** with it.

Wrong: Larry is the most tallest boy in our school.

Right: Larry is the **tallest** boy in our school.

 Oral Drill

A. Give the three forms of comparison.
   1. soft   3. smooth   5. beautiful
   2. tall   4. green   6. cool

B. Give the correct form of each word in parentheses. Tell how to spell it.
   1. This is the (small) house I have ever seen.
   2. This pie is (sweet) than that one.
   3. Mount Hermon is the (high) mountain in Palestine.
   4. Am I (old) than you?

5. You must be (considerate) than you have been.
6. This coin is (valuable) than that one.

C. Correct the mistakes.

1. A ladybug is more small than a Japanese beetle.
2. My grandfather is the most old man in our church.
3. Of my two brothers, Frank is the oldest one.

> **Written Practice**

A. Write the three forms of comparison for each adjective.

1. small   4. pleasant
2. sweet   5. quick
3. high   6. beautiful

B. Write the correct adjective in parentheses.

1. Harold is (taller, tallest) than his brother.
2. The living room feels (colder, coldest) than the kitchen.
3. Mount Everest is the (higher, highest) mountain in the world.
4. Of the two brothers, John is (taller, tallest).
5. Sunday was the (clearest, most clear) day of the week.
6. Yesterday it was (clearer, more clear) than it is today.
7. Is the soup (hot, hotter)?
8. "Jesus wept" is the (shorter, shortest) verse in the Bible.
9. Her deed of kindness was the (thoughtfullest, most thoughtful) thing anyone had done for the old man.

10. The weather is (milder, more mild) today than yesterday.

> **Review and Practice**

A. Write the correct word for each blank.
   1. Adjectives modify —— and ——.
   2. Adjectives tell wh——, wh——, h—— ————, and wh— —— ——.
   3. The three little words **a,** ——, and —— are also adjectives. They are called ——.

B. Diagram these sentences. Be especially careful with adjectives, direct objects, and predicate nouns.
   1. Our little dog followed the old man.
   2. Their curious raccoon can open most latches.
   3. The flower was a big red rose.
   4. Howard's black horse ate the sweet hay.

> **Challenge Exercise**

Find a poem that has many descriptive adjectives. Copy it, and underline all the adjectives that tell **what kind of.**

82. Using Adjectives That Compare

Some adjectives have a spelling change when **er** or **est** is added. Learn to spell these forms of comparison correctly.

If an adjective ends with **y** after a consonant, change the **y** to **i** before adding **er** or **est.**

happy	happ**i**er	happ**i**est
heavy	heav**i**er	heav**i**est

If an adjective ends with a single consonant after a short vowel, double the final consonant before adding **er** or **est.**

thin	thi**nn**er	thi**nn**est
big	bi**gg**er	bi**gg**est

If an adjective ends with **e,** drop the **e** before adding **er** or **est.**

late	lat**er**	lat**est**
nice	nic**er**	nic**est**
large	larg**er**	larg**est**

The dictionary shows how to spell adjective forms of comparison. If it does not show a spelling with **er** or **est,** use **more** and **most** to make the forms of comparison.

Oral Drill

A. Give the three forms of comparison.

1. sad
2. nice
3. tiny
4. blue
5. happy
6. powerful

B. Give the correct form of each word in parentheses. Tell
   how to spell it.
   1. Martha is (close) to the door than I am.
   2. Abigail is (thin) than Eva.
   3. Of all the stories, this one is (sad).
   4. The baby is (happy) when you play with him than
      when you try to read a book.
   5. Of all the papers, this one is (late).

C. Correct the mistakes.
   1. Gold is heavyer than lead.
   2. Paul is the most strongest boy in our class.
   3. We have a more farther distance to school than you do.
   4. Jane was glader to get home than I was.
   5. This box is the largeest one here.

> Written Practice >

A. Write the three forms of comparison.
   1. nice   5. careful
   2. thin   6. pleasant
   3. late   7. happy
   4. heavy   8. lazy

B. Write the correct form of each word in parentheses.
   1. This is the (pretty) rose I have ever seen on the bush.
   2. She is the (tiny) baby I have ever held.
   3. Samuel is (careful) than he was before he broke the
      eggs.
   4. Jason is (tall) for his age.
   5. Sarah is (thin) than she used to be.
   6. Which of the five children finished in the (short)
      time?

C. Write the correct adjective in parentheses.
1. Of the three boys, Mark is the (faster, fastest) runner.
2. Of the two girls, Lillian is (taller, tallest).
3. Judy has the (clearer, clearest) soprano voice of all the girls.
4. These flowers are (beautiful, more beautiful).
5. They are (beautifuller, more beautiful) than they were last year.
6. I think this flower is the (beautifullest, most beautiful) one in the garden.
7. Texas is (larger, more large) than California.
8. The Dead Sea is (lower, more lower) than the Mediter- ranean Sea.

D. Use these adjectives in sentences of your own.
1. louder   3. bluest
2. hottest   4. sweeter

> Review and Practice >

A. Write the correct form of the verb in each sentence.
1. Fred (go) to the store yesterday.
2. Bill (think) he will be able to go sledding.
3. Had all the students (finish) by recess time?
4. Susan has (ride) her bike to school many times this year.
5. Mary (do) the cleaning every day.

B. Write the eight forms of the verb **be.**

C. List fifteen helping verbs. Do not list the forms of **be.** Keep each set together.

83. Irregular Adjectives That Compare

You have learned that the forms of comparison of some adjectives are made by adding **er** and **est**. Other adjectives show comparison by using **more** and **most** with them.

Some adjectives have irregular forms of comparison. Look at these common irregular forms.

good	better	best
bad	worse	worst
little	less	least
much	more	most
many	more	most

Study the following sentences.

Wrong:

Harold feels gooder than he did last week.

He said it was the baddest sickness he had ever had.

Carl ate lesser cake than I did.

John ate the mostest cookies of all.

Right:

Harold feels **better** than he did last week.

He said it was the **worst** sickness he had ever had.

Carl ate **less** cake than I did.

John ate the **most** cookies of all.

When only one thing is described, use adjectives from the first column in the list above: **good, bad, little, much, many.**

When two things are compared, use adjectives from the second column above: **better, worse, less, more.**

When three or more things are compared, use adjectives from the third column: **best, worst, least, most.**

Do not use **more** and **most** with the irregular forms of comparison.

Wrong: A soft answer is more better than angry words.

Right: A soft answer is **better** than angry words.

 Oral Drill

A. Give the three forms of comparison.

   1. good   3. many   5. much

   2. little   4. bad

B. Give the correct form of each word in parentheses.

   1. Noah lived through the (bad) flood in history.

   2. This loaf looks (good) than that one.

   3. Her picture is the (good) one of all.

   4. Most girls eat (little) food than boys.

   5. Sue ate the (little) soup of all.

   6. There are (many) berries in your bucket than in mine.

   7. Who has the (many) berries of all?

   8. There is (much) water in the pond now than there was yesterday.

   9. Today it has the (much) water it has had all week.

  10. Which cow gives the (much) milk?

C. Correct the mistakes.

   1. Her report was more better than his.

   2. This apple tastes gooder than that one.

   3. This flood is worser than the one last year.

   4. That is the muchest water I have ever seen.

   5. The Taylors had the worstest damage of all our neighbors.

> Written Practice >

A. Write the correct adjectives.
1. I think ice cream is (gooder, better) than jelly beans.
2. Jason feels (better, more well) now than he did this morning.
3. Of the two girls, Julie is the (better, best) writer.
4. Jacob has the (worse, worst) handicap of anyone in school, but he works the (more, most) cheerfully of all.
5. Jerry spent the (less, least) possible time on his homework, and he got the (more, most) wrong answers of all.

B. For each sentence, write the correct form of the adjective in parentheses.
1. (good) You did —— work. Mary did —— work than John. Joe did the —— work of all.
2. (little) We had —— rain last summer. Monroe County received —— rain than we did. Perry County had the —— rain of all.
3. (bad) Nancy has a —— scratch on her face. The scratch on her leg is —— than the one on her face. The scratch on her arm is the —— one of all.

> Review and Practice >

A. Write the subject pronouns.

B. Answer these questions.
1. What kind of words do adjectives modify?
2. What four questions do adjectives answer?
3. Which three adjectives are the articles?

[Handwritten note:] Read English L. 84
Write a story about
something that happened
at school...
What did we do?
Why did we do it?
Did you learn anything?
[SKIP everything else]

C. Write the correct adjectives.
    1. Who is the (faster, more faster) runner, you or Will?
    2. Jane was (thoughtful, more thoughtful) than Susan.
    3. Julie is the (shorter, shortest) one of the four girls.
    4. Nelson is (taller, tallest) than Jay.

84. Writing a Story

You have learned that a paragraph tells about one topic, or main idea. A story also tells about just one main idea. The main idea of a story is called the **theme.**

When you write a story, you first need to decide what the theme will be. Then make a list of the details you will use. Arrange the details in the correct order so that your story will make sense and be easy to understand.

Write a sentence to introduce your theme in an interesting way. Then, using your list, write the details of the story in proper sentences. Remember not to write too many short, choppy sentences. Avoid run-on sentences or sentences that are too long.

Write with clear, descriptive words, using sentences that show action and feeling. Do not write unimportant details. When you have finished, stop! Do not write about things that do not add to the theme.

Give your story a good title. The title should give a clue to what the story is about. It should be interesting so that others will want to read the story.

It is a good idea to skip every other line when you first write a story so that you have room to make changes later. Proofread your story. Did you use sentence variety and descriptive words? Did you use proper capitalization and punctuation? Make the corrections, and then copy the story neatly on a clean sheet of paper.

Remember: A story should be about one theme, and it should give its details in proper order.

Oral Drill

Carefully read John 6:1–14. Then answer the questions below in complete sentences. You may use more than one sentence to answer a question, but try to be brief and clear.

1. Why was a crowd following Jesus?
2. Where had Jesus gone? What was He doing?
3. What did He ask Philip?
4. What did Andrew say?
5. What did Jesus say the people should do?
6. What miracle did He perform?
7. What amazing thing happened after everyone had eaten enough?

Written Practice

In your own words, write the story found in John 6:1–14. Begin with this sentence: **One day Jesus used a boy's lunch to feed about five thousand people.** Then write a story with sentences that answer the questions in Oral Drill. Make your story only one paragraph long.

Rewrite your story, joining or dividing sentences so that they are not all the same length. Make other changes so that the story is interesting and pleasant to read. Give your story a good title.

Review and Practice

A. Rewrite each phrase so that it uses a possessive noun as an adjective.
   1. the nest of the rabbits
   2. the shoe of the horse

B. Write the missing words.

Singular	Singular Possessive	Plural	Plural Possessive
1. mouse	——	——	——
2. wagon	——	——	——

C. Choose the correct words in parentheses. After each answer, write **C** for contraction or **P** for possessive pronoun.
   1. We enjoy playing with (their, they're) kittens.
   2. (Their, They're) really growing fast.
   3. (Your, You're) sister likes the black one.
   4. (Its, It's) fur is soft and fuzzy.
   5. (Its, It's) time to go home now.

D. Write the correct words.
1. A topic sentence (may, must not) give details about the main idea of a paragraph.
2. It is not —— to copy someone else's writing and use it as our own.
3. It is all right to copy key —— that give main —— when taking notes.
4. Letters that are written to show friendship are called —— letters.

---

85. What to Write in a Friendly Letter

You have learned that a friendly letter has five parts: heading, greeting, body, closing, and signature. The body is the most important part because it contains the message you are sending. But have you ever started a letter and not been able to think of much to write? There are many good things to write in friendly letters.

Write about things that have happened to you or your family. Tell about a trip you took or about things you did or learned in school. Give interesting descriptions. Tell about a storm in your area or about something interesting that happened in your church or neighborhood. Give enough details so that your friend can "see" what you are talking about.

Describe how you feel about things that happened. Tell about things that you know will interest your friend. Ask questions that show you are interested in him, and answer any question that your friend asked you in a letter. Try to write about pleasant things and to write in a pleasant way.

Your letter should sound as if you were right there talking to your friend.

> **Example:** We had a bad ice storm. Our electricity was off for three days. (not enough details)

> **Better:** Last Monday we had a bad ice storm. The rain froze as it fell until everything was covered with a layer of ice. Father said it was a quarter inch thick on our car! The sparkling ice made things really beautiful, but it also broke down many tree branches and electric wires. Our electricity was off for three days. You can imagine how glad we were to have electric lights again!

Sometimes there are special reasons for writing a letter. You may write to give someone help and encouragement. Maybe you want to give or accept an invitation. If someone did something thoughtful for you, you can write a letter to thank him.

Write kindly and courteously. Make your letter easy to read by writing neatly and correctly. In all your letters, write to others as you would have them write to you.

Oral Drill

A. Review the five parts of a friendly letter and how they should be written.

B. Discuss some things you could write about for each suggestion in Written Practice.

Written Practice

Write a friendly letter, using one of the suggestions below. After the teacher has checked your letter, you may want to recopy it and actually send it to someone.

1. Write to an older person in your church. Describe school happenings. Tell about your friends. Describe some beautiful things of nature you have seen lately.

2. Write to someone your age from another school. Tell about the things you are studying at school. Describe your friends and your teacher. (Remember to be kind and courteous when writing about other people. Follow the Golden Rule.)

3. Write a letter inviting one of your friends to your house for a meal or inviting someone to your church for a service. Tell when you want him to come. Give the date and the time. Tell about some things you plan to do when he comes.

Review and Practice

Write the correct words.

1. You must move your ——— in order to speak clearly.
2. You should ——— the whole book before you give a book report.

3. A book report (should, should not) tell everything that happened in the book.
4. You should use good ——— when you speak or read orally.
5. The main idea of a story is its ———.
6. For an oral book report, you should write down only the ——— points that you will tell about.

---

86. Chapter 7 Review

> Oral Drill

A. Answer these questions.
1. What parts of speech do adjectives modify?
2. What questions do adjectives answer?
3. What are the articles?
4. What part of speech are articles?

B. Say and spell the missing words.

Singular	Singular Possessive	Plural	Plural Possessive
1. horse	———	———	———
2. mouse	———	———	———
3. sheep	———	———	———
4. baby	———	———	———

C. Give two forms of comparison for each adjective. Tell how to spell them.
1. happy   4. good
2. wise   5. big
3. helpful

D. Give the proper form of comparison for each sentence.
1. Mary is (tall) than Martha.
2. This is the (bad) storm we have had all summer.
3. This kitten is the (small) one in the nest.
4. Of the two boys, Frank is the (tall) one.
5. These bananas are (ripe) than those.
6. Jesus is the (good) friend we have.

E. Answer these questions.
1. What should you check when you proofread your stories?
2. When you give an oral book report, how much of the story should you tell?

> Written Practice

A. Diagram these sentences.
1. The selfish little girl was pouting.
2. My brother rode the large brown horse.
3. Jesus is our kind Shepherd.
4. The hungry kittens were drinking the warm milk.
5. Those yellow flowers are Mother's daffodils.

B. Write the missing words.

Singular	Singular Possessive	Plural	Plural Possessive
1. deer	——	——	——
2. boy	——	——	——
3. fox	——	——	——
4. child	——	——	——
5. woman	——	——	——

C. Find each word that needs an apostrophe, and write it correctly.
1. The childrens books are on their desks.
2. Arnolds father drove Brother Philips car.
3. The two boys bicycles are parked outside.
4. Anns sister is wearing her mothers coat.
5. The mens shirts are on those racks.

D. Write **true** or **false** for each sentence.
1. You should practice giving an oral book report to one of your parents, brothers, or sisters.
2. You should write down everything you plan to say in an oral book report.
3. A good book report gives only the main facts from the book.
4. A book report should leave the listeners in some suspense so that they will want to read the book.

E. Copy each adjective, and write its two forms of comparison.
1. thin   4. little
2. good   5. much
3. bad

F. Write the correct form of each word in parentheses.
1. Richard is (heavy) than Philip.
2. Ralph is the (tall) boy in the room.
3. Baby Amy is (happy) than she had been.
4. This cake is the (good) one of the three I have tasted.
5. They have (many) stamps than we do.
6. His fever is (bad) today than it was yesterday.
7. (Its, It's) time to go.

8. (Their, They're) books are blue.

9. (Your, You're) not ready to go.

10. (Its, It's) door is open.

G. Write the correct words.

1. What are the five parts of a friendly letter?

2. In a friendly letter, write about things that have happened to —— or your ——.

3. When you proofread your stories, you should check for good —— in words and sentences. Also check for correct ——, punctuation, and ——.

The Snow

Last night when we were sound asleep,
The snow fell **fast**, the snow piled **deep.**
When morning came and we looked **out,**
The snow was lying all **about.**

The wind was blowing **high** and **low,**
And wrinkling **up** the pure white snow;
And **everywhere** that we could see,
We found that God made mystery.

—*Marguerite Church Clark* (adapted)

Adverbs tell **how, when,** or **where.**
In the poem, which words in bold print
tell **how**? Which ones tell **where**?

Chapter 8
Adverbs

Adverbs tell *how*, *when*, and *where*.

WORKED

How

carefully

carelessly

When

early

now

late

Where

there

outside

inside

87. Adverbs

Adverbs are another part of speech. They are words that modify, or add to, verbs by telling **how, when,** and **where.**

> Mother spoke **softly.**
> The children worked **outdoors yesterday.**

Many adverbs end with **ly.** In the following sentences, find four adverbs that end with **ly,** and two that do not end with **ly.**

> The kitten cried sadly.
> The smoke rose slowly upward.
> We opened the box carefully.
> Tom stood up quietly.

Some adverbs are made by adding **ly** to adjectives.

> calm—calmly　　bitter—bitterly　　rapid—rapidly

Adverbs are diagramed on slanted lines beneath the verb.

> The rain poured down suddenly.

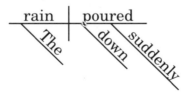

Remember: Adverbs modify verbs. They tell **how, when,** and **where.** Many adverbs end with **ly.**

A. Tell which words are adverbs. Say whether each one tells **how, when, or where.**
   1. My little sister sang joyously.
   2. That horse ran fast yesterday.
   3. The sun shone brightly today.
   4. The children played happily outside.

B. Diagram these sentences at the chalkboard.
   1. Helen came yesterday.
   2. Susan is here now.
   3. We listened carefully.

C. These sentences have adjectives that should be adverbs. Read each one, changing the incorrect adjectives to adverbs.
   1. The doctor worked careful.
   2. He spoke soft as he worked.
   3. Those girls can write neat.
   4. You did your work correct.

> Written Practice >

A. Copy the adverbs in these sentences. After each adverb, write whether it tells **how, when, or where.**
   1. The wind blew furiously.
   2. Father is coming inside now.

   3. James worked carefully yesterday.

   4. Do your lesson heartily.

   5. The children are eating outdoors today.

   6. We shall build the shed here.

B. Diagram these sentences.

   1. Our goat ran around wildly.

   2. The sun shone brightly yesterday.

   3. The apostles preached faithfully.

   4. Students should listen attentively.

C. Rewrite the following sentences, changing the adjectives that should be adverbs. Underline the words you changed.

   1. The two hungry dogs ate swift.

   2. The angry man waved his hands furious.

   3. Father spoke calm to him.

> **Review and Practice**

A. Write the correct words for these sentences.

   1. —— are words that modify nouns and pronouns.

   2. —— are words that modify verbs.

   3. Adjectives tell ——, ——, —— ——, and —— —— ——.

   4. Adverbs tell ——, ——, and ——.

   5. The articles are ——, ——, and ——.

   6. Articles are (adjectives, adverbs).

B. Copy each word in bold print. After it write **adj.** if it is an adjective, or **adv.** if it is an adverb.

   1. A **strong** wind blew **fiercely.**

   2. The waves roared **loudly** around the **small** ship.

   3. The **twelve** disciples cried **out.**

4. The Lord came **soon** and helped His **fearful** disciples.
5. Jesus calmed the **fierce** storm **suddenly.**
6. **Our** Saviour cares for us **today.**

---

88. Adverbs in Sentences

Adverbs may come before or after the verb in a sentence. They may come at the beginning, in the middle, or at the end of a sentence.

Slowly he closed the door.
He **slowly** closed the door.
He closed the door **slowly.**

Steadily he worked at the lock.
He worked **steadily** at the lock.
He worked at the lock **steadily.**

Tomorrow we shall paint the fence.
We shall paint the fence **tomorrow.**

How, when, and **where** are also adverbs.

How are you?
When are you coming?
Where is my cap?

Not, never, ever, always, and **hardly** are adverbs.

This is **not** a cold land.
It **never** snows here.
It **always** rains in November.
It **hardly ever** rains in July.

Diagram an adverb under the verb it modifies, no matter where it is in the sentence. The first three examples near the beginning of the lesson would all be diagramed as shown here.

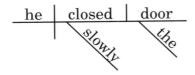

> **Remember:** Adverbs may come at the beginning, in the middle, or at the end of a sentence. **How, when,** and **where** are adverbs. **Not, never, ever, always,** and **hardly** are adverbs.

Oral Drill

A. Tell which words are adverbs.
1. We never have many floods here.
2. Cautiously the little animal crept away.
3. Cheerfully the birds sang.
4. They are not working hard today.
5. Where is your coat?
6. When are you going?
7. We hardly know them.
8. Always do good work.

B. On the chalkboard, diagram the sentences in Part A.

> Written Practice >

A. Copy all the adverbs in each sentence.
1. Then the children came in.
2. Soon the little wild ducks were swimming around.
3. The children were not working lazily.
4. Always trust and obey.
5. Never shirk your duty.
6. Do not write carelessly.
7. She may not go along.
8. The eager pupils studied their lessons diligently.
9. Where are they today?
10. When did you arrive?
11. How do you work?
12. We should always help our friends gladly.

B. Diagram these sentences. One sentence has a direct
object, and one has a predicate noun.
1. She slowly got up.
2. Yesterday we went.
3. Now Raymond is mowing the
lawn.
4. The baby smiled brightly today.
5. The Lord is always our God.

C. Write three sentences of your own that begin with
adverbs.

D. Write sentences using the following adverbs.
1. not   3. never
2. always   4. hardly

> **Review and Practice**

A. Write definitions for these parts of speech.
   1. noun   4. adverb
   2. pronoun   5. adjective
   3. verb

B. Name the four kinds of sentences.

C. Write the correct words.
   1. Of all the boys, Alvin is (taller, tallest).
   2. Of my two brothers, Karl is (taller, tallest).
   3. Carrie is the (older, oldest) girl in my class.
   4. This berry is the (most large, largest) one I picked.
   5. These are the (most thinnest, thinnest) sheets of paper
      I have ever seen.

> **Challenge Exercise**

   Write a sentence about each picture. Use descriptive
adjectives and adverbs. Draw a circle around each adjective,
and a box around each adverb in your sentences.

89. Telling How to Do Something

Your parents and teachers tell you how to do many things. When you are older, you yourself will have many opportunities to tell someone else how to do something. Therefore, you should learn to explain things clearly and correctly.

First, know how to do it yourself. Think what steps must be taken, and arrange the steps in a sensible order.

When you talk to a group, speak clearly and distinctly. Do not rush, but take time to say things plainly and properly. Do not fill in pauses with **ah** or **uh.** Give your thoughts in complete sentences.

Look at the listeners, and talk directly to them. Do not look out the window or stare at the back wall or at your feet. Smile pleasantly and use good posture.

Use pictures, diagrams, or objects to make your instructions clear and interesting. Whenever possible, **show** how to do what you are describing. For example, if you are telling how to draw a tree, have a pencil or a piece of chalk in your hand, and show how to draw each step.

Making a Penny Seem to Rise

1. Set a cup on a table.
2. Put a penny in the bottom of the cup.
3. Ask another person to look at the penny and keep watching it as he slowly backs away. He should stop when the penny is just hidden by the rim of the cup.
4. Slowly pour water into the cup.
5. The penny will seem to rise so that the other person can see it again.

When you have finished, summarize what you have said by repeating the main points in order. This will help to make the explanation stick in the minds of your listeners.

Remember: When you give directions orally, tell the main points in the proper order. Demonstrate what you are explaining, if possible. Be sure to speak slowly and distinctly enough to be understood easily. End with a summary of the main points.

> Oral Drill

Tell how the order in this set of directions could be improved.

Washing Dishes

Look at the dirty dishes with a smile. Say to yourself, "This is a big stack of dishes, but I shall make them clean and shining. I shall do my job quickly, cheerfully, and well."

Begin your task at once. Stack the dishes neatly. Then begin to wash them. First, get warm, soapy water.

When you have finished, you will have the joy of a job well done. Thank the Lord that you are well, able, and strong enough to do your share of the work.

Sing good, cheery songs as you work. Chase away any thought of pity by saying this verse to yourself: "In every thing give thanks."

> Written Practice >

A. Write a list of main ideas in proper order to explain how to do one of the following activities.
   1. How to draw a simple picture of a tree, cat, or dog.
   2. How to clear the table after a big meal.
   3. How to clean your own bedroom.
   4. How to paint a table or a chair.
   5. How to make a kind of cookie or candy that you like.
   6. How to wash a big dog.

B. Give an oral explanation to the class, using your list from Part A for your notes.

> Review and Practice >

Answer these questions in complete sentences.
   1. What is spoken English called?
   2. What should you check for when you proofread a story?
   3. What are some rules for giving an oral book report?

90. Adverbs That Compare

Like adjectives, adverbs can be used to make comparisons. Adjectives compare things, but adverbs compare actions. Study the list on the next page.

late	later	latest
low	lower	lowest
quickly	more quickly	most quickly

When using an adverb to describe only one action, use the simple form.

Ellen came **late.**
Frank can run **swiftly.**

When using an adverb to compare two actions, add the suffix **er** or use the word **more.**

Carol came **later** than Ellen.
Amos runs **more swiftly** than Frank.

When using an adverb to compare three or more actions, add the suffix **est** or use the word **most.**

Karen came the **latest** of all the girls.
Douglas can run the **most swiftly** of all the boys.

For most one-syllable adverbs and some two-syllable adverbs, make the forms of comparison by adding **er** or **est** to the simple form. For most other adverbs, use **more** and **most** to compare two or more actions.

hard	harder	hardest
early	earlier	earliest
loudly	more loudly	most loudly

Do not add **er** or **est** to an adverb and also use **more** or

most with it. Do not use the **est** form when comparing only two actions.

> **Wrong:** Bob runs more faster than Joe.
> **Right:** Bob runs **faster** than Joe.
>
> **Wrong:** Jerry runs the most fastest of all.
> **Right:** Jerry runs the **fastest** of all.
>
> **Wrong:** Of the two boys, John ran fastest.
> **Right:** Of the two boys, John ran **faster.**

A few adverbs have irregular forms of comparison.

well	better	best
badly	worse	worst
little	less	least
much	more	most
far	farther	farthest

> Oral Drill

A. Give the forms of comparison of each adverb.

1. wisely
2. soon
3. cheaply
4. late
5. near
6. quickly

B. Correct the mistakes.
1. Of the two brothers, Alvin works hardest.
2. David runs the most fastest of all the boys.
3. Jane sang loudlier than Joan.
4. Of the four girls, who awoke the earlier?
5. Who can draw best, Carrie or Lucy?
6. John was here more oftener than Jerry.

> Written Practice

A. Copy each adverb, and write the forms of comparison.
   1. badly   4. far   7. happily
   2. well   5. soon   8. painfully
   3. little   6. near

B. Write the correct words.
   1. Who spoke (louder, more louder), Saul or David?
   2. Who ran (faster, fastest), Ahimaaz or Cushi?
   3. Of the two towns, Bethlehem was (nearer, nearest) to Jerusalem.
   4. Trudy did (better, best) today than she did yesterday.
   5. Of the five students, Daniel works the (more diligently, most diligently).

C. Write the correct form of each adjective or adverb in parentheses.
   1. Today Luke feels (well) than he did yesterday.
   2. Jesus asked, "Lovest thou me (much) than these?"
   3. Of the four teams, ours had the (many) points.
   4. I have (little) milk in my glass than you do.
   5. Who walked (far), you or Grant?
   6. Of all the girls in class, Sharon spoke (quickly).
   7. Hugh writes (neatly) than Howard.

> Review and Practice

A. Diagram these sentences. (Hint: **Flying squirrel** and **tree frog** are compound nouns.)
   1. Rhode Island is the smallest state.
   2. The brown flying squirrel glided down gracefully.
   3. Tree frogs are trilling their cheery songs now.

B. Write the correct words.
1. Adjectives modify ——— and ———.
2. Adjectives tell ———, ———, ——— ———, and ———
——— ———.
3. Adverbs modify ———.
4. Adverbs tell ———, ———, and ———.
5. Many (adjectives, adverbs) end with **ly.**

---

91. Using *Good* and *Well*

The words **good** and **well** are easily confused. Learn to use them correctly.

Good is an adjective. It tells **what kind of** and describes nouns.

A **good** tree produces **good** fruit.

Good may be in the predicate after a form of the verb **be.**

The bread is **good.**
These stories are **good.**

Well is used mainly as an adverb to tell **how.**

Sarah sews **well.**
Clean the sink **well.**

Well may also be an adjective meaning **healthy.**

Charles is **well** again.
Soon the sick calf was **well.**

Some people use **good** when they should use **well.** Study the following sentences.

Wrong:

> Laura was sick, but she is good again.
> Jesus touched the leper and made him good.
> Sue can draw good.
> Do your lessons good.

Right:

> Laura was sick, but she is **well** again.
> Jesus touched the leper and made him **well.**
> Sue can draw **well.**
> Do your lessons **well.**

Remember: Good is an adjective. **Well** is an adverb when it tells **how. Well** is an adjective when it means **healthy.**

 Oral Drill

Choose **good** or **well** for each blank. If you choose **good,** tell which noun it modifies or say that it follows a form of **be.** If you choose **well,** tell whether it is an adverb that tells **how** or an adjective that means **healthy.**

1. This apple is ———.
2. Ruth can write very ———.
3. We used ——— soap.
4. Larry is not feeling ——— today.
5. This book is ———.
6. I cannot sew very ———.
7. My big brother drives ———.
8. You are pale and do not look ———.

9. Roger reads ———.
10. Mother made a ——— pie.

> Written Practice

A. Write **good** or **well** for each sentence.
1. We learned our lessons ———.
2. That was a ——— lesson.
3. Are you sick or ———?
4. Everything God made was ———.
5. You have done ——— work in the garden.
6. The visitor could not speak English ———.
7. The old bread was not very ———.
8. Susie made a ——— cake.
9. Be a ——— pupil.
10. ——— cakes sell ———.

B. Answer these questions in complete sentences.
1. When is **well** an adverb?
2. When is **well** an adjective?
3. What part of speech is **good**?

> Review and Practice

Write the following sentences correctly.
1. The children was playing tag at recess.
2. The bell rung too soon.
3. I have tore my dress.
4. Myron and me tied the dog.
5. Them there apples are well.
6. My aunt can draw good.
7. John tripped me and James.
8. James and me could see that John was sorry.

> Challenge Exercise >

Find information on a plant or animal in an encyclopedia, and write a descriptive paragraph about it. You may use one of the following ideas.

pitcher plant	camel
dandelion	palm tree
leopard	anteater

92. Negative Words

Negative words mean **no.** They change a sentence so that it has an opposite meaning. These are some common negative words.

no	never	hardly
not	nobody	barely
none	nothing	scarcely

Contractions with **not** are also negative words.

isn't	couldn't	won't
haven't	can't	

The negative word **no** is an adjective. **Not, never, hardly, barely,** and **scarcely** are adverbs.

Do not say things like "I can't see nothing." Such a sentence is incorrect because two negative words must not be used together. Use only one negative word in a sentence.

Words like the four following ones are not negative words. Each may be used with a negative word.

any	anything	someone	ever

In the following sentences, all the negative words are in bold print. Notice the two negative words in each sentence that is marked **Wrong.**

Wrong: He **doesn't** want **no** candy.
Right: He **doesn't** want any candy.
Right: He wants **no** candy.

Wrong: We **couldn't hardly** find the way.
Right: We could **hardly** find the way.
Right: We **couldn't** find the way.

Remember: Do not use two negative words together in one sentence.

Give two ways to correct each sentence.
1. There isn't no sin in heaven.
2. We won't never die in heaven.
3. He doesn't hardly know what to do.
4. We didn't find scarcely any berries.
5. They can't hardly see it.
6. I didn't do none of the dishes.
7. Jerry didn't go nowhere last night.
8. Jason didn't see nobody at the school.
9. The teacher hasn't given us no homework.
10. Haven't you never seen a killdeer?

Written Practice

Copy the negative word in each sentence. Then copy the correct word in parentheses.

> **Example:** Haven't you finished (any, none) of your homework?
> **Answer:**   Haven't, any

1. I couldn't hear (nothing, anything) they were saying.
2. It seemed that the noise wasn't (ever, never) going to stop.
3. Don't you want (no, any) cookie?
4. I (can, can't) scarcely hear what you are saying.
5. Didn't you (ever, never) see a bear?
6. Didn't (nobody, anybody) come while I was gone?
7. God doesn't (ever, never) sleep.

8. There isn't (no, any) sadness in heaven.
9. God doesn't (ever, never) tell a lie.
10. I (can, can't) hardly see in this dark corner.

Review and Practice

A. Write correctly each word that should be capitalized.
 1. the red sea is between africa and arabia.
 2. the mediterranean sea almost surrounds the countries of italy and greece.
 3. the owner of that house lives in richmond, virginia, at the corner of grove avenue and plum street.

B. Write the correct form of comparison for each word in parentheses.
   1. This watermelon is (sweet) than the other one.
   2. I think studying about insects is (interesting) than studying about motors.
   3. This is the (steep) hill I ever climbed.
   4. Sandra awoke the (early) of all the girls.
   5. His bruise hurt (painfully) than mine did.

C. Copy all the adverbs in these sentences. After each adverb, write whether it tells **how, when,** or **where.**
   1. The water was running rapidly.
   2. Birds were chirping cheerfully.
   3. Down fell the old oak.
   4. We will walk quietly today.

D. Write **good** or **well** for each sentence.
   1. —— is an adjective when it means **healthy.**
   2. —— is always an adjective.
   3. —— is an adverb when it tells **how.**
   4. The students can sing ——.
   5. Mother's soup is very ——.
   6. Is Martha —— today, or is she still sick?

---

93. Rhyme in Poetry

Rhyming words are words whose endings sound alike. They help to make a poem pleasant and appealing.

The endings of rhyming words do not need to be spelled alike, but they must sound alike. In most rhyming words, only one syllable rhymes, as in **plain—grain** and **assign—combine.** Sometimes two or more syllables rhyme, as in **seven—heaven** and **wearily—cheerily.**

In poetry, two lines rhyme with each other if they end with rhyming words. There are many different rhyming patterns. In some poems, every line rhymes. In other poems, every other line rhymes. Whatever the rhyming pattern, it is usually followed in each stanza of a poem.

Study the rhyming patterns in the following stanzas.

Lines 1 and 2, and lines 3 and 4:

I know not by what methods **rare;**
But this I know: God answers **prayer.**
I know that He has given His **Word,**
Which tells me prayer is always **heard.**

Lines 1 and 3, and lines 2 and 4:

If you've tried and have not **won,**
Never stop for **crying;**
All that's good and great is **done**
Just by patient **trying.**

Only lines 2 and 4:

Courtesy is beautiful,
Courtesy is **kind,**
Keeping others' happiness
Constantly in **mind.**

Remember: Rhyming words help to make a poem pleasant and appealing.

A. Tell which lines rhyme in the following stanzas.

1. How do you like to go up in a swing,
     Up in the air so blue?
   Oh, I do think it the pleasantest thing
     Ever a child can do!

2. Last night when we were sound asleep,
   The snow fell fast, the snow piled deep.
   When morning came and we looked out,
   The snow was lying all about!

B. Use rhyming words to finish the following poem.

To the First Robin

Welcome, welcome, little stranger;
Fear no harm and fear no ___1___.
We are glad to see you ___2___,
For you sing, "Sweet spring is near."

Now the white snow melts ___3___;
Now the flowers blossom gay.
Come, dear bird, and build your ___4___,
For we love our robin ___5___.

                    —*Louisa May Alcott*
                    (Written at eight years of age)

> **Written Practice**

A. Write rhyming words to fill in the blanks. Then copy all the sets of rhyming words in each poem.

The Brown Thrush

There's a merry brown thrush sitting up in a ___1___ ;
He's singing to me! He's singing to me!
And what does he say, little girl, little boy?
"Oh, the world's running over with ___2___ !
   Don't you hear? Don't you ___3___ ?
   Hush! Look! In my tree
   I'm as happy as happy can ___4___ !"

—Lucy Larcom

The Postman

The whistling postman swings along.
   His bag is deep and wide,
And messages from all the world
   Are bundled up ___5___ .

The postman's walking up our street;
   Soon now he'll ring my bell.
Perhaps there'll be a letter stamped
   In Asia. Who can ___6___ ?

—Author unknown

B. Write a four-line poem about a blue jay or some other bird. Make at least two lines rhyme.

Write the correct words.
1. A paragraph must tell about —— topic only.
2. Each —— in a poem begins with a capital letter.
3. Name the five parts of a friendly letter.
4. When you explain how to do something, it is better to —— how instead of just telling how.
5. You should —— how to do a thing before you try to tell someone else how to do it.

---

94. Rhythm in Poetry

God put rhythm into the world when He made it. Our hearts beat in rhythm. Ocean waves roll in rhythm. Rhythm is part of the beauty that God made for us to enjoy.

Good poems also have rhythm. Rhythm helps the words of a poem to flow smoothly. It also adds feeling to the poem. Fast-moving rhythm is cheerful and gay. Slow-moving rhythm is sober and sad. The kind of rhythm helps to bring out the meaning of the poem.

Rhythm in poetry is made of a regular pattern of **accented** and **unaccented** syllables. Accented syllables are said with more force than unaccented syllables. Look at the following lines. The accented syllables are marked with ′, and the unaccented syllables with ˘.

˘ ′ ˘ ′ ˘ ′ ˘ ′
A bunch of gold-en keys is mine
˘ ′ ˘ ′ ˘ ′ ˘ ′
To make each day with glad-ness shine.

Rhythm is also made of a regular number of syllables in each line. In the example above, each line has eight syllables.

Different patterns of rhythm are used in different poems. In one common pattern, the first syllable is unaccented, the second syllable is accented, the third syllable is unaccented, and so on. The two lines shown above follow this pattern.

In another common pattern, the first syllable is accented, the second syllable is unaccented, the third syllable is accented, and so on. Notice the accents in these lines, and count the syllables.

′ ˘ ′ ˘
Leaves were bud-ding,
′ ˘ ′ ˘
Birds were sing-ing,
′ ˘ ′ ˘
Fawns were feed-ing,
′ ˘ ′ ˘
Spring was spring-ing.

In another pattern, an accented syllable is followed by two unaccented syllables. This is a delightful rhythm pattern.

′ ˘ ˘ ′ ˘ ˘
Winds through the ol-ive trees
′ ˘ ˘ ′
Soft-ly did blow.

Poetry with good rhythm sounds beautiful if it is read or recited in a meaningful, expressive way. It is good to feel the rhythm, but it is more important that the listeners understand the meaning of the words.

> **Remember:** Rhythm helps the words of a poem to flow smoothly. Rhythm in poetry is made of a regular pattern of accented and unaccented syllables and a regular number of syllables in each line.

 Oral Drill

A. Read the poems below. On the chalkboard, mark the accented and unaccented syllables of the first two or three lines in each poem. How many syllables are in each line?

Trees

I think that I shall never see
A poem lovely as a tree.

A tree that looks at God all day,
And lifts her leafy arms to pray;

A tree that may in summer wear
A nest of robins in her hair.

Poems are made by fools like me,
But only God can make a tree.

—*Joyce Kilmer*

Dandelion

There's a pretty little fellow,
And he dresses all in yellow,
And he lives among the grasses tall and green;
In the springtime, bright and early,
With his yellow hair all curly,
On the lawns and in the meadows he is seen.

He's a cheerful little fellow,
In his pretty coat of yellow,
And he nods a cheerful greeting as we pass;
Very soon his yellow head
Will be silvery instead,
But we'll find him there next year among the grass.

—Muriel Lancaster

Dare to Do Right

Dare to do right! Dare to be true!
You have a work that no other can do;
Do it so bravely, so kindly, so well,
Angels will hasten the story to tell.

—George Lansing Taylor

B. Answer the following questions about the poems in
   Part A.
   1. Which poem has the liveliest rhythm pattern?
   2. Which poem is more sober and thoughtful?
   3. Are there any sad poems in this part?

C. Read each poem chorally with rhythm and expression to
   bring out the meaning.

> **Written Practice**

A. Copy the first line of each song. Mark the rhythm pattern, and write the number of syllables after the line. Also write which lines rhyme in each song.

> **Example:** Je-sus loves me! this I know,
> For the Bi-ble tells me so.
> Lit-tle ones to Him be-long,
> They are weak but He is strong.
>
> **Answer:** Je-sus loves me, this I know,   7
> rhyme: lines 1 and 2, and lines 3 and 4

1. Let us ev-er love each oth-er
   With a heart that's warm and true,
   Ev-er do-ing to our broth-er
   As to us we'd have him do.

2. This is my Fa-ther's world,
   And to my list'ning ears,
   All na-ture sings, and 'round me rings
   The mu-sic of the spheres.

3. I am so glad that our Fa-ther in heav'n
   Tells of His love in the Book He has giv'n;
   Won-der-ful things in the Bi-ble I see;
   This is the dear-est, that Je-sus loves me.

B. Write a short poem of your own. You may use these beginning lines for ideas.

> I saw a lovely rainbow
> God made one summer day . . .
>
> I like to play out in the barn,
> Up in the fragrant hay . . .

Review and Practice

Write the correct words.

1. The —— sentence tells what a paragraph is about.
2. Sentences in a paragraph may be written in the order of t—— or the order of i——. Some paragraphs describe p—— in a certain order, and some give e——.
3. Give the main —— in order when you give an oral explanation.
4. Poetry usually has —— and ——.

---

95. Chapter 8 Review

Oral Drill

A. Answer these questions.
   1. What part of speech do adverbs modify?
   2. What do adverbs tell?
   3. Many adverbs end with what two letters?
   4. When is **well** an adjective?
   5. What part of speech is **good**?

B. Give two ways to correct each sentence.
   1. He doesn't hardly know the way.
   2. I don't have no pencil.
   3. We can't scarcely finish in time.
   4. Judy didn't see no robins.

C. On the chalkboard, mark the rhythm of the first line of this poem. Tell which lines rhyme. Read the poem chorally with expression.

> I have the fin-est moth-er
>   That an-y boy could have;
> She cleans-es all my scratch-es,
>   And binds them up with salve.

D. Give the answers.
  1. Do all lines in every poem rhyme?
  2. How many patterns of rhythm did you study?
  3. Some kinds of rhythm help a poem to sound ———. Other kinds help a poem to sound ———.
  4. How should poetry be read?

> Written Practice

A. Fill in the blanks.
  1. Adverbs are words that modify ———.
  2. Adverbs tell ———, ———, and ———.

B. Write the correct words.
  1. Of the two girls, Judy can read (better, best).
  2. Of all the girls, Jane works (faster, fastest).
  3. She works (more rapidly, most rapidly) than Joan.
  4. Charles worked (harder, more hard) than Samuel.

C. Write the correct form of each word in parentheses.
  1. She did her work (well) than he did.
  2. This job was done (badly) than that one.

D. Diagram these sentences.
  1. Soon Robert ran by.

2. We will not come soon.

3. How did you come?

4. We always sing heartily.

E. Write **good** or **well** for each sentence.

1. These carrots are ———.

2. She does not feel ———.

3. Alice does ——— work.

4. Nellie sews ———.

5. God is ——— to all.

F. Copy the negative word in each sentence. Then copy the correct word in parentheses.

1. I didn't see (anything, nothing) in the box.

2. It seems he doesn't (never, ever) miss a problem.

3. Didn't (anybody, nobody) come to help you?

4. There isn't (no, any) duck on the pond.

5. I (can't, can) hardly see what you are holding.

6. We (will, won't) scarcely have enough pins.

G. Write **true** or **false** for each sentence.

1. Showing how to do something is better than just telling how to do it.

2. You should keep looking at your hands or the floor when you speak to a group.

3. Pictures, diagrams, or objects will make your explanations clear and interesting.

4. If you are not sure how to do something, you should still explain it as well as you can.

H. For each number, write whether line **a** or **b** has better rhythm. (Hint: Numbers 1, 3, 5, and 7 should have 8 syllables each. Numbers 2, 4, 6, and 8 should have 6 syllables each.)

Evening Song

1. a. I hear no voice, I feel no touch,
   b. I hear no loud sound, I feel no touch,

2. a. I see no glory bright;
   b. I see no light bright;

3. a. But yet I understand that God is near
   b. But yet I know that God is near

4. a. In darkness as in light.
   b. In the nighttime as in light.

5. a. He stays ever by my side,
   b. He watches ever by my side,

6. a. And listens to my whispered prayer;
   b. And hears my whispered prayer;

7. a. The Father for His little child
   b. The Father for His small child

8. a. Both by day and by night doth care.
   b. Both day and night doth care.

I. Fill in the blanks with suitable rhyming words.

Homes for All

The dog has a kennel, the pig has a sty,
The rabbit a burrow (I don't know just __1__);
The bee has a hive, and the bird has a __2__,
For Bossy, the cow, a good barn is the best.
The horse has a stable, the chicken a pen,
The cat has a mat, but a wolf has a __3__;
A cave for a bear, and a hole for a mouse,
But I am so glad that I live in a __4__!

—*Mabel Watts*

A Wonderful Nose

The elephant's nose is a cleaner that blows
The dust that collects on his back;
A hand it may be, picking leaves from a tree,
Or a mower for grass in his track.

The elephant's nose is a pump and a hose
To suck up a drink from a pool;
It's a good sprinkler, too, for a bath or shampoo—
So truly, a flexible tool.

The elephant's nose is a club for his foes.
With one stroke a man it can kill.
But if you're his friend, he may use his trunk's end
To pat you with kind, gentle skill.

Punctuation marks make a difference. Notice
how they help you to understand the poem.

Chapter 9
Punctuation

96. End Punctuation

When we speak, the look on our face and the tone of our voice help to explain what we mean. Often our voice rises to a higher pitch when we ask a question. When we are thrilled about something, we look excited and speak in excited tones. But in writing we cannot use our face or voice to make the meaning clear. We need to use punctuation marks instead.

Study the following rules for punctuation marks at the end of sentences.

1. **A statement ends with a period.** It is a sentence that states a fact. A statement gives information.

    Roger has found the ball.

2. **A command also ends with a period.** A command is a sentence that tells you to do something.

    Wait for us at the door.

3. **A question ends with a question mark.** It is a sentence that asks for information.

    Where did you pick these lovely asters?

4. **An exclamation ends with an exclamation mark.** It is a sentence that shows strong feeling.

    How glad I was to see him!

> **Remember:** A statement and a command end with a period. A question ends with a question mark. An exclamation ends with an exclamation mark.

Oral Drill

Tell what kind of sentence each of the following is. Tell what end punctuation each sentence should have.

1. Did you see that butterfly
2. It was a monarch
3. Stand very quietly
4. What beautiful wings he has

5. We must cross the Mississippi River to reach the Ozark Mountains of Missouri
6. Will our friends be waiting for us
7. Michael Sattler was born in Baden, Germany
8. Oh, what a strong faith he must have had

Written Practice

A. Copy these sentences, and punctuate them correctly.

1. God is our refuge and strength
2. Whom shall I send
3. Oh, how I love thy law
4. Trust and obey
5. Michael Sattler was a leader of God's people in a time of great persecution
6. How much church history do you know
7. I read the true story about John Olesh of Yugoslavia

8. Have you read that story
9. What an interesting book it is
10. I will see if I can get it for you

B. Copy this paragraph, dividing it into six sentences. Use capital letters and end punctuation correctly.

These flowers are very lovely do you know what kind they are I have seen them somewhere before can they be asters how many kinds of flowers there are what beautiful things our God has made

> Review and Practice >

A. Write the eight forms of the verb **be** and fifteen other helping verbs.

B. Copy each verb phrase, and underline the main verb.
1. Arnold is building a birdhouse.
2. Where have you been?
3. The boys had been playing softball.

C. Copy the negative word in each sentence. Then copy the correct word in parentheses.
1. Doesn't he know (anything, nothing) about the book?
2. We (could, couldn't) hardly see in that fog.

97. Abbreviations

An abbreviation is a shortened form of a longer word. Abbreviations help to save time and space when we write. They may be used in taking notes and in everyday writing, but most abbreviations should not be used in stories and reports. An abbreviation usually ends with a period.

Abbreviations may be used in addresses.

St. for Street	**Rd.** for Road
Ave. for Avenue	**Rte.** for Route

Some abbreviations are correct in all writing. Four of these are abbreviations of titles before names. Two others are abbreviations used in telling time.

Mr. for Mister	**St.** for Saint
Mrs. for Mistress	**A.M.** for "before noon"
Dr. for Doctor	**P.M.** for "after noon"

The abbreviation **St.** is used in many place names, such as **St. Louis.** Notice that **Street** and **Saint** have the same abbreviation.

The title **Miss** is not an abbreviation. It does not end with a period.

Names may be abbreviated by using initials.

J. D. Smith   Abram **R.** Martin

The names of most months and all the days of the week may be abbreviated.

Sun. for Sunday	**Thur.** for Thursday
Mon. for Monday	**Fri.** for Friday
Tues. for Tuesday	**Sat.** for Saturday
Wed. for Wednesday	

Jan. for January
Feb. for February
Mar. for March
Apr. for April
(May, June, and July
are seldom abbreviated.)
Aug. for August
Sept. for September
Oct. for October
Nov. for November
Dec. for December

December 2008

ROD AND STAFF PUBLISHERS, INC.
Bible-based Textbooks, Books and Periodicals for all ages,
Sunday School Materials, and Tracts

Abbreviations may be used for words of measurement.

in. for inch   **pt.** for pint
ft. for foot   **qt.** for quart
yd. for yard   **oz.** for ounce
mi. for mile   **lb.** for pound
doz. for dozen   **mo.** for month

Oral Drill

A. Tell what each abbreviation means.

1. lb.	4. ft.	7. yd.	10. in.
2. St.	5. A.M.	8. P.M.	11. Mrs.
3. Mr.	6. Dr.	9. doz.	12. qt.

B. Give the correct abbreviation for each word.
   1. The name of each month except May, June, and July.
   2. The name of each day of the week.
   3. quart   7. inch
   4. foot   8. yard
   5. Mistress   9. month
   6. Miss   10. dozen

>  **Written Practice** >

A. Write the abbreviation for the name of each month. If a month name is not usually abbreviated, write the whole word.

B. Write the correct abbreviation for each day of the week.

C. Write the correct abbreviation for each word.
1. dozen   5. Road   9. yard
2. inch   6. Street   10. pint
3. ounce   7. Avenue   11. Route
4. foot   8. Saint   12. Mister

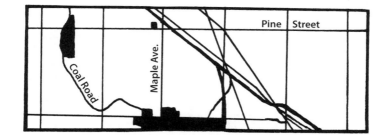

D. Write the meaning of each abbreviation.
1. oz.   5. ft.   9. A.M.
2. P.M.   6. St.   10. Rd.
3. yd.   7. pt.   11. in.
4. mi.   8. qt.   12. Mr.

E. Follow the directions.
1. Write a sentence that contains a title such as **Mr.**, **Mrs.**, or **Dr.**
2. Write your address. Abbreviate words like **Route, Street,** and **Road.**

> **Review and Practice**

Write the correct word for each sentence.

1. The smoke (raises, rises) from the chimney.
2. Shep will (lay, lie) down.
3. Please (set, sit) the vase on the counter.
4. Mother (lets, leaves) us make cookies.
5. (Can, May) I go outside?
6. Jesus (taught, learned) the disciples how to pray.
7. The Lord has done all things (good, well).

---

98. Telling a Story

The rules for telling a story are similar to those for writing one. Know the theme and the details you will use, and tell the details in the right order. Do not add extra details or things not related to the theme of the story.

For a long story, you may list the main points on an index card or a small piece of paper. You may also write down a few important names or phrases. Do not write every word of the story on your notes.

When you tell the story, begin with a smile and keep a pleasant look on your face. Hold your notes at your side, and look at them only when you need them. Look at your audience, not down at the floor or out the window.

Stand straight on both feet, and be relaxed. Do not squirm or make other unnecessary movements. Do not move your hands except to make meaningful gestures.

Do not hurry, but take your time. It won't take as long as you think! Speak loudly and clearly enough so that the person farthest away can hear you easily.

Do not fill in pauses with **ah** or **uh.** Do not overuse expressions such as **like, and then,** and **you know.** When the story is finished, use a good ending. You do not need to say "That's the end."

Remember: When you tell a story, know the main points well and give them in proper order. Face the audience, speak clearly, and use good posture. Do not use unnecessary words.

Tell which sentences in the following story do not belong. Pick out the unnecessary words.

A Surprise

Our teacher wants us to keep our desks neat and clean. My chair is separate from my desk this year. I like it that way. One day at two o'clock, she said, "Everyone put your hands on your desk." Then she inspected each desk to see if it was clean. Every desk was in order. So she gave us all like a package of Life Saver candy, you know, as a reward. Some teachers inspect desks like twice every week.

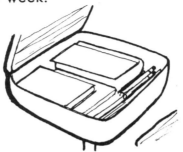

> Written Practice

Choose one of the following things, and prepare to tell a story about it. List the main points of the story and any important names or other facts you want to remember. Be sure to have all the facts in order.

Practice telling the story to someone in your family. Your story should be one or two minutes long. Tell the story in class when your teacher asks you. Then give your notes to your teacher to check.

1. A story from long ago that one of your grandparents or another older person has told you.
2. Something that happened to you.
3. Something that happened to a person in your family or to someone else you know.

> Review and Practice

A. Write the correct words.
   1. Indent the —— line of a paragraph.
   2. You must move your —— to speak clearly.
   3. You should use good —— when you speak or read orally.
   4. (Every, Not every) line of a poem rhymes.
   5. Rhythm is made of —— and —— syllables.

B. Copy the following sentences. Write one of these abbreviations above each word to label its part of speech: **n., pron., v., adj., adv.**
   1. A lovely wild duck was swimming gracefully.
   2. The white snow sparkles brilliantly.
   3. She gave me a pretty pink rose.

99. Commas

Commas help us to write clearly. They also help us to understand what others write. We should pause when we come to a comma, but we should not come to a complete stop as we do for a period. Study the following rules for using commas.

1. **Use commas to separate items in a series.** The items may be words or phrases. A comma is placed after each item except the last one, which comes after the word **and.**

   > Dogs, cats, raccoons, and mice all make interesting pets.
   > The girls washed the dishes, swept the floor, and baked a cake.

   Without commas, we would have to use many **and**s between the items in a series. Using commas is better than saying **and** so often.

   > We have pencils and tablets and erasers and crayons.
   > We have pencils, tablets, erasers, and crayons.

2. **Use a comma after *oh, well, yes,* and *no* when these words come at the beginning of a sentence.**

   > Oh, look at that bird!
   > Well, we shall see.
   > Yes, he will be there.
   > No, it is too late.

3. Use a comma to set off a noun of direct address.
A noun of direct address names the person to whom one is speaking.

> Alice, your brother is ill.
> Harold, clean the chalkboard.
> Will you come with us, Nancy?
> Yes, Thomas, you may go outside.

Remember: Use commas to separate items in a series. Use a comma after **oh, well, yes,** and **no** at the beginning of a sentence. Use a comma to set off a noun of direct address.

> Oral Drill

Tell which words need commas after them.
1. Mother put flour sugar shortening eggs and flavoring into the cake.
2. Mr. Bates traveled to Japan Korea China and India.
3. Charles walked forward broke into a run and leaped into the water.
4. Arthur did you feed the pigs?
5. Would you like to go with us Jane?
6. Yes Julie that is an excellent idea!

> Written Practice

A. Copy each sentence, and add the missing commas.
1. Well we shall try again.
2. Harold may we help you?
3. Yes you may clip the stems gather the clippings and throw them away.

4. Bob raises tulips petunias and daffodils in his garden.
5. We sing pray and listen in church.
6. My son forget not my law.
7. Lord who shall abide in Thy tabernacle?
8. Do you like chocolate cake John?
9. Yes Mother I like chocolate cake very much.
10. In the pantry is the dessert Mary.
11. Martha please bring the cake the peanuts and the ice cream.

B. Write a sentence about this picture. You should name the girl and give a list of the things she is using to bake a cake.

> **Review and Practice** >

A. Diagram these sentences. (**Porcupine fish** is a compound noun.)
1. A large porcupine walked quietly by.
2. It had long, sharp quills.
3. The animal ate and left.
4. Porcupine fish have sharp spines.
5. They can inflate their bodies.
6. Did you ever see a porcupine fish?

B. Copy the direct objects and predicate nouns in these sentences. Label each one **DO** or **PN.** Remember that direct objects follow action verbs.
1. My uncle visited my grandfather.
2. My uncle is a grandfather.
3. Jonathan mailed two packages.
4. Fluffy is our cat.

C. Write the abbreviations for these.

1. inch   4. November
2. pound   5. foot
3. Monday   6. after noon

---

100. Commas in Addresses and Dates

Commas help to make writing clear. In this lesson you will study the rules for using commas in addresses and dates.

1. **Place a comma between the name of the street and the name of the city or town when they are together in a sentence.**

> Dr. Johnson's office is on Apple Street, Philadelphia.
>
> Last summer the Smiths moved to Maple Avenue, Boston.

2. **Place a comma between the name of the city or town and the name of the state, province, or country.**

> Chicago, Illinois   Winnipeg, Manitoba
> Houston, Texas   London, England

3. Place a comma after each item in a complete address when it is part of a sentence.

My address was Water Street, London, England, for many years.

4. Place a comma after the day of the year in a date. If the date is in a sentence, also place a comma after the number of the year, except when it comes at the end of the sentence.

My father's birthday is May 10, 1955.
On July 4, 1776, the Declaration of Independence was signed.

Remember: Commas must be used to separate items in addresses and dates.

 Oral Drill

Tell which words or figures need commas after them.
1. Market Street Lancaster
2. Smith Road Newton
3. Helena Montana
4. Abraham Lincoln was born near Hodgenville Kentucky on February 12 1809.
5. On November 4 1842 Abraham Lincoln was married to Mary Todd.

Written Practice

A. Copy each sentence, and add the missing commas.
1. On January 21 1525 an important meeting took place in Zurich Switzerland.
2. Felix Manz died in Zurich Switzerland on January 5 1527.
3. On January 17 1706 Benjamin Franklin was born in Boston Massachusetts.
4. Send your order to Rod and Staff Publishers, Crockett Kentucky by May 9.
5. His address was Arlington Illinois.
6. On October 19 1879 Thomas Edison tested the first successful electric light.

B. Copy and complete this sentence: **My address is . . .**

Review and Practice

A. Write the correct form of each word in parentheses.
1. It is (cold) today than it was yesterday.
2. This basket is (full) than that one.
3. Last year we picked the (many) tomatoes we had ever picked.
4. This is the (valuable) diamond in the museum.

B. Copy each sentence. Add commas, capital letters, and end punctuation where they are needed.
1. alice irene betty and i will clean the room
2. in the afternoon the girls sold beans carrots cabbage and flowers
3. brother aaron is this book yours
4. the pencils tablets and erasers are on the table

5. do we have enough supplies jerry
6. no rhoda but there are some more in the closet
7. john and martha have visited museums in richmond boston and chicago

---

101. Making Introductions

Did you ever want to be friendly to a stranger but did not know how to get acquainted? This lesson has some suggestions that should help you.

Remember that a stranger may feel as timid as you do. You can soon get acquainted and feel comfortable if you learn how to introduce yourself and others.

Do not be afraid of making mistakes. Be yourself and be kind, and the mistakes will not matter too much. Others make mistakes too. If a mistake is made, never laugh unkindly.

To know whose name you should say first in introductions, remember the rules of respect. Ladies come before gentlemen, the elderly come before the younger, and your mother comes before any of the rest. As you make an introduction, address each person by name when you speak to him.

1. To introduce a man and a woman or a boy and a girl, say the woman's or girl's name first.

> Mary, this is Carl Weaver. Carl, this is Mary Smith.

2. To introduce a younger person and an older person, say the older person's name first.

Grandmother, this is my friend John Benson. John, this is my grandmother.

3. To introduce anyone to your mother, say *Mother* first.

Mother, this is my friend Jerry Miller. Jerry, this is my mother.

4. To introduce two boys, two girls, two men, or two women of about the same age, say either name first.

5. To introduce yourself to a stranger, say "Hello" and give your name.

Hello. My name is Alta Harding. May I ask your name?

Remember: In introductions be courteous and respectful.

Do unto others as you would have them do unto you.

Oral Drill

A. Tell which rule is followed in each introduction.

1. Mother, this is my teacher, Sister Mildred. Sister Mildred, this is my mother.
2. Mrs. Smith, this is my cousin Susie Step. Susie, this is Mrs. Smith, our nearest neighbor.
3. Hello. My name is Nathan Yoder. May I ask your name?
4. John, this is my friend Philip Reed. Philip, this is my classmate John Eaton.
5. Mrs. Smith, this is Mr. Taylor. Mr. Taylor, this is Mrs. Smith.

B. Tell whose name should be said first in the following introductions.

1. Your cousin, who is a boy, and your classmate, who is a girl.
2. Your mother and your teacher.
3. Your father and your teacher, who is a woman.
4. Your father and your teacher, who is a man about the same age.

C. Make an introduction in class, using real names. You may get ideas from Part B.

Written Practice

A. Write what you would say in the following introductions, using correct punctuation and capitalization. Use real names in numbers 1 and 2. Remember to use a comma after each noun of direct address as you learned in Lesson 99.

1. Your classmate, who is a boy, and your grandmother.
2. Your aunt and your minister.
3. Your cousin Ruth and your friend Jane, who are about the same age.

B. Write what you would say to introduce yourself to a stranger.

> Review and Practice

A. Write the correct words.
   1. The —— sentence tells what a paragraph is about.
   2. You should not write ——, choppy sentences or sentences that are too ——.
   3. You need a leader for good —— reading.
   4. You must —— how to do something before you can show others how to do it.
   5. When you prepare to tell a story, you (should, should not) write down everything you plan to say.

B. Diagram the skeleton and the direct object or predicate noun in each sentence. Above each verb, write **A** for action or **B** for being. Above each direct object or predicate noun, write **DO** or **PN** to tell which it is.
   1. Ezekiel was a prophet.
   2. Ezekiel rebuked the false prophets.
   3. Jesus raised a young man.
   4. Jesus was a young man.
   5. Jesus is our Saviour.
   6. God sent the Saviour.

102. Direct and Indirect Quotations

Sometimes in writing we want to repeat the exact words that someone has said. By using a **direct quotation,** we can show that someone is speaking.

A direct quotation repeats the exact words that a person said. It is put inside quotation marks (" "). In the following sentences, notice the words inside quotation marks. They are the exact words of the speakers.

> Father said, "Charles has chicken pox."
> "I shall bring the book," said Gerald.
> Jesus said, "I am the light of the world."

Sometimes we want to tell what someone said without repeating his exact words. Then we use an **indirect quotation.** In the following sentences, notice that quotation marks are not used with indirect quotations. Also notice the word **that,** which is often used with indirect quotations.

> Father said **that** Charles has chicken pox.
> Gerald said **that** he will bring the book.
> Jesus said **that** He is the light of the world.

Remember: A direct quotation repeats the exact words of a speaker. A direct quotation is placed inside quotation marks. An indirect quotation tells what someone said without repeating his exact words. Quotation marks are not used with indirect quotations.

Oral Drill

A. Tell whether each sentence has a **direct quotation** or an **indirect quotation.**

   1. Lester told us that he is very tired.

   2. Lester said, "I am very tired."

   3. Ruth exclaimed, "The cows are out!"

   4. Ruth said that the cows are out.

   5. The woman asked if I know her son.

   6. The woman asked, "Do you know my son?"

B. Change these sentences to direct quotations. Leave out the word **that.**

   1. My sister said that Thomas likes spinach.

   2. Thomas replied that she likes it too.

   3. The little boy said that the roof is on fire.

Written Practice

A. Write **direct** or **indirect** to tell what kind of quotation each sentence has.

   1. Our teacher told us that we should always write our names clearly.

   2. My teacher said, "Practice good posture."

   3. He asked, "Can you help us?"

   4. Sarah said that she would help us.

   5. "Where did you find it?" asked Mother.

   6. Mark said that it was on the front lawn.

B. Rewrite each sentence, changing the direct quotation to an indirect quotation.
   1. Jesus told the woman, "Go, call thy husband."
   2. The woman said, "I have no husband."

Review and Practice

A. Write each sentence correctly in two ways.
   1. Father didn't cut no wood.
   2. Haven't you never been to the park?

B. Copy each sentence, and add the correct punctuation and capital letters.
   1. on july 19 1924 their home on woolton road berlin ohio was destroyed by fire
   2. norman do you still live on pringle street avoca indiana
   3. i was born on august 24 1996 in cottonwood arizona

   4. was your father born in kitchener ontario on january 1 1974

C. Write a short paragraph about yourself. Tell when and where you were born. Give both of your parents' names. Give your home address. Tell the names of your school and your church.

103. Direct Quotations: Quotation Last

Direct quotations can be written in different ways. Sometimes the quotation comes last in a sentence. Sometimes it comes first.

> Jesus said, "Seek, and ye shall find."
> "Seek, and ye shall find," said Jesus.

In this lesson you will work with sentences in which the quotations come last.

In a sentence with a direct quotation, the first word must begin with a capital letter. The first word of the direct quotation must also be capitalized.

> **T**he Lord said, "**W**hom shall I send, and who will go for us?"
> **T**hen said I, "**H**ere am I; send me."

A comma separates the direct quotation from the rest of the sentence. The direct quotation ends with a period, question mark, or exclamation mark according to the kind of sentence it is.

> Mother asked, "Where did you find it**?**"

Quotation marks are placed before and after the exact words of the speaker. They go **after** the end punctuation mark.

> Susan asked, "How soon will we begin**?**"
> Betty answered, "We shall begin right away**.**"
> Susan exclaimed, "All right, let's get started**!**"

> **Remember:** A sentence with a direct quotation begins with a capital letter. The direct quotation also begins with a capital letter. A comma separates the direct quotation from the rest of the sentence. The quotation marks are placed after the end punctuation mark.

Tell where capital letters, commas, and quotation marks are needed. Also give the correct end punctuation.

1. a certain blind man cried jesus, thou Son of David, have mercy on me
2. the people exclaimed keep still
3. the blind man cried all the more thou Son of David, have mercy on me
4. then jesus asked him what do you want me to do to you
5. he answered lord, that I may receive my sight
6. jesus said receive your sight
7. jesus said your faith has saved you

> Written Practice

A. Copy each sentence, using capital letters where they are needed. Also add the missing commas, quotation marks, and end punctuation.

1. God said let there be light
2. mary said my soul doth magnify the Lord
3. a voice said saul, saul, why persecutest thou me
4. john the Baptist cried behold the Lamb of God
5. abraham replied my son, God will provide Himself a lamb for a burnt offering
6. an angel called lay not thine hand upon the lad
7. the disciples asked when shall these things be

B. Write two sentences about this picture, using direct quotations. Tell what the children might be saying.

> Review and Practice

A. Write the plural form of each noun.
1. glass   4. baby
2. boy   5. calf
3. trio   6. ox

B. Write the past tense of each verb.
1. pray   4. show
2. send   5. say
3. lead   6. lose

C. Write the correct words.
1. Maria can draw (good, well).
2. Michael's story is (good, well).
3. We are glad Sister Anna is feeling (good, well) again.

104. Direct Quotations: Quotation First

You have worked with sentences in which the direct quotation comes last. In this lesson you will study sentences in which the direct quotation comes first.

Whenever a quotation is written, the exact words of the speaker always begin with a capital letter.

> "Come unto me, all ye that labour and are heavy laden," said Jesus.

The words outside the quotation marks belong to the rest of the sentence. These words do not begin with a capital letter unless they are proper nouns.

> "We have found the Messias," said Andrew.
> "Come and see," Philip said.

A comma usually separates a direct quotation from the rest of the sentence. If the direct quotation is a question or an exclamation, a question mark or an exclamation mark is used instead of a comma.

> "I am the way," said Jesus.
> "What seek ye?" Jesus asked.
> "Behold the Lamb of God!" called John.

Direct quotations should always be written inside quotation marks. The quotation marks are placed before the first word of the direct quotation and **after** the punctuation mark at the end.

> "Master, where dwellest thou?" they asked.

Do not forget to put a period at the end of a sentence with a direct quotation.

> "Whence knowest thou me?" Nathanael asked.

> **Remember:** A direct quotation must begin with a capital letter. If the quotation comes first in a sentence, a comma usually separates it from the rest of the sentence. If the quotation is a question or an exclamation, a question mark or an exclamation mark is used instead of a comma.

Oral Drill

Tell where quotation marks and other punctuation marks should go. Tell which words need to be capitalized.

1. arise, and go toward the south said the angel
2. go near the chariot said the Spirit
3. understandest thou what thou readest asked philip
4. how can i, except some man should guide me asked the man
5. i believe that Jesus Christ is the Son of God said the eunuch
6. behold the man cried pilate
7. what shall i do with Jesus he asked

Written Practice

A. Copy each sentence, and add the missing quotation marks.

1. I surely hope it rains, said Father.
2. We need rain, replied Mother.
3. Did he see you? asked Ralph.
4. Hold on tight! cried Joe.

B. Copy each sentence. Add commas and quotation marks where they are needed.

1. We will buy this book Mother decided.
2. I will find a smaller one said the man.

C. Copy these sentences, and add the missing commas, quotation marks, question marks, and exclamation marks.

1. I heard a lion Bruce exclaimed.
2. Is a lion really a cat asked Elsie.
3. Yes, a lion is in the cat family Ervin replied.

D. Copy each sentence, and add quotation marks and any other missing punctuation marks. Use capital letters where they are needed.

1. have you finished your work sister martha asked
2. i shall be glad to help said our neighbor
3. would you like some cake margaret asked
4. we have already had enough everyone agreed

> **Review and Practice**

Copy each sentence, and add all the missing punctuation, including end punctuation. Use capital letters where they are needed.

1. may I help you this morning asked the clerk
2. john replied yes i would like to buy some bread
3. the clerk said we have plenty of fresh bread today
4. the bread smells delicious exclaimed john
5. john asked what is the price of the bread
6. it is ninety cents a loaf answered the clerk
7. john said that he would like to buy four loaves

105. Conversation in Stories

Many stories have conversation between two persons. The conversation tells us what they said, and it also helps to **show** what they did instead of just telling it. A story with conversation is more interesting than one without it.

When conversation is written in a story, each person's speech is placed in a separate paragraph.

A light shone from heaven. Saul fell down and heard a voice asking, "Saul, Saul, why do you persecute me?"

Saul answered, "Who are You, Lord?"

The Lord answered, "I am Jesus whom you are persecuting. It is hard for you to kick against the pricks."

Trembling and astonished, Saul asked, "Lord, what do You want me to do?"

Jesus answered, "Arise and go into the city, and it shall be told you what you must do."

Direct quotations are used in written conversation. The quotation marks show what each speaker said. When a speaker says more than one sentence in the same paragraph, the quotation marks are placed before his first sentence and after his last one. Quotation marks are not needed before and after every sentence.

Wrong:

> The Lord answered, "I am Jesus whom you are persecuting." "It is hard for you to kick against the pricks."

Right:

> The Lord answered, "I am Jesus whom you are persecuting. It is hard for you to kick against the pricks."

Conversation makes stories more interesting. Learn to write it correctly.

> **Remember:** Conversation makes stories more interesting. When you write conversation, start a new paragraph each time the speaker changes.

 Oral Drill

A. Look in your reading book for a story that has conversation. Notice how a new paragraph begins every time a different person speaks. Find some quotations that are more than one sentence long.

B. In this lesson, read the story about Saul in parts. One student can be the storyteller. Another student can read all the words that Saul said, and a third can read all the words that Jesus said.

> Written Practice >

Copy this story. Add quotation marks, and start a new paragraph each time the speaker changes. Your story should have four paragraphs when it is finished.

Naaman and his servants came to Elisha's house because Naaman had leprosy. Elisha sent a message to Naaman. He said, Go and wash in the Jordan River seven times, and you will be healed. Naaman said angrily, Why should I wash in the Jordan? I may as well wash in our rivers at home! His servants asked, If the prophet had told you to do something great, wouldn't you have done it? Why not do this little thing and be cured of your leprosy?

Naaman obeyed, and he was healed. How thankful he was to be well again! Naaman said, Now I know that there is no God in all the earth but in Israel.

> Review and Practice >

Write the answers.
1. —— is a special kind of writing that is pleasing to the ear.
2. List four ways to develop paragraphs.
3. When you read orally, pause at each —— and stop at each ——.
4. When you prepare to give an oral book report, write only the —— —— on an index card.
5. When you introduce a girl to your mother, say ("Mother," the girl's name) first.

106. Descriptive Words in Poetry

Good poems have words and phrases that are full of meaning. They are so descriptive that they bring clear pictures into our minds. It is as if the poet were an artist painting pictures with words.

One way that poets paint good word pictures is by making special comparisons. Some comparisons say that one thing is **like** or **as** something else.

The dog's coat was **like a wet mop.**

We know a dog's coat is not exactly like a wet mop. But the comparison helps us to imagine what it was like. Now look at the comparisons in the lines below.

I wandered lonely **as a cloud**
    That floats on high o'er vales and hills.

How good to lie a little while
    And look up through the tree!
The sky is **like a kind, big smile**
    Bent sweetly over me.

The snow is **like a blanket** that
    God spreads across the land.

Other comparisons do not use the words **like** or **as.** They say that one thing **is** something else. In such a description, an interesting word picture compares one thing to another.

In the following stanza, a child is compared to a lamb. It does not say that the child is **like** a lamb, but it says, "I **am** Jesus' lamb." We know that a child is not really a lamb. But this comparison puts a picture in our minds that helps us understand how Jesus cares for us.

I am Jesus' little lamb;
Ever glad at heart I am.
Day by day, at home, away,
Jesus is my staff and stay.

To what does this stanza compare Jesus? It says that
He **is** my staff and stay. This means that Jesus protects us
in much the same way that a shepherd's staff protects his
sheep. He is our stay because He supports us and keeps us
in the right way.

> **Remember:** Good poems use descriptive words and phrases to
> paint word pictures. One way they describe things is by making
> comparisons.

 Oral Drill

A. Answer the questions about the following poems. Then
   read each poem, using good expression.

Look and Listen

Look and listen! Autumn's here.
Hills are hazy, skies are clear.
Birds are leaving, southward bound.
Goldenrod in bloom is found.
Brittle cornstalks and crisp leaves
Rustle in the gentle breeze.
Brooks run slowly, locusts hum,
Thus proclaiming, "Autumn's come."

1. What adjectives describe the following things?

   hills, skies, cornstalks, leaves, breeze

2. What descriptive verbs are used to tell what the following things do?

   cornstalks and leaves, brooks, locusts

3. What adverb tells how brooks run?

4. With what kind of sentence does the poem begin?

Motor Cars

From a city window, 'way up high,
I like to watch the cars go by.
They look like burnished beetles black
That leave a little muddy track
Behind them as they slowly crawl.
Sometimes they do not move at all,
But huddle close with hum and drone
As though they feared to be alone.
They grope their way through fog and night
With the golden feelers of their light.

—*Rowena Bastin Bennett*

5. What comparison describes what cars look like from a skyscraper window?

6. What comparison describes the headlights of the cars?

7. What descriptive verb shows how cars move along a city street?

8. What descriptive verb tells how the cars crowd together on city streets?

9. Which lines rhyme?

B. Complete the following sentences with comparisons of your own.

   1. James was running like ———.

   2. This bed is as hard as ———.

> **Written Practice** >

A. Answer the questions about this poem.

Words

Words are like kites—
    We send them away
On the wing of the air
    When we speak or we pray.

Words fly away
    For good or for ill,
But we can't pull them in,
    Like kites, at our will.

1. What comparison describes words?
2. What descriptive word is used with **air** in the first stanza?
3. What descriptive verb in the second stanza tells what words do?
4. What does the second stanza say we cannot do with our words?
5. Which lines rhyme?

B. Copy each sentence, and complete it with a comparison of your own.
1. The cat sprang as swiftly as ———.
2. The blanket was soft like ———.
3. I felt as happy as ———.

C. Copy a stanza from a poem that uses descriptive comparisons. Underline the words that make the comparisons. Then read it to the class with good rhythm and expression.

 Review and Practice

A. Name the five parts of a friendly letter.

B. Fill in the blanks.
1. —— makes stories more interesting.
2. Good poems use —— words and phrases.

C. Copy these sentences. Place capital letters and quotation marks where they are needed, and start a new paragraph when there is a different speaker.

> Father asked, where are the kittens? didn't you feed them last night, Susie? Susie replied, they were on the back porch when I fed them last night. I don't know where they are now.

---

107. Chapter 9 Review

 Oral Drill

A. Spell the abbreviations for the names of the days of the week.

B. Spell the abbreviations for the names of the months. If a month name is not usually abbreviated, spell the whole word.

C. Give the correct punctuation for each sentence.
1. Jane have you read the book *Thrilling Escapes by Night*
2. What an interesting story it is

3. Yes I have read that book Martha
4. Robert lived in Baltimore Maryland until October 20 1989
5. The queen of Sheba said The half was not told me
6. Blessed be the Lord thy God she exclaimed
7. Jesus said Go and teach all nations, baptizing them in the name of the Father the Son and the Holy Ghost

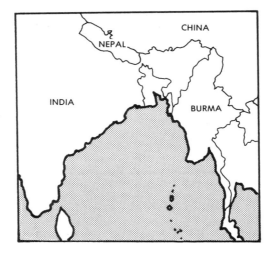

D. Answer the following questions.
1. What kind of words and phrases are used in good poems?
2. What do poets use to paint good word pictures?

> **Written Practice**

A. Write the correct abbreviations.
1. January
2. Wednesday
3. before noon
4. foot
5. quart
6. pint
7. Avenue
8. Friday
9. September
10. yard

B. Copy each sentence, and add the missing punctuation.
1. Mr Holton is this your car asked Henry
2. I want to send Jane a card for her birthday, August 21 2008
3. Mr N B Doles and Mr J T Ellis visited Sunnyside Church on Sunday
4. Can you find it asked Louis
5. Yes I think so Larry replied
6. The three boys are Jonathan Dale and Brian

C. Write **T** for true and **F** for false.
1. When telling a story, you should hurry so that you finish in time.
2. You should have good posture and a pleasant expression when you give an oral report.
3. You should move your hands most of the time while you are giving an oral report.
4. When you introduce anyone to your mother, you should say **Mother** first.
5. When you prepare to tell a story, you should write every word in your notes.
6. You should use the words **and then, you know, uh,** and **anyways** while you think what to say next.
7. You should introduce a younger person and an older person by saying the older person's name first.
8. You should introduce a man and a woman or a boy and a girl by saying the man's or boy's name first.

D. Using real names, write what you would say to introduce the following people.
1. Your cousin, who is a boy, and your grandfather.
2. Your friend and your mother.

E. Copy the following story. Add the missing punctuation marks, and divide paragraphs correctly.

Yesterday was very warm and sunny, and I rode our pony around on the lawn said Albert How did you get up on her asked Joel I led her to a fence and climbed on her back from there replied Albert Weren't you afraid asked Joel She is so gentle that I did not fear she would try to run away from me We have many good times with her, and we always try to treat her kindly answered Albert

F. Answer the questions about the poem.

Dandelion

"O dandelion, yellow as gold,
What do you do all day?"
"I just wait here in the tall green grass
Till the children come out to play."

"And what do you do when your hair is white
And the children come out to play?"
"They take me up in their dimpled hands
And blow my hair away."

1. Which descriptive phrase tells what color the dandelion is?
2. What two adjectives describe the grass? What word describes the children's hands?
3. The seeds of the dandelion are compared to what?
4. What are the two pairs of rhyming words?

Common Prepositions

about	below	in	through
above	beneath	inside	to
across	beside	into	toward
after	between	near	under
among	by	of	up
around	down	off	upon
at	during	on	with
before	for	outside	
behind	from	over	

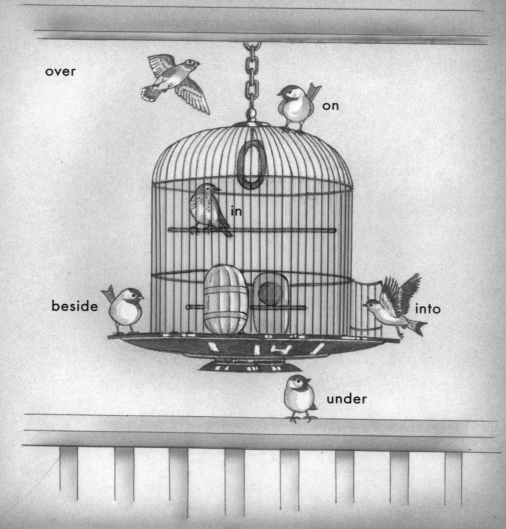

over

on

in

beside

into

under

Chapter 10
Prepositions and Conjunctions

Conjunctions join words, phrases, and sentences.

108. Prepositions

A **preposition** is a part of speech. It is a connecting word that begins a phrase. Most prepositions are small, simple words. You met some prepositions in Lesson 66 when you studied object pronouns. Now you will meet more prepositions and learn more about them.

Here are some common prepositions. Memorize them.

> **across, after, around, before, behind, down, for, from, in, near, on, over, to, up, under, with**

To find a **prepositional phrase,** first find the preposition. Then find the **object of the preposition** by asking **whom** or **what** after it. The object of the preposition is always a noun or a pronoun.

> The house is **near** the *bridge*.
> The ducks swam across the pond.

In the first sentence above, the preposition is **near.** To find the object, ask "near whom or what?" The answer is **bridge,** so **bridge** is the object of the preposition. All the words between the preposition and its object are part of the prepositional phrase. So the phrase in this sentence is **near the bridge.**

The prepositional phrase in the second sentence is not marked. See if you can find it yourself.

The words between the preposition and its object are adjectives that modify the object of the preposition. Many prepositional phrases have adjectives, but not all of them do.

> Who will come **with me**?

In this sentence, the preposition is **with** and the object is **me.** There is no adjective in the prepositional phrase.

Prepositional phrases may be in different places in a sentence. They may come at the beginning, in the middle, or at the end.

> **During the night** I heard an owl.
> The boy **with red hair** is my brother.
> We worked **in the garden.**

Remember: A preposition is a connecting word that begins a phrase. The object of a preposition is a noun or a pronoun.

A. Read the prepositions on the chart at the beginning of this chapter.

B. Practice saying by memory the prepositions listed in this lesson.

C. Write each prepositional phrase on the board. Underline the preposition and its object. Then read the whole phrase.
  1. He showed me the card from his aunt.
  2. After the storm the road was blocked.
  3. The dog on the porch watched us carefully.
  4. Near the house we found a rabbit hole.
  5. John painted the fence in the morning.
  6. A large white bird flew over the pond.
  7. Trust in the Lord.
  8. How sweet the Name of Jesus sounds!

> **Written Practice**

A. Copy each prepositional phrase. Underline the preposition and its object.
   1. The envelope on the table contains money.
   2. We were working with my grandfather.
   3. The day after the fire was very busy.
   4. The path down the hill was steep.
   5. In the evening we heard a whippoorwill.
   6. Flowers are growing under the trees.
   7. In my Father's house are many mansions.
   8. In Thee, O Lord, do I put my trust.
   9. God is a very present help in trouble.

B. Use these prepositional phrases in sentences of your own. Underline the phrase in each sentence you write.
   1. around the lake   3. behind the door
   2. under a mossy log   4. over the fence

C. Write the list of sixteen prepositions from the lesson. Memorize them.

> **Review and Practice**

Copy each sentence, and add the missing capital letters and punctuation marks. Remember to use a comma after a noun of direct address.
   1. saul saul why do you persecute me asked a voice
   2. who are You lord asked saul

3. the voice answered i am jesus whom you are persecuting
4. lord what do You want me to do asked saul
5. arise and go into the city said the lord
6. ananias came and said brother saul the lord jesus has
   sent me

---

109. Prepositional Phrases
Used as Adjectives

A phrase is a group of words that work together as one part of speech. Sometimes a prepositional phrase modifies a noun just as adjectives do.

When a prepositional phrase modifies a noun, it is called an **adjective phrase.** Adjective phrases usually tell **which** or **what kind of.** An adjective phrase must come right after the noun it modifies.

The school **near the lake** is large.

Near the lake is an adjective phrase. It tells **which** school. The sentence does not tell about the school **near the town** or **in the woods,** but the school **near the lake.** The phrase **near the lake** comes right after the noun **school.** It modifies the noun **school** by telling **which.**

Mother made a yellow cake **with white icing.**

With white icing tells **what kind of** cake. It tells **what kind of** in the same way that **yellow** does. The phrase **with white icing** comes right after the noun **cake.**

> **Remember:** Prepositional phrases can be used as adjectives that tell **which** or **what kind of.** An adjective phrase comes right after the noun it modifies.

Read each adjective phrase, and tell what noun it modifies.

1. The dog with curly hair chased a rabbit.
2. A fox with a bushy tail is watching.
3. Here is a letter for my sister.
4. The cat behind the bush is our neighbor's.
5. The barn across the road is burning!
6. Our Father in heaven loves you and me.
7. The mercies of the Lord are new every morning.

> Written Practice >

A. Copy each adjective phrase. After it write the noun it modifies.
1. The letter from Paraguay is Susan's.
2. The cat is watching the bird on the wall.
3. A picture in this book shows various animals.
4. Here is a card for you.
5. The boy across the room is my brother.
6. John caught the chicken with red feathers.
7. The weeds near the road had turned brown.
8. Please water the flowers behind the house.

9. The girl before me was my cousin.
10. I lost the book with the blue cover.
11. The giant across the valley was Goliath.
12. David was a man after God's own heart.

B. Use the following adjective phrases in sentences of your own. Remember that each phrase must come right after the noun it modifies.

1. near me
2. with the blue dress

3. from my aunt
4. for me

> Review and Practice >

A. Fill in the blanks. Choose from these words: **nouns, person, place, pronoun, verb, action, being, adverb, name.**

Parts of Speech

A noun is a __1__ word.
   To save time and space,
A __2__ relieves it
   By taking its __3__ .

A __4__ may be active
   And do many things,
But when it shows __5__ ,
   No action it brings.

To tell about __6__
   Is an adjective's task;
An __7__ tells **how,**
   When, or **where,** if we ask.

B. Copy the two adverbs in each sentence.
1. The mailman will soon be here.
2. Yesterday the mailman came late.
3. Stephen quietly finished his assignment today.

---

110. Prepositional Phrases Used as Adverbs

Prepositional phrases that modify nouns are called adjective phrases. A prepositional phrase that modifies a verb is called an **adverb phrase.** Adverb phrases tell **how, when,** and **where.**

a. The fan blades whirled **with great speed.**

> The phrase **with great speed** is used as an adverb to modify **whirled.** It tells **how** the blades whirled.

b. We worked hard **in the morning.**

> The phrase **in the morning** modifies the verb **worked.** It tells **when** we worked. (Do you see the adverb that tells **how** we worked?)

c. The wagon rolled **down the hill.**

> The phrase **down the hill** modifies the verb **rolled.** It tells **where** the wagon rolled.

An adverb phrase may come at the beginning or at the end of a sentence. The adverb phrase still modifies the verb, no matter where it is found in the sentence.

The moon and stars shine **at night.**

At night the moon and stars shine.

The phrase **at night** modifies the verb **shine.** It tells **when** about **shine,** whether the phrase is at the beginning or at the end of the sentence.

Remember: Prepositional phrases can be used as adverbs that tell **how, when,** and **where.** Adverb phrases may come at different places in a sentence.

 Oral Drill

A. Read each adverb phrase, and give the verb it modifies.
1. In a dark corner we found an old book.
2. We discussed the problem at our meeting.
3. After the meeting we walked home.
4. With a small lantern, Harold climbed the stairs.
5. The Lord is in His holy temple.
6. Let all the earth keep silence before Him.
7. Strength and beauty are in His sanctuary.
8. In the beginning God created the heaven and the earth.
9. John the Baptist preached in the wilderness.
10. He prepared the way before Jesus.

B. Do the following with the sentences in Part A.
   1. In sentences 1 and 3, move each adverb phrase to the end of the sentence. Say the new sentence.
   2. In sentences 2 and 9, move each adverb phrase to the beginning of the sentence. Say the new sentence.

C. Give sixteen prepositions by memory.

> Written Practice >

A. Copy each adverb phrase. After it write the verb or verb phrase that it modifies.
   1. My little dog was waiting near the road.
   2. Father left with the other man.
   3. Up the steep path we climbed.
   4. We should wait for the others.
   5. In the morning the workers began.
   6. Abraham sat in the tent door.
   7. Before long he saw three men.
   8. Inside the tent Sarah prepared food.
   9. Abraham showed kindness to the strangers.

B. Rewrite each sentence, moving the adverb phrase to the beginning of the sentence.
   1. A cow lay contentedly under the trees.
   2. The whippoorwill sings in the evening.

C. Rewrite these sentences, moving the adverb phrases to the end of the sentences.
   1. Over the fence the startled deer leaped.
   2. Down the road we could see fire engines.

> **Review and Practice**

A. Copy the direct object or predicate noun in each sentence, and write **DO** or **PN** after it. The verb will help you decide.
   1. Bernice cleaned the windows.
   2. Brother Albert is my teacher.
   3. Sister Sarah will draw a picture on the board.

B. Write the three forms of comparison for these adjectives and adverbs.
   1. thin   4. powerful
   2. good   5. painfully
   3. bad   6. soon

> **Challenge Exercise**

Find and write all the adverb phrases in Psalm 23. Write the verb that each phrase modifies.

---

111. Dividing a Longer Story Into Paragraphs

A story may be several paragraphs long. Each paragraph should tell about only one topic. Ideas not related to the topic sentence should be left out or put into a different paragraph.

Genesis 28 tells the story about Jacob's ladder. We can divide this story into five paragraphs. The first paragraph tells about Jacob being sent on a journey (verses 1–5). Verses 6–9 can be left out because they tell about Esau. The second paragraph describes Jacob's dream (verses 10–12). The third paragraph tells what God said to Jacob (verses 13–15). The fourth paragraph shows what Jacob did when he awoke (verses 16–19). The last paragraph tells what promises Jacob made to God (verses 20–22).

With a little practice, you will soon learn to divide stories into proper paragraphs.

> **Remember:** Each paragraph of a story should tell about one topic only.

 Oral Drill

A. The following paragraph is part of the story from Genesis 28. Tell where to divide the paragraph. Tell which is the topic sentence of each paragraph, and find one sentence that does not belong.

> Isaac sent Jacob on a journey to Padan-aram to find a wife. Isaac said, "Go to the house of Bethuel and take a wife of the daughters of Laban. May God Almighty bless you as He blessed Abraham." Jacob stopped at a certain place for the night. I don't like to be outside alone in the dark. While he slept, he had a dream. He saw a ladder reaching from earth to heaven, and the angels of God were ascending and descending on it. God Himself was at the top of the ladder.

B. This paragraph is from Genesis 28:13–15. The topic sentence is missing. Give a good topic sentence for the paragraph.

> He said that He would give the land of Canaan to Jacob and his children. He said that Jacob's children would multiply and spread abroad in the earth. God promised to keep Jacob safe from harm and bring him back to the land of Canaan.

> Written Practice

A. This story should be divided into three paragraphs. Copy the three sentences that should begin the paragraphs. (They are the topic sentences.)

My Pet Animals

I have a poodle whose name is Nick. He follows me everywhere I go, and I always like to have him with me. Around his neck he wears a silver collar with his name on it. I have a white kitten. She is so much like a ball of snow that I named her Snowball. She and Nick are great friends. They often eat out of the same dish without quarreling. Another pet I have is a Shetland pony. I like her even more than Nick or Snowball. Her name is Midnight. She has this name because she is as black as night. I enjoy going about the farm, and Midnight is always willing and ready to carry me on her back.

B. Here are the main points for the story in Genesis 28:16–22, but they are in question form. Answer the questions in complete sentences. Then divide your sentences into two groups, and use them to write two paragraphs. Use descriptive words and good sentence variety.

1. How did Jacob feel when he awoke?
2. What did Jacob say about God when he awoke?
3. What did Jacob do because God was there?
4. What did Jacob name this place?
5. To whom did Jacob make a vow?
6. What things did Jacob say in his vow?
7. How much of his possessions did Jacob promise to give to God?

> Review and Practice >

A. Write **true** or **false** for each sentence.
   1. Copying someone else's writing word for word is a good way to make a report.
   2. When taking notes, it is good to copy key words that give main ideas.
   3. You should proofread a story before you write it.
   4. A book report should make others want to read the book.
   5. You should write every word in your notes when you prepare to tell a story.
   6. You should speak clearly and use good posture when giving an oral report.
   7. One good way to describe things is to use comparisons.

B. Copy the two prepositional phrases in each sentence. After each phrase, write the noun, verb, or verb phrase that it modifies. Also write whether it is an **adj.** or an **adv.** phrase.

1. A great crowd of people had come after Jesus.
2. Jesus stood beside the sea and taught the Word of God.
3. Jesus went up the mountain and prayed to God.
4. The disciples in the ship were rowing across the sea.
5. Jesus walked upon the water and came toward the ship.

---

112. Diagraming Prepositional Phrases

Prepositional phrases can be diagramed. Since they are used as adjectives and adverbs, they are diagramed in much the same way as other adjectives and adverbs. The prepositional phrase **on a long trip** is diagramed like this.

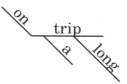

On the diagram above, the preposition is written on a slanted line. The object of the preposition goes on a level line connected to the slanted line. The adjectives go on slanted lines beneath the object of the preposition.

The prepositional phrase is placed beneath the word it modifies. The following example shows how to diagram an adjective phrase that modifies a noun.

The animal **in the box** was eating.

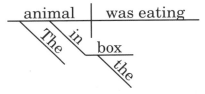

An adverb phrase is diagramed below the verb it modifies.

We hoed **in the morning.**

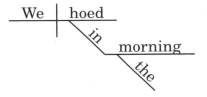

Remember that an adjective phrase always comes right after the noun it modifies. Phrases used as adjectives usually tell **which** or **what kind of.**

An adverb phrase may come at the beginning or at the end of a sentence. Phrases used as adverbs tell **how, when,** and **where.**

 Oral Drill

Diagram these sentences at the chalkboard.
1. A crooked old tree stood near the fence.
2. Our ducks are swimming across the pond.

3. The cow with a white face is not here.
4. With a great crash, the large tree fell.
5. Elijah was a prophet of God.
6. The man with him was Elisha.

> Written Practice >

A. Write the word that is modified by each phrase in bold print.

Examples: a. Aaron fell **down the stairs**.
b. I saw a deer **with a fawn**.

Answers: a. fell
b. deer

1. The books fell **off the table.**
2. The books **on the table** are new.
3. The flowers **in the garden** are yellow.
4. **With great speed** the blades whirled around.
5. The whippoorwill **in the woods** sang all night.
6. The heavens declare the glory **of God.**
7. In them hath He set a tabernacle **for the sun.**
8. Let us give thanks **to the Lord.**

B. After your answers in Part A, write whether each prepositional phrase is an **adj.** or an **adv.** phrase.

C. Copy the word that is modified by each phrase in bold print, and write what part of speech it is.

Example: The sheets **on the line** have been washed.
Answer: sheets—noun

1. Mary is carrying a pail **in her hand.**

2. The pigs **in the pen** have just been fed.
3. Snow still lies **on the roof.**
4. The snow **on the ground** has already melted.
5. The pig **near the fence** turned up its nose.
6. Those trees **in the woods** are quite tall.

D. Diagram these sentences.
1. Down the lane the frisky puppy scampered.
2. A small face peeked around the hedge.
3. The boat by the lake leaks.
4. Mother told a story about Samuel.

5. The clock upon the shelf struck.
6. The new clock sat on the shelf.
7. This vase came from Norway.
8. The vase from Norway broke.

Review and Practice

A. Write the correct word: **good** or **well.**
   1. This orange is ———.
   2. Dorcas was not feeling ——— yesterday.
   3. Sarah can sew ———.

B. Copy these sentences. Use correct capitalization and punctuation.
   1. mary did you finish your lesson sister anita asked
   2. have you read the new library book
   3. some holidays in the united states are new year's day memorial day independence day labor day columbus day thanksgiving day and christmas

C. Use these phrases in sentences of your own.
   1. up the steep hill   3. with blond hair
   2. under the sofa   4. with a fawn

113. Prepositions and Adverbs

Some words can be either prepositions or adverbs. The part of speech depends on how the words are used in sentences.

Study the following sentences. The word **inside** is a preposition in the first sentence and an adverb in the second sentence.

> We played **inside** <u>the house</u>. (preposition)
> We played **inside.** (adverb)

How can we tell the difference? This is not hard if we remember: **A preposition always has an object.** It is always followed by a noun or a pronoun that the preposition connects to another word in the sentence. A preposition cannot stand alone (without an object). It always comes at the beginning of a phrase.

In the first sentence above, **inside** begins the phrase **inside the house.** So **inside** is a preposition. It does not stand alone.

Also remember: **An adverb never has an object.** It does not begin a phrase, but it stands alone.

In the second sentence above, **inside** stands alone. It does not begin a phrase. So **inside** is an adverb.

Do not use an unnecessary preposition at the end of a **where** sentence. If the preposition has no object, leave the preposition off.

> **Wrong:** Where did the twins go to?
> **Right:**   Where did the twins go?

> **Wrong:** I don't know where they are at.
> **Right:**   I don't know where they are.

Remember: A preposition always has an object. An adverb
stands alone. We should not use unnecessary prepositions.

A. Tell whether the word in bold print is a preposition
   or an adverb. If it is a preposition, also give the whole
   phrase.
   1. The water was deep, but we waded **through.**
   2. Dust collected **beneath** the table.
   3. The children ran **outside.**
   4. The children ran **outside**
      the house.
   5. **Down** came the large bird.
   6. **Inside** we were warm and dry.
   7. **Inside** the hut we were warm
      and dry.

B. Read these sentences, leaving out any unnecessary
   prepositions.
   1. Where did Dennis go to?
   2. Where is Susan at?
   3. Is she inside?
   4. Where are the baby's toys at?
   5. Are they here?

> Written Practice

A. Write **adv.** or **prep.** to tell whether each word in bold print is an adverb or a preposition.
1. The men left **before** midnight.
2. No one told me that **before.**
3. The plane hovered **above** the water.
4. Jesus is in heaven **above.**
5. Jesus is **above** all.
6. **Up** flew the chaff.
7. **Away** it blew.
8. **Down** poured the rain.
9. **Down** the chute came the beans.
10. The dog ran **after** the cat.
11. She went first and he came **after.**
12. Dust collects **under** the beds.
13. The ship struck an iceberg and went **under.**
14. We sat on the ends, and Nancy sat **between.**
15. **Across** the plain ran the buffalo.
16. **Among** the bushes we found a frog.

B. Rewrite the incorrect sentences. Do not copy prepositions that should be left out.
1. Where are you at?
2. Where did you go to?
3. Where is Billy at?
4. Is he inside?

C. Diagram these sentences.
1. We coasted down the hill.
2. Down we fell.
3. You will stay behind.
4. You must stay behind us.
5. Come with me.
6. Come inside.

Review and Practice

A. Write words to fill in the blanks.
  1. A noun is the name of a ——, ——, or ——.
  2. A pronoun takes the place of a ——.
  3. A verb shows —— or ——.
  4. An adjective tells ———, ———, ——— ———, or
     ——— ——— ———.
  5. The adjective articles are ——, ——, and ——.
  6. An adverb tells ——, ——, or ——.
  7. A —— is a connecting word that begins a phrase.

B. Write the eight forms of the verb **be.**

C. Copy all the verbs in these sentences. Underline the helping verbs.
  1. The horse was trotting around the pasture.
  2. Leaves fall to the ground during autumn.
  3. Has Joel been helping you with the chores?

D. Write the correct words in parentheses.
  1. Who writes (better, best), Jean or Jeffrey?
  2. Of all the boys, Roy finished (more quickly, most quickly).
  3. We walked (farther, more farther) than they did.
  4. I feel (better, more well) than I did before.
  5. Who has (less, least) work, Mother or I?

114. Conjunctions

A conjunction is one of the eight parts of speech. A conjunction is used to join other words or groups of words. Three of the most common conjunctions are **and, but,** and **or.** Learn them.

Conjunctions help us to combine sentence parts. A conjunction can join two simple subjects.

> My little <u>brother</u> got lost.
> His <u>friend</u> got lost.
> My little <u>brother</u> **and** his <u>friend</u> got lost.

A conjunction can join two simple predicates (verbs).

> We <u>caught</u> the turtle.
> We <u>ate</u> the turtle.
> We <u>caught</u> **and** <u>ate</u> the turtle.

A conjunction can join two whole sentences.

> The children knew the song.
> They did not sing it.
> <u>The children knew the song</u>, **but** <u>they did not sing it</u>.

In the last sentence above, notice the comma just before **but.** When a conjunction joins two sentences, a comma usually comes before the conjunction.

Remember: A conjunction is a word that joins words or groups of words. Three common conjunctions are **and, but,** and **or.** When a conjunction is used to join two sentences, a comma usually comes before the conjunction.

 Oral Drill

A. Find each conjunction. Tell whether it joins **simple subjects, simple predicates,** or **sentences.**
   1. David saw the coin and picked it up.
   2. We planned a picnic, but it rained.
   3. Beetles or crickets were singing.

B. Join the following sentences. Use a different conjunction in each one.
   1. The thunder crashed. I was not afraid.
   2. The thunder crashed. A jet flew overhead.
   3. The thunder crashed. The lightning flashed.

C. Join these sentences, making the shortest possible sentence from each pair.
   1. We studied the question. We wrote the answer.
   2. Frank is coming. Bert is coming.
   3. The rain fell. The wind blew.

D. In each sentence, tell which word needs a comma after it.
   1. The dog bit me and the cat scratched me.
   2. Mother comforted me and she bandaged my sores.
   3. Father spanked the dog and he scolded the cat.
   4. Nancy drew a girl but Edith drew animals.

Written Practice

A. Copy the conjunction in each sentence. After the conjunction, write **subjects, predicates,** or **sentences** to tell what it joins.

1. The dog and cat hurt me.
2. It rained or snowed.
3. James picked the pansies and mowed the lawn.
4. The ram charged forward, but the ewes stayed behind.
5. The sparrows and swallows sang.

B. Copy the word that needs a comma after it, and add the comma.

1. She studies Spanish and he is learning English.
2. Larry sat still but Lester squirmed.
3. Lucy wrote stories but Margaret wrote poems.
4. You should study diligently or you might fail.
5. Maybe you cannot do it fast but you can do it well.

C. Make the shortest possible sentence from each pair of sentences. Use suitable conjunctions, and put commas where they are needed.

1. Get your work done. You cannot go along.
2. Henry did not come. James did not come.
3. Mary mowed the grass. Mary raked the yard.
4. The sun shone. The breeze blew.
5. Be careful. You will get hit.
6. Karen ran. She missed the bus.
7. He called. They answered.

Review and Practice

A. Copy and complete this chart.

Present	Past	Future
1. ——	helped	——
2. walk	——	——
3. ——	——	will draw
4. ring	——	——

B. Copy each prepositional phrase. Write the noun or verb that each phrase modifies.
1. Titus walked around the house.
2. The oak near the road is dead.
3. In the morning Mr. Brown milks his cows.

---

115. Parts of Speech Review

There are eight parts of speech in all. You have studied seven of them. The one you have not studied is the interjection. You will learn about it later.

You are now ready to look at each word in a sentence and tell what part of speech it is. You can use the following abbreviations for labeling the parts of speech.

noun—n.	adverb—adv.
pronoun—pron.	preposition—prep.
verb—v.	conjunction—conj.
adjective—adj.	

Use the following steps when you decide what part of speech each word in a sentence is.

1. Find and label the main verb and any helping verb.
2. Find the subject. Decide whether it is a noun or a pronoun, and label it correctly.
3. Find and label the other nouns and pronouns. These may be direct objects, predicate nouns, predicate pronouns, or objects of prepositions.
4. Look for adjectives that modify the nouns, and label them.
5. Find all the adverbs that modify the verb, and label them.
6. Find and label any prepositions.
7. Find and label any conjunctions.

Oral Drill

A. Name the seven parts of speech that you have studied, and define each of them.

B. Tell what part of speech each word is in the following sentences. Follow the steps in the lesson.
   1. The bells rang loudly.
   2. The little children were talking excitedly.
   3. Several small fish swam lazily in the cool water.
   4. We searched carefully, but we did not find the little turtle.
   5. We should go before dark.
   6. Lot escaped from Sodom with his two daughters.
   7. Lot's wife turned and looked back.
   8. She turned into a pillar of salt.

C. At the chalkboard, diagram sentences 1, 2, and 3 of Part B.

Written Practice

A. Match the parts of speech to the definitions.

    a. noun   d. adjective   f. preposition

    b. verb   e. adverb   g. conjunction

    c. pronoun

1. A word that shows action or being.
2. A connecting word that begins a phrase.
3. A word that joins words or groups of words.
4. A word that takes the place of a noun.
5. A word that names a person, place, or thing.
6. A word that describes a verb by telling **how, when,** or **where.**
7. A word that describes a noun by telling **which, whose, how many,** or **what kind of.**

B. Copy each sentence, and label the parts of speech.

            pron. conj. adj. n. prep. adj.   n.

Example: She and the girl with dark hair

               v.   v.   adv.

          have gone out.

1. Charles and Peter flew in a large airplane.
2. The dog with her is a pretty collie.
3. She is patting him on the head.
4. At dawn we started out.
5. Quickly they ran to the river.
6. The dog ran after the cat.
7. The Lord is clothed with majesty.
8. My God is the rock of my refuge.

C. Diagram these sentences.
1. Several lively red squirrels scampered in the trees.
2. Amos tumbled off the wagon.
3. The letter on the table was opened.

> **Review and Practice**

A. Write **statement, question, command,** or **exclamation** for each sentence. Write the correct end punctuation.
1. Do men gather grapes of thorns, or figs of thistles
2. Consider the lilies of the field
3. God has made everything beautiful in its time
4. O that there were such an heart in them, that they would fear me

B. Write the correct words.
1. We (raise, rise) corn in our garden.
2. Mary's father (lays, lies) bricks at work.
3. (Set, Sit) the chairs in a circle.
4. Did Mother (let, leave) the card on the table?
5. Albert (don't, doesn't) have his work finished.
6. Mother will (teach, learn) Joanna how to sew.

---

116. Writing a Story From a Poem

Sometimes a story is told in the form of poetry. Instead of being written in paragraphs, the story is arranged in stanzas that have rhythm and rhyme. The descriptive words in a poem help to tell the story in an interesting way.

The story that a poem tells can be written in paragraphs as stories usually are. To do this, first write down the main idea in each stanza of the poem. Do not copy word for word, but copy only key words that give the main ideas.

Make sure your ideas are in order. Then write complete sentences for your story, using the main ideas in your list. You may get ideas for descriptive words from the poem.

Divide your story into paragraphs in a sensible way. Write about only one main idea in each paragraph. When you have finished, your paragraphs should tell the same story as the poem.

A Lesson From a Horse

Old Jim was such a faithful horse,
But he was growing old;
And Uncle Lem made up his mind,
The horse should not be sold,
But turned out in the pastureland
To roam and feed at will,
Or rest beneath a shady tree
Down by the waters still.

Lem loved his faithful servant, Jim,
And watched him day by day;
And when he whistled for his horse,
Jim gave an answering neigh.
One day the horse had disappeared,
And Lem went out to see
What had become of faithful Jim;
Where could the creature be?

Lem thought of an abandoned well
    Which had uncovered been;
He hurried down the path to see—
    Yes! Jim had fallen in!
If he should try to pull him out,
    A leg might broken be,
So he would go and fetch his gun
    And end Jim's misery.

He brought his gun, but couldn't bear
    To shoot old faithful Jim,
So brought his shovel and his pick
    With which to bury him.
He took a shovelful of dirt
    And rolled it in the well;
It rolled onto the horse's back
    And to the bottom fell.

As fast as every load was sent,
    Old Jim would stamp it down;
And as they both thus worked away,
    At last the well was gone!
Out jumped the horse, all whole and sound,
    Kicked up his heels and ran.
Let's get from out this simple tale
    A lesson, if we can.

When people try to crush us down
    And cover us with dirt,
Let's stamp it underneath our feet
    And never let it hurt.
Let's be like Jim and rise above
    The troubles that beset;
If we are on the side of right,
    We'll gain the victory yet.

Oral Drill

Read the poem, and discuss the story it tells. Then answer the following questions.

1. Why did Uncle Lem decide to turn the horse into the pasture?
2. Why did Uncle Lem like this horse?
3. Why did the horse disappear one day?
4. Why didn't Uncle Lem pull him out?
5. What did Uncle Lem do next?
6. Why didn't Uncle Lem use his gun?
7. What did Uncle Lem decide to do next?
8. What happened when Uncle Lem threw dirt into the well?
9. What lesson can we learn from this story?
10. What adjectives in the poem are used to describe the horse? What other adjectives that describe the horse does the poem make you think of?
11. What words could you use to describe Uncle Lem?

Written Practice

Make a list of the main ideas in the poem about the horse. Be sure your list is in order. Then, using your list of main ideas, rewrite the poem in the usual story form and in your own words. Write only on every other line so that you can make changes later.

In your story, remember to write sentences of different lengths, using colorful, descriptive words. Proofread the story, and then recopy it neatly. Write a good title for your story.

> Review and Practice >

Write the correct words.
1. You should —— the whole book before you write a book report.
2. A book report (should, should not) tell about everything in the book.
3. Letters that are written to show friendship are called —— letters.
4. Using —— in stories makes them more interesting.
5. Each paragraph must tell about —— topic only.
6. Stories should be divided into proper ——.

117. Chapter 10 Review

> Oral Drill >

A. Name the part of speech described by each phrase.
   1. A word that modifies a noun.
   2. A word that joins words or groups of words.
   3. A word that modifies a verb.
   4. A connecting word that begins a phrase.

B. Give three conjunctions.

C. Give ten words that can be prepositions.

D. Read each prepositional phrase. Say the preposition and its object. Tell which word the phrase modifies. Tell whether it is an **adjective phrase** or an **adverb phrase.**

1. Inside the tent Sarah laughed.
2. She did not believe the words of the Lord.
3. In good time God's promise was fulfilled.
4. The tent in the background is made of goats' hair.
5. The bottle of skin was leaking.

E. Tell the part of speech that each word is in Part D.

F. On the chalkboard, diagram the sentences in Part D.

G. Combine these sentences in the shortest way possible. Use fitting conjunctions. Tell whether the conjunctions in your new sentences join **subjects, predicates,** or **sentences.**
1. The flowers in the garden grew.
   The flowers in the garden bloomed.

2. The children peeled the peaches.
   Mother canned them.

3. John broke the window.
   James broke the window.

H. Tell whether each word in bold print is a preposition or an adverb. Give the object of each preposition.
1. **Inside,** the children played quiet games.
2. **Inside** the shop three boys worked with hammers and saws.

Written Practice

A. Copy each prepositional phrase. Underline the preposition and its object.
1. The letter on the table is yours.
2. My dog lives under the porch.
3. After the fire we started cleaning up.

4. The work began in the morning.

5. I saw a giraffe with a very long neck.

B. Write the word that is modified by each phrase in bold print. After each word, write **N** for noun or **V** for verb.
   1. I have a cat **with green eyes.**
   2. Jim jumped **off the haystack.**
   3. **After dark** we went outside.
   4. The dog **with long ears** is mine.
   5. The house **across the road** was sold.
   6. The fox hid **behind the bush.**

C. After each answer in Part B, write **adj.** for adjective phrase or **adv.** for adverb phrase.

D. Diagram these sentences.
   1. The frisky colt galloped around the pasture.
   2. Around the corner we saw the children.
   3. A story from the Bible was told.
   4. The cookies in the jar were eaten.

E. Rewrite the incorrect sentences, leaving out the unnecessary prepositions.
   1. Where is Shirley at?
   2. Is she outside?
   3. I wonder where Jason is going to.
   4. Is he coming here?

F. Copy the sentences, and label the parts of speech.
   1. We stayed inside.
   2. The children played inside the playhouse.
   3. Down the hammer came and hit my thumb.
   4. The nails went into the board.
   5. The deer in the field ran swiftly.

G. Copy the conjunction in each sentence. Write whether it joins **subjects, predicates,** or **sentences.**
1. April or May may be warm.
2. We sing and pray at church.
3. We wanted to buy peaches, but the market had none.

H. Combine these sentences in the shortest way possible. Use suitable conjunctions. Remember to use commas correctly.
1. We tried to call her. She did not answer.
2. She may have been away. She may have been outside.
3. I swept the floor. Mary dusted the furniture.
4. Mother washed windows. Carol washed windows.
5. Father drove the tractor. The boys picked up stones.

I. Write **preposition** or **adverb** for each word in bold print.
1. Our airplane flew **across** the water.
2. **In** the meadow was a small stream.
3. The children jumped **across.**
4. One little girl fell **in.**

J. Write the correct words.
1. A long (poem, story) should be divided into proper paragraphs.
2. Each paragraph in a story should tell about ―――― topic.
3. A poem that tells a story is divided into ―――― rather than paragraphs.
4. To write a story from a poem, first make a list of the ―――― ideas.

Love

Love will make us well-behaved
In each word and deed;
It will think of others first,
To their needs give heed.

Love will keep us sweet and kind
When we're treated wrong;
Then we still can praise the Lord
With a happy song.

Every line of poetry is capitalized.

Chapter 11
Capitalization
and Dictionary Use

118. Capitalization

We want our writing to be as clear and easy to read as possible. Capitalizing words correctly helps to make our writing clear. Capital letters are signals that show certain things. They show when a new sentence is beginning. They also show when a specific person, place, or thing is being talked about.

Here are four rules for capitalization that you will practice in this lesson.

1. Capitalize the first word of every sentence.

> **A** friend in need is a friend indeed.
> **Who** then indeed is willing?
> **Follow** me.
> **What** hath God wrought!

2. Capitalize the first word in every line of poetry.

> **Whether** the task be great or small,
> **Do** it well, or not at all.

3. Always capitalize the pronoun **I.**

> Yea, though **I** walk through the valley of the shadow of death, **I** will fear no evil.

4. Capitalize all names of God and all pronouns that refer to Him.

> The **Lord** is with **His** people.
> The **Creator** of heaven and earth is **He.**
> We have found the **Messiah.**
> Quench not the **Spirit.**

> *Other examples:* the **Holy Ghost,** the **Father,** the **Son,** the **Comforter, Christ, Jehovah**

> **Remember:** Capitalize the first word of every sentence, the
> first word in every line of poetry, the pronoun **I,** and all nouns or
> pronouns that refer to God.

 Oral Drill

Tell which words should be capitalized, and why. Some
words should be capitalized for two reasons.

1. jesus loves me, and i love him.
2. i will praise him as long as i live.

3. god is so mighty, great, and strong;
   he loves the good and hates the wrong.
   his love is wonderful and pure;
   his Word is true and very sure.

4. all the apostles of jesus were disciples, but not all
   the disciples were apostles. a disciple was simply a
   follower of jesus. an apostle was someone who had seen
   jesus and received a special assignment from him.

5. follow the path of jesus,
     walk where his footsteps lead;
   keep in his beaming presence,
     ev'ry counsel heed;
   watch while the hours are flying,
     ready some good to do;
   quick, while his voice is calling,
     yield obedience true!

6. god is three in one: the father, the son, and the holy
   ghost.
7. have you thanked god today?

 Written Practice

A. Copy this poem, using correct capitalization.

1. oh, what a happy soul am i!
   although i cannot see,
   i am resolved that in this world
   contented i will be.

2. how many blessings i enjoy
   that other people don't!
   to weep and sigh because i'm blind,
   i cannot and i won't.

   —Fanny Crosby

B. Find each word that needs a capital letter, and write it correctly.

1. i love the lord. i shall praise him as long as i live.
2. god loved us so much that he gave his only begotten son to die for us.
3. since god is with me, what have i to fear?

Review and Practice

A. Review the rules in Lesson 28, "Common Nouns and Proper Nouns." Then write correctly each word that should be capitalized.

1. the israelites crossed the red sea and the Jordan river.
2. god miraculously parted the water of the sea and the river.
3. jesus died on good friday and rose again on easter.
4. on ascension day he ascended to prepare a place for us.

5. have you ever visited yellowstone national park?
6. james and donna go to barre christian school.
7. in arizona you can see the grand canyon, which is a place of beautiful scenery.
8. the great victoria desert in australia was named after queen victoria.
9. mount st. helens in washington has erupted several times since 1980.
10. lake louise is a beautiful lake in canada.
11. the continent of antarctica is a huge cold wasteland.
12. our school is the pine shore christian school.
13. the desert called death valley was named by some pioneers who got lost and almost died in it.

B. Copy these sentences. Use capital letters and punctuation where needed.
1. father said that many people do not think about jesus as they should on christmas
2. uncle ben aunt miriam and i visited brother noah on wednesday, october 17
3. are any rivers in north america larger than the mississippi river asked conrad
4. president roosevelt signed a law saying that thanksgiving day should be held on the fourth thursday in november

C. Make the shortest possible sentence from each pair of sentences. Use a different conjunction in each one.
1. Harold ran fast. William ran faster.
2. Susan fed the chickens. Susan gathered the eggs.
3. Write carefully. You may misspell a word.

---

119. Capitalizing Names and Titles

The name of a specific person must be capitalized because it is a proper noun. A person's initials must be capitalized too.

    John E. Martin   J. Henry Taylor

Sometimes a title is used before a person's name. Capitalize a person's title when it comes before his name.

Mr. James King   **President** Lincoln
Mrs. Leon Hunt   **Uncle** Joseph
Miss Jane Good   **Aunt** Eva
Brother Nelson   **Doctor** Lee
Sister Sarah   **Queen** Mary

The name of a specific place or thing is also a proper noun, and so it must be capitalized. Review the capitalization rules that you studied in Lesson 28, "Common Nouns and Proper Nouns."

Main Street
Lincoln Building
Sharon Christian School
Thanksgiving Day

Do not capitalize words like **school, street, mountain, river,** and **ocean** unless they are part of a proper noun.

> We saw a wide **river.**
> We crossed the **Mississippi River.**

Remember that the names of the seasons are not capitalized.

spring	fall (autumn)
summer	winter

Capitalize the first word, the last word, and all important words in the title of a book, poem, story, or song. Do not capitalize the articles **(a, an,** and **the)** or a conjunction or preposition with fewer than four letters, unless it is the first or last word in the title.

Kitten in the Well	A Home for Grandma
God Cares for Timothy	The Bible Smuggler
Abide With Me	Jesus, Still Lead On

Remember: Capitalize proper nouns and any title used before a person's name. Capitalize the first word, last word, and all important words in the title of a book, poem, story, or song.

Oral Drill

Tell which words should be capitalized, and why.

1. my teacher is brother edgar l. charles.
2. samuel f. b. morse invented the telegraph.
3. queen mary was the queen of scotland.
4. doctor barnes called for miss levan.
5. brother daniel read *the man in bearskin* to us.
6. i received the books *five loaves and two small fish,*
   trouble at windy acres, and *home fires at the foot of*
   the rockies from sister esther.
7. last spring we visited aunt may in portland, maine.

Written Practice

A. Find the words that need capital letters, and write them
   correctly.

1. fanny j. crosby wrote the song "to god be the glory."
2. p. p. bliss wrote the words and the music to the song
   "wonderful words of life."
3. mrs. ruth k. jones and miss helen h. long moved to
   hagerstown, maryland, last fall.
4. last december mr. george heath gave a speech here.
5. brother john e. kauffman preached at weavers church
   on sunday.
6. i plan to give a book report on
   the lim family of singapore.
7. the students in brother jerry's
   class must read the book *science*
   and the bible.
8. i was born that winter on a monday
   in january.
9. what a lovely time of year autumn is!

The LIM FAMILY of Singapore

B. Use the words **spring, summer, autumn,** and **winter** in sentences of your own.

> Review and Practice

A. Copy the negative word in each sentence. Then copy the correct word in parentheses.
   1. Don't you want (no, any) milk?
   2. Didn't you (ever, never) plant watermelons?

B. Copy these poems correctly.
   1.   **the months**
      thirty days hath september,
      april, june, and november.
      all the rest have thirty-one
      save the second month alone,
      to which we twenty-eight assign
      till leap year gives it twenty-nine.

   2.   **gladness every day**
      on sunday i am happy,
         on monday full of joy,
      on tuesday i have peace within
         that nothing can destroy.
      on wednesday and on thursday,
         i'm walking in the light.
      oh, friday is a heaven below,
         and saturday's always bright!

C. Write a sentence telling when each of the following holidays takes place. Match the days to the correct times. Be sure to use capital letters correctly.

Examples: Good Friday takes place in the spring.
Labor Day comes in September.

Holiday	**Time**
1. father's day	a. january
2. christmas	b. november
3. easter	c. december
4. new year's day	d. spring
5. thanksgiving day	e. june

D. Write ten prepositions.

---

120. Writing a Story About a Personal Experience

Our lives are filled with interesting experiences, and we enjoy telling about them. Perhaps we moved into a new house, or we saw a great storm, or someone in our family was seriously ill or injured. Maybe we saw a barn burn down, or we went on a trip to Canada.

Even everyday things are worth writing about. Our family may have watched a beautiful sunset together, or people from a distant state or country may have visited in our home. Maybe we learned how to do a new kind of work, or we made an interesting discovery about a bird or something else in nature. We all have worthwhile things to write about.

Follow these rules for writing a story. First, write the main idea that your story will be about. Then write a list of details that you may use in your story. Write plenty of details so that you can choose only the best ones.

Organize your list of details in the order of time. The first thing that happened should come first, the second thing second, and so on. If any details do not fit into the story, leave them out.

Then write your story. Put the details in order as you have planned. Give your story a good title.

Check for proper spelling, correct punctuation, and good English. Then rewrite the story neatly and correctly.

Remember: When you write a story, first make a list of details and put them in order. Proofread your story when it is finished.

A. Help to make a list of details about something that happened at school. Your teacher can list them on the chalkboard. Decide which details should be crossed out, and arrange the rest of them in the proper order.

B. Tell which sentences do not belong in this story because they do not tell about the main idea.

My parents took us to the zoo one day last summer. We saw some strange and interesting animals. One time we went to visit a cave too.

The elephant house was quite fascinating. There were five elephants. In one stall was a mother elephant with her baby. It was a huge baby! One elephant was spraying water from his trunk. Another elephant took peanuts from our hands with his trunk and put them in his mouth. In some countries, elephants are used for dragging logs out of the forest.

We saw camels too. Some camels had only one hump and some had two. They were kept in an area that looked like a desert. We studied deserts in school this year. The camels seemed to feel at home there. I would have liked to ride one.

I liked the monkey jungle best. It seemed that monkeys were everywhere! Most monkeys have tails, but apes

Corel

do not. One baby monkey was swinging on a vine. Another baby monkey was being spanked by his mother. The monkeys peeled bananas and ate them. I wished I could take a baby monkey home for a pet!

We ate lunch in the picnic area at the zoo. Before we ate, Father thanked the Lord for the beautiful things He made for us to enjoy.

C. Tell which is the best title for the story in Part B. Tell why the others are not suitable.
   1. The Monkey Jungle
   2. Our Visit to the Zoo
   3. Animals at the Zoo

> Written Practice

A. Write a list of details about an experience in your life. Arrange the details in the order they happened, and leave out any that do not belong. You may choose one of the following topics or make up your own.
   1. A time when I was afraid
   2. A lesson I learned the hard way
   3. An accident that happened to me
   4. An unusual day at school
   5. The first day of school
   6. A sad experience
   7. An interesting experience I had last summer

B. After your teacher has looked over your list, write your story. Give it a good title.

> Review and Practice

Write the correct answers.
   1. The —— sentence tells what a paragraph is about.
   2. Each —— in poetry begins with a capital letter.
   3. You should use good —— when you speak or read orally.
   4. You should pause briefly at each ——.
   5. Give three ways to develop paragraphs.

121. Using the Telephone

It is important to be courteous when you use the telephone. One way to be courteous is to speak clearly and listen carefully. In this way, you can give and receive messages accurately.

When you make a call, be sure to dial the right number. If you do not know the number, find it in the telephone directory, or ask someone to find it for you. Dialing a wrong number through haste or carelessness is not courteous.

If you are calling and no one answers right away, let the telephone ring at least seven times. When someone answers, say "Hello." Then tell who you are and why you are calling.

Speak into the mouthpiece of the receiver, and hold the other end lightly against your ear. Be sure to speak distinctly. Speak loudly enough so that the other person can easily hear you, but do not shout into the mouthpiece.

When you answer the telephone, say "Hello" and tell who you are. If the caller wants to speak to someone else who is there, say, "Just a minute; I'll call him (or her)." If the caller wants to speak to someone who is not at home, ask whether you may take a

message. If a message is given, listen carefully and write it down accurately. Ask questions if you do not understand something.

Unless for a good reason you must end the conversation, let the person who called say "Good-bye" first.

Remember: When you are using the telephone, be courteous and respectful.

Think what you would do in each of the following cases, and be ready to do it in class. Use toy telephones if you have them.

1. Betty calls and asks to speak to your older sister, who is at home.
2. Mrs. Smith asks for your mother, who is not at home.
3. Mr. Fields asks for your father. Father is at the office, and his telephone number is 442-5386.
4. The neighbor lady asks to speak to your mother, but she cannot leave her work at the time.

> **Written Practice**

A. List five things you should do that show courtesy when using the telephone.

B. In two or three sentences, tell how you should take a message that is given to you on the telephone.

> **Review and Practice**

A. Write the missing words.
  1. You must move your ——— in order to speak clearly.
  2. For good choral reading, you need a ———.
  3. At a ———, you should let your voice drop and pause a little longer than at a comma.
  4. Before giving a book report, you should ——— the whole book.
  5. Give the main ——— in order when you give oral directions.

B. Copy these sentences, and add the missing capital letters and punctuation marks.
  1. do you know what the mediterranean sea is called in the bible
  2. on monday, september 2 1999 i began attending orchard valley christian school
  3. for the first telegraph message, samuel f b morse said what hath god wrought!
  4. this message was sent from washington, d.c., to baltimore maryland
  5. cyrus w field and william thompson helped to get a telegraph cable laid across the atlantic ocean
  6. the united states and canada laid thousands of miles of telegraph cables
  7. countries like england france germany russia and spain also made vast telegraph systems

122. Using the Dictionary

The dictionary is a very useful book. It shows the pronunciations, meanings, and spellings of the words we read and write. Learn to use the dictionary well, and use it often.

Each word listed in a dictionary is called an **entry word.** The entry words are arranged in alphabetical order to help us find them easily. **Guide words** at the top of each page also help us find words quickly. The guide words show the first and last entry words on a dictionary page.

After each entry word comes the **phonetic spelling,** which shows in phonetic symbols how the word is pronounced. Some words may be pronounced more than one way.

The dictionary also gives **definitions,** which tell what the entry words mean. You will do more work with definitions in the next lesson.

Guide Word

Entry Word

Phonetic Spelling

Definition

blue jay

blue•jay (blü•jā), *n.* A noisy, chattering North American bird with a crest and a blue back.

bod•y (bod'•ē), *n.* 1. The whole part of a person, animal, or plant. 2. Mass: *A lake is a body of water.* 3. The main part of a letter that gives the message.

both•er (both'ər), *v.* 1. Take trouble; concern oneself: *Don't bother about the noise.* 2. Annoy: *Hot weather bothers me.*

bowl (bōl), *n.* A hollow, rounded dish, usually without handles.

buy

bright (brīt), *adj.* Giving much light; shining.

burn (bėrn), *v.* Injure by fire or heat.

bus•y (biz•ē), *adj.* Having plenty to do; working; active.

but•ter•fly (but'•ər•flī), *n.* An insect with a slender body and two pairs of large, usually brightly colored, wings.

but•ton (but'•n), *n.* A round, flat piece, usually of metal or plastic, fastened on garments to keep them closed. *v.* Fasten the buttons of.

buy (bī), *v.* Get by paying.

Oral Drill

A. Tell how to put each group of words in alphabetical order.

1. carrot	2. appear	3. been
apple	away	being
banana	aster	bear

B. Use the phonetic spelling and the pronunciation key in your dictionary to help you pronounce each word correctly.

1. route	4. creek	7. our
2. mischief	5. ration	8. either
3. less	6. often	9. knee

C. Say **yes** or **no** to tell whether each word would be on a dictionary page with these guide words on it.

Guide words: **elk...emu**

1. embark	3. eleven	5. emery
2. enclose	4. empire	6. egg

D. Use guide words to find these words quickly. Pronounce each one correctly, and give its first meaning.

1. lapse	3. ague	5. thrall
2. digress	4. jetty	6. joggle

E. Look up these words, and tell whether each pair is pronounced alike.

1. berry—bury
2. hour—our
3. poor—pore

Written Practice

A. Write these ten words in alphabetical order.

strait   straw   stuff   strike   strict,
stain   steep   stock   stir   strew

B. Write these words in alphabetical order. If you do it correctly, the words will make a sentence.

the   began   a   yesterday   water   beaver   damming

C. Write the phonetic spelling for each word.
   1. idea   3. apostle
   2. gesture   4. draught

D. For each word, write **yes** or **no** to tell whether it would come on a dictionary page with these guide words.
   Guide words: **prank...pretty**
   1. preen   4. pond
   2. pride   5. post
   3. pray   6. press

preen

Review and Practice

A. Write correctly each word that needs a capital letter.

   1.   **the months**
      january brings the snow;
      makes our feet and fingers glow.
      february brings the rain;
      thaws the frozen lake again.

2. march brings breezes loud and shrill;
   stirs the dancing daffodil.
   april brings the primrose sweet;
   scatters daisies at our feet.

3. may brings flocks of pretty lambs
   skipping by their fleecy dams.
   june brings tulips, lilies, roses;
   fills the children's hands with posies.

4. hot july brings cooling showers,
   apricots, and gillyflowers.
   august brings the sheaves of corn;
   then the harvest home is borne.

5. warm september brings the fruit;
   hunters then begin to shoot.
   fresh october brings the pheasant;
   then to gather nuts is pleasant.

6. dull november brings the blast;
   then the leaves are whirling fast.
   chill december brings the sleet,
   blazing fire, and winter treat.

   —Sara Coleridge

B. Answer the following questions in complete sentences.
   1. When is **well** an adverb?
   2. When is **well** an adjective?
   3. What part of speech is **good**?

C. Copy the conjunction in each sentence.
   1. Daniel and Matthew like to fish.

2. Listen carefully, or you will not understand your assignment.
3. Fred wanted to go, but he was not ready.

> Challenge Exercise

Use a dictionary to find answers to these questions.
1. Where might you go to see a gibbon?
2. When might you wear a mackintosh?
3. Which of the following name things to eat or drink?

avocado	sari	pekoe
marl	mango	tome
piazza	cress	pemmican

---

123. Spellings and Meanings in the Dictionary

A dictionary can help you to spell words correctly. Keep a dictionary handy whenever you are doing a school lesson. If you are not sure how to spell a word, look it up.

Also use the dictionary to find the meanings (definitions) of words. You should do this whenever you meet words whose meanings you do not know.

Because some words have more than one meaning, the dictionary may list more than one entry, or it may give several definitions under the same entry word. Be sure to find the meaning that fits the word as it is used in the particular sentence you are reading.

Look at this entry for **domestic.** Can you tell which definition is the right one for each sentence below?

> **do·mes·tic** (də·mes′·tik), *adj.* 1. Tame; not wild.
>   2. Having to do with the home or household.
>   *n.* Household servant.

1. A cow is a **domestic** animal.
2. Joseph was a **domestic** under Potiphar.
3. Mothers have many **domestic** duties.

Another thing the dictionary shows is what parts of speech a word can be. In sentence 2 above, **domestic** is used as a noun. The noun meaning of **domestic** is "household servant." Both the meaning and the part of speech are correct for the way **domestic** is used in the sentence. So you can be sure that is the right definition.

Oral Drill

A. Look in a dictionary, and tell how to spell these words correctly.

1. doller   3. beleive   5. fourty
2. develope   4. supose   6. personul

B. Give several different meanings for each word. Give the part of speech for each meaning.

1. pitch   2. lash   3. tender

Written Practice

A. Correct these misspelled words.

1. surprize   2. covetious   3. actial

B. Write two different meanings for each word.
   1. bread   2. pass   3. host   4. even

C. Choose and write the correct word for each sentence. Check a dictionary if you are not sure.
   1. A (gored, gourd) looks like a squash.
   2. He had a small (brews, bruise) on his cheek.
   3. The eagle (preys, prays, praise) on small animals.
   4. We shall (urn, earn) the money ourselves.
   5. She has very (fare, fair) skin.

D. Name the part of speech for each word in bold print as it is used in that sentence.
   1. **Pitch** the ball to me.
   2. Noah covered the ark with **pitch.**
   3. We saw a black **bear.**
   4. The donkey could hardly **bear** the load.
   5. Sally liked her job of being a baby **tender.**
   6. The **tender** meat was delicious.

E. Write the letter of the correct meaning for each word in bold print.

   a. Put or place. (verb)
   b. Become solid. (verb)
   c. Group of things that belong together. (noun)
   d. Firmly fixed; established. (adjective)

   1. Please **set** the plant on the shelf.
   2. There is no **set** way to solve every problem.
   3. Concrete must be smoothed before it **sets.**
   4. The boys played with a **set** of building blocks.

> Review and Practice

A. Diagram these sentences.
   1. Some lizards live in the desert.
   2. Many other animals live and grow there.
   3. Cacti can store water in their stems.

B. Below are the titles of some songs written by Isaac Watts, who lived in England long ago. Write each title correctly.
   1. o god, our help in ages past
   2. joy to the world, the lord is come
   3. when i survey the wondrous cross
   4. am i a soldier of the cross?
   5. the lord my shepherd is
   6. jesus shall reign

C. Write three kinds of information that a dictionary gives.

D. Write a sentence about this picture. Give the boy a name, and tell what tools and materials he is using to build a birdhouse.

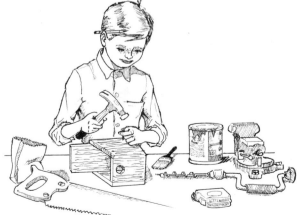

> **Challenge Exercise** >

See if you can find the answers to these questions in a dictionary.

1. Is a **barnacle** a kind of bird or a sea animal?
2. Is a **battering-ram** an animal or a machine?
3. Is a **pastern** part of an animal or a place where animals stay?
4. Does **nebulous** mean cloudy or empty?
5. Which words name an animal or a bird?

monk	fisher	dodo
mussel	gusset	merganser
egret	mongoose	dodder

dodo *or* dodder?   monk *or* mongoose?

6. Do **flammable** and **inflammable** have similar or opposite meanings?
7. In what country is the **Zuider Zee** found?
8. Is the **Zuider Zee** a gulf or a road?
9. **Canberra** is the capital city of what country?
10. When did the **Hittite** civilization exist?

124. Synonyms, Antonyms, and Homophones

The English language has a great variety of words. Learning about words helps us to be exact in our writing. In this lesson you will study words with similar meanings, words with opposite meanings, and words that sound alike.

Synonyms are words with similar meanings.

> **Big** means about the same as **large.**
> **Big** and **large** are synonyms.

Here are two more pairs of synonyms.

> aid—help   order—command

Antonyms are words with opposite meanings.

> **Hot** means the opposite of **cold.**
> **Hot** and **cold** are antonyms.

hot

Here are two more pairs of antonyms.

> up—down   short—tall

cold

Homophones are words that are pronounced the same but are spelled differently. They have different meanings.

> **Dear** and **deer** are homophones.
> I have a **dear** baby sister.
> We saw a **deer** running through the field.

Knowing about synonyms, antonyms, and homophones will help you to be an interesting speaker and writer.

 Oral Drill

A. Find synonyms for these words in your dictionary.
   1. weary   2. often   3. plain

B. Give an antonym for each of the following words.
   1. early   2. rough   3. calm   4. feeble

C. Tell whether the words in each pair are **synonyms** or **antonyms.**
   1. red—ruddy   4. short—tall
   2. climb—rise   5. under—beneath
   3. slow—fast   6. hot—cold

D. Spell the correct homophones.
   1. We (rowed, road, rode) (their, they're, there) on (our, hour) horses.
   2. (Sum, Some) of (their, they're, there) (pares, pairs, pears) are ripe.
   3. (Won, One) must (knead, need) the (bread, bred) well.
   4. There were no (brakes, breaks) on the (slay, sleigh).
   5. We went (to, two, too) (hour, our) grandmother's house.
   6. My cousins went (there, they're, their) (to, two, too).

> Written Practice

A. Write **S** or **A** to tell whether the words in each pair are synonyms or antonyms.
   1. small—large   5. easy—difficult
   2. down—up   6. night—day
   3. swift—fast   7. old—ancient
   4. enemy—foe   8. told—said

B. Write the correct homophones.
1. The (son, sun) (shone, shown) (threw, through) the (missed, mist).
2. (Write, Right) a letter to (your, you're) friend.
3. She (blue, blew) the (seeds, cedes), and they (flew, flue) away.
4. The artist painted a (seen, scene) showing a (grate, great) (waste, waist) region.
5. We stayed (there, they're, their) (to, two, too) long, and then we were late.

C. Write a more exact synonym to replace each word in bold print.
1. The colts **run** around the pasture.
2. The pie tasted **good.**
3. The rose was **pretty.**
4. The **little** child couldn't reach it.

D. Rewrite these sentences, using an antonym to replace each word in bold print.
1. We wore **warm, heavy** clothes on the **cold** day.
2. We traveled **swiftly down** the path.
3. The **cloudy** day made the children feel **gloomy.**

> Review and Practice

A. Name the part of speech for each word in bold print.
1. **Hammer** the nails in tightly.
2. Father used a **hammer** to open the lid.
3. We should have **neat** desks.
4. The children had a **quarrel.**
5. Mother said, "Do not **quarrel.**"
6. Remember to speak **kindly.**

7. Keep love **in** your heart.
8. Tell the visitors to come **in.**
9. Sing **and** pray every day.
10. **We** will praise the Lord.

B. Write whether each word in bold print is a **direct object** or a **predicate noun.**
1. Anita is my **cousin.**
2. Anita saw my **cousin.**
3. Jerry has a **puppy** too.
4. Philip was a **disciple.**
5. Jerry brought his **rabbit** to school.

C. Write the meaning of each word in bold print as it is used in the sentence.
1. The **sage** gave good advice.
2. Grandmother likes to use **sage** in cooking.

---

125. Being Clear and Specific

When we are talking to someone, we can stop and explain things that our listener does not understand. But we cannot do that when we write our thoughts on paper. Therefore, we must be clear and specific so that the reader can easily understand what we mean. Clear and specific writing is not easy, but we can learn to do it by diligent work.

Through our five senses, we learn about many things in our Father's world. We can write interesting descriptions by using exact words that tell how things look, sound, taste, smell, or feel. Sounds can be made more real with words like **crashed, hummed, croaked, swished, rustled,** and **tapped.** Tastes or smells can be described as **sweet, sour, salty, bitter, spicy,** and **delicious.** An object can feel **soft, fuzzy, sharp, round, rough,** or **cool.** A person's inner feelings might be described as **happy, cross, discouraged, afraid, or cheerful.**

Descriptive adjectives and adverbs help to make sentences clear and exact. As an example, look at the following sentence. How could we make it more specific?

> The boy sat in a chair.

We could use adjectives to tell what kind of chair it was. Was it a rocking chair, a blue wooden chair, a large overstuffed chair, or a folding chair? We could also use adverbs to tell how the boy sat. Did he sit quietly, wearily, restlessly, or contentedly?

Often the word **good** is used instead of a more exact adjective. **Good** can mean many things. A **good** apple might be a **ripe** apple. A **good** story might be a **true** or **interesting** story. A **good** lesson might be an **important** or **valuable** lesson.

Descriptive verbs also help us to be more specific. The word **walked** has many interesting synonyms. Use the most exact one for what you are describing. A crippled person might **hobble** or **limp.** A tired person might **trudge.** A feeble person might **totter,** and a proud person might **swagger.**

Remember: Write with clear, specific words. Use descriptive verbs, adjectives, and adverbs.

A. Give some adjectives that describe different kinds of dogs.

B. What adjectives describe different kinds of trees?

C. Give a more descriptive word for each word in bold print.

   1. This book is **good.**
   2. I ate a **good** peach.
   3. The flowers smell **nice.**
   4. Cinnamon has a **nice** flavor.
   5. The angry cat **made a noise** like a goose.
   6. I felt **awful** after I ate too much candy.
   7. I felt **awful** when I heard that a robber was out.

D. Tell how each sentence could be made more clear and specific.
   1. The funny thing was filled with different kinds of stuff.
   2. The place is not far from here.
   3. There was a cabin near the road.
   4. Charles is like that.

> Written Practice >

A. List five adjectives that describe different kinds of packages.

B. Write a more descriptive word to replace each word in bold print. You may use a dictionary.
1. The pie smelled **nice.**
2. Mary is a **nice** friend.
3. The teacher read a **good** story.
4. We had a **good** English lesson this morning.
5. We **walked** on a trail through the woods.
6. The feeble old man **walked** up the drive.
7. The **large** building seemed to touch the sky.
8. A **small** mouse scurried across the floor.
9. The old man was feeling **bad.**
10. This blanket feels **good.**

C. Rewrite these sentences, adding words or phrases to make them more clear and specific.
1. There was food to eat.
2. The man was standing in the lane.
3. The teacher was carrying a bag.
4. Peter looked at the crab.

> **Review and Practice**

Write the correct words.
1. When you introduce anyone to your mother, say (the other person's name, "Mother") first.
2. Good poems use —— words.
3. When speaking on the telephone, give messages —— and receive them ——.
4. The person who called should usually be the first to say "——."

126. Bible Poetry

The Bible has poetry in it. In fact, several books in the Bible are made almost entirely of poems. The largest book of poetry is the Book of Psalms. Other books of poetry are Job, Proverbs, Ecclesiastes, and the Song of Solomon. There is much for us to learn from Bible poetry. It teaches us many things about God's care for us and about right living.

Poems in the Bible do not rhyme. Some words in Bible poems do rhyme in the original language, but the rhyme was lost when the poems were translated into English. Bible poems do not have regular rhythm either. The lines do not contain the same number of syllables, and they do not have a pattern of accented and unaccented syllables.

Bible poetry is full of descriptive words. It is excellent poetry even without rhyme and rhythm. Bible poetry uses highly expressive language.

Many words of comparison are found in Bible poems. Some comparisons say that one thing is **like** or **as** another.

> And he shall be **like a tree** planted by the rivers of water (Psalm 1:3).
>
> **As cold waters to a thirsty soul,** so is good news from a far country (Proverbs 25:25).

Other comparisons say that one thing **is** another.

> The Lord **is** my **shepherd** (Psalm 23:1).
> A wholesome tongue **is a tree of life** (Proverbs 15:4).

Although Bible poetry does not rhyme in sound, many of the lines "rhyme" in meaning. One way they do this is by repeating the same thought in different words.

The heavens declare the glory of God;
And the firmament sheweth his handywork (Psalm 19:1).

Let another man praise thee, and not thine own mouth;
A stranger, and not thine own lips (Proverbs 27:2).

Remember: Bible poetry uses descriptive language in a special way.

> Oral Drill >

A. Tell how to divide Psalm 1:1 into lines of poetry. Write the lines on the board. How should each line begin?

B. In each set below, tell which lines have "rhyming" thoughts.

1. The Lord hath been mindful of us:
   He will bless us;
   He will bless the house of Israel;
   He will bless the house of Aaron (Psalm 115:12).

2. It is a good thing to give thanks unto the Lord,
   And to sing praises unto thy name, O most High:
   To shew forth thy lovingkindness in the morning,
   And thy faithfulness every night (Psalm 92:1, 2).

C. Find the comparing words in the following lines.
   1. Keep me as the apple of the eye, hide me under the shadow of thy wings (Psalm 17:8).
   2. For the Lord God is a sun and shield (Psalm 84:11).
   3. The righteous shall flourish like the palm tree: he shall grow like a cedar in Lebanon (Psalm 92:12).

Written Practice

A. Write these lines from Psalm 23 in the way we usually write poetry.

> the Lord is my shepherd;
> i shall not want.
> he maketh me to lie down in green pastures:
> he leadeth me beside the still waters.

B. Look up the following references, and finish the comparisons.
1. Gird up thy loins now like a —— (Job 40:7).
2. But made his own people to go forth like —— (Psalm 78:52).
3. A merry heart doeth good like a —— (Proverbs 17:22)
4. The words of the wise are as —— and as —— fastened by the masters of assemblies (Ecclesiastes 12:11).
5. Love is strong as ——; jealousy is cruel as the ——: the coals thereof are —— of —— (Song of Solomon 8:6).

Review and Practice

Fill in the blanks.
1. —— is a special kind of writing that is pleasing to the ear.
2. Rhythm is made of a pattern of —— and —— syllables.
3. Poems in the Bible do not have —— or ——.
4. Bible —— uses descriptive language in a special way.

> Challenge Exercise >

Look through the Book of Exodus. Which chapter has the poem or song that the children of Israel sang after the Lord brought them safely through the Red Sea?

Can you find other poetry in books of the Bible that are not considered poetic books?

---

127. Chapter 11 Review

> Oral Drill >

A. Tell which words need capital letters.

my friend

before i go to bed at night,
   i like to kneel and pray;
And it is very nice to know
   That god hears what i say.

i always tell him, "Thank You, God,
   For all Your gifts to me."
i like to tell him everything,
   For he's my Friend, you see.

i never need to be afraid,
   For god is always near;
i always try to please my Friend;
   And then i never fear.

—*Lela Birky*

B. Give the correct capitalization for this story.

somebody must stop first

susie and sophie were quarreling. "you did it!" sophie exclaimed.

"no, i didn't!" said susie. the words were growing angrier every minute.

susie's lips suddenly closed tightly, and she would not speak.

"why do you keep still, susie, when sophie keeps on quarreling?" asked another girl.

"mother said that somebody must stop first," susie replied. "i'll stop first, and then the quarrel will be over more quickly."

C. Choose the correct meaning for each word in bold print.

      a. Fill up so as to prevent passage. (verb)
      b. Solid piece of material such as wood. (noun)
      c. Length of one side of a city square. (noun)

1. Lee played with his **blocks.**
2. Walk one **block;** then take the next street left.
3. A traffic jam **blocks** the roads.

D. Give the letter of the correct pronunciation.
1. mischief   a. mis'·chif   b. mis'·chef
2. berry   a. bir'·y   b. ber'·ē   c. bur'·ē

E. Give a synonym, an antonym, and a homophone for each of the following words.
1. weak   3. new
2. fair   4. right

gnu

F. Give the missing words.
   1. The words in a dictionary are entered in —— order.
   2. The —— —— helps us to pronounce an entry word correctly.
   3. Words with similar meanings are ——.
   4. Words with opposite meanings are ——.
   5. Words that are pronounced alike but spelled differently are ——.

G. Give four things you should do to show courtesy when you use the telephone.

H. Tell where to divide these verses into lines with "rhyming" thoughts.
   1. Serve the Lord with gladness: come before his presence with singing (Psalm 100:2).
   2. Make no friendship with an angry man; and with a furious man thou shalt not go (Proverbs 22:24).

> Written Practice

A. Copy the poem, and use correct capitalization. Include the author's name.

my shadow

i have a little shadow
   that goes in and out with me,
And what can be the use of him
   is more than i can see.
he is very, very like me
   from the heels up to the head;
and i see him jump before me
   When i jump into my bed.

—*robert louis stevenson*

B. Write correctly each word that needs to be capitalized.
   1. my address is mill st., akron, ohio.
   2. mrs. c. f. miller moved to lexington ave., stone mountain, georgia, last spring.
   3. mrs. mary m. dobbins from pinecraft, florida, visited our school on march 6, 2008.
   4. no, mary, i hadn't heard that story before.

C. Write each list in alphabetical order.

1. altar	2. maple	3. spring
animal	meaning	speak
active	measure	symbol
amber	market	spade

D. Write the words that would come on a dictionary page with these guide words.

   leader . . . letter

lemon	lesson	lentil
latter	lid	leopard

E. For each pair of words, write **S, A,** or **H** to tell whether they are synonyms, antonyms, or homophones.
   1. angry—cross
   2. by—buy
   3. street—road
   4. threw—through
   5. small—tiny
   6. rich—poor
   7. kind—cruel
   8. road—rode

F. Write the correctly spelled word in each pair. Check the dictionary if you are not sure.
   1. recieve—receive
   2. veil—viel
   3. Israel—Isreal
   4. ofen—often
   5. misspell—mispell
   6. horizon—horizen

G. Find and write one meaning for each word.
  1. buoyancy   2. marten   3. cowslip   4. zest

H. Copy the phonetic spelling for each word.
  1. ewe   2. material   3. lemur

I. Write **true** or **false** for each sentence.
  1. If you are not sure of a telephone number, you should dial the number you think is right.
  2. When talking on the telephone, you should always speak clearly and distinctly.
  3. If a message is given, you should listen carefully and write it down accurately.
  4. If a caller wants to speak to someone who is there, you should ask, "What do you want?"
  5. If someone calls and asks a question, you should answer his question and say "Good-bye."

J. Write a more descriptive word for each word in bold print.
  1. Thank you for the **good** dinner.
  2. With shining eyes, Timothy **said,** "I would really like that!"
  3. The boy **walked** across the room as quietly as he could.

K. Look up the following verses, and finish the comparisons.
   1. He moveth his tail like a ——— (Job 40:17).
   2. He maketh the deep to boil like a ——— (Job 41:31).
   3. Shall thy jealousy burn like ———? (Psalm 79:5).
   4. Their contentions are like the ——— of a ——— (Proverbs 18:19).

L. Read this paragraph, and follow the directions below.

White and Purple Violets
Flowers of Beauty and Surprise
Shooting Seeds

Violets are among the most popular spring flowers. They grow in many places around the world. Antarctica is covered with ice though. In early spring, violets bloom in colorful clusters. There are yellow and white violets, but most people like the blue and purple ones best. Violets have a most interesting way of spreading their seeds. When the seed pods are ripe, they burst open and the seeds shoot out. Violet seeds can land as far as fifteen feet away! Dandelion seeds float with the wind. God surely made an interesting beauty when He made the violet.

1. Copy the best title.
2. Copy the first three words of the topic sentence.
3. Copy the first three words of each sentence that does not belong.

Index

V

W